Chance Survivor

Chance Survivor

Andrew Karpati Kennedy

Old Guard Press

Published in the United Kingdom in 2012 for Old Guard Press
by Shearsman Books Ltd
50 Westons Hill Drive
Emersons Green
BRISTOL
BS16 7DF
to whom permissions enquiries should be directed.

ISBN 978-1-84861-190-0

Cover: (top) Photograph of deportation train (courtesy of the
Wiener Library) and (bottom) the Wills Building,
University of Bristol, copyright © 2010, Tupungato.

Contents

PART I

1. Prelude

Shining pebbles in the grey asphalt, light in the grey, grey, endless grey. Lean out of the pram, drag a stick along that hard grey stony street, scrape and listen to the scraping sound. Not so boring when scraping. I like the iron fence, my stick makes a lovely loud sound on the iron bars. I don't like the endless grey.

Stop that. Sit up.

Nasty Hilda. Not nasty, lovely in the morning. Why angry? Why stop? I am bored. Jump out and run, run away. Or lie down and sing. Or scrape louder and let her shout.

Stop that. And sit up. We're going to the meadows, you'll love that, you always do. See the green fields and see the stork and the water mill. Spoilt boy! Soft fingers pull me up, soft but hard. Softer in the bath, her fingers on my skin in the warm water. Mummy never does that.

Where is Mummy?

Gone out.

Why?

She's busy shopping.

Why?

We're going to the meadows.

I don't want to go.

To the water mill!

I don't want to go.

What do you want then?

Nothing.

What?

Why are we here? Where is Mummy?

Now it's green, not grey. Jump out and run from her. Run, run, run. Green, all green. Then black, see, black mud on shoes, black legs and knees. Where is Hilda, where is she? Black mud on my hands, my face. Dripping mud. Where is she? Run and run. Shout. Nobody can hear me. Nobody can see me. Run and run. Shout again. Sing.

The sun is gone.

Scream.

The earth is dark.

Scream.

They left me.

Scream.

9

They want me to die.

It's all right little boy, I am here.

   Scream.

You're not hurt.

   Scream.

You're all right, perfectly all right, silly.

   Scream.

Now stop crying.

   Scream.

Do you want to go home?

   Scream.

Mummy will be back soon.

   Scream.

What do you want?

   Scream.

Do you want to see the stork then? Long, long red beak—eating a green frog?

   Yes!

*

The gipsy comes for boys who cry too much. She comes and wraps you in her great big black shawl. Then she puts you in her big wicker basket. And off you go, the gipsy will take you away.

The soldiers come and play music for good boys. Listen to the trumpet. Listen and look at them—there on the bandstand, see? You like it in the park, don't you? You are a very lucky boy to have a bandstand just outside your house. Do you want to sing to the music? All right, go on singing.

That's the king, you see? Look at his golden crown. And that's the queen. And those are angels—little girls with wings. Tomorrow we are going to see them in the theatre. You can watch them play, yes, it's called a theatre. Yes, yes, you will see the witch too, the big black hunchbacked witch.

Leave that doll alone. Put it down. Boys don't play with dolls. Now look what you have done. You've made a hole in her head. What will your sister say?

Leave those ripe tomatoes alone. Now look what you've done, pushed them off the shelf, squashed them all. What a mess.

Drop that thing at once. It's a cigarette. Of course you can't eat it, stupid boy, spit it out or you'll be sick. And you make me sick.

*

2. Late Baptism in a Sheltered World
Székesfehérvár, Western Hungary, 1934–35

Among my earliest memories, aged over three, that screaming stands out: the fear of getting lost again and again, and later the fear of someone else getting lost, usually a child, always someone I love. That fear has never left me. Another lasting memory is the scolding that followed the cuddling and spoiling of a child in a life of comfort amounting to luxury. We were then living in the old city of Székesfehérvár, the early medieval capital of Hungary, not far from Lake Balaton, where we moved from my birthplace, Györ, before I was one year old. My father, I was made to understand early, was a gentleman of standing, manager of the Credit Bank, seldom seen except in the evening when he lifted me up and kissed me, sometimes scraping me with his stubble. He never stayed long. Neither did my mother spend a lot of time with me, or with my older sister Eva; I missed my mother but, it was later explained, it was not expected at the time for a mother to pick up or hold and hug a child too often—the experts on child care advised against such indulgence. To show too much affection was not good for a child either; if the child cried, let him cry. So my mother kept 'disappearing' while I kept a wary watch on her movements, wanting to know where exactly she was going, when she was coming back, and how soon. I wanted her to promise that she would return soon. By contrast Hilda, our Austrian governess, was always around and thus a very important person, mixing tenderness with severity. She was physically close. It was incomprehensible that she could desert me—letting me get lost in that field—an event I could not forget though I forgave her in return for a whole lot of other adventures.

Trips out to the country, presumably just nearby fields, had many delights. The stork could be watched preening itself, perhaps it would really catch a frog that wriggled in that long red beak. I liked the funny clapping noises of the stork. Then there was the watermill, its giant wheel turning and churning with a clatter as in the German song that Hilda had been singing to us. There was also the old smithy—the heat of its forge and the terrific sound of hammer blows or the quiet shoeing of a horse; I wondered why it didn't hurt the horse as it stood there patiently enduring the operation. Not far away, in a whitewashed thatched cottage a friendly peasant woman, enormous and loud-voiced, sold us fresh eggs, which at Easter were beautifully painted in elaborate patterns. She always petted and praised us, which was pleasing up to a point but I had already developed a touch of reserve about familiarity from strangers, perhaps as a side-effect of all those warnings about the gipsy who would come and grab the naughty boy.

Anything away from the grey asphalt, where I had to spend too much time, was fun—short trips and longer trips. Some friends sent a carriage to collect us for a tea party; the climax was the journey home in the dark, listening to a pair of horses galloping, their smell and the coachman's shouts adding to the excitement. The carriage lamps swung and flickered in tune with the horses' feet hitting the ground. In winter a horse-drawn sledge took us out to the snow-covered hills. Wrapped up in thick striped travel rugs on top of extra pullovers, we picked hips like cherries. But the trip ended all too soon with fussing about the children getting cold; so back in time for rice pudding and bed. We also visited strange houses where I could investigate strange objects to satisfy my curiosity: a silver cigarette case, a paper-weight with a theatre of moving figures inside the glass or a musical box that played a haunting tune when I touched it. 'Put that back at once' came the familiar command. Trips further afield included a journey to the big lake (Balaton) on doctor's orders, it was explained to me, for a change of air to get over my severe whooping cough. I considered the cough was well worth having for the reward of an extra holiday: croissant-like pastry for breakfast served on an embroidered cloth by a pretty chamber maid and dinner starting with hot chicken soup poured out of a shiny silver spout. And then the doctor came daily to tickle me with his funny instrument, sticking another instrument in my mouth and a thermometer in my bottom, poking my chest, nodding and grunting. Meanwhile, out on the lake a sea plane would take off; I wanted to fly in it but they would not let me, they would never let me do the things I most wanted to do. Paddling in the lake was also forbidden though the water remained shallow, with tempting long mudflats as far as the eye could see.

On a summer journey to Bled (in Slovenia), all I wanted was to be rowed to the magic island. There it was, twinkling lights at dusk, far away but inviting. 'No', came the answer, 'impossible!' I think I wanted to row to that island every day. I somehow got it into my head that it was the island of the dead, and that's why they would not let me go there; I was not in the least afraid, thinking that the dead would not mind my company.

Inside the church they poured cold drops of water on my head from a silver cup while a man in black went on mumbling something nobody could understand. Then they started singing to organ music. There was more mumbling, more smiling. The man in black took out a big book and scribbled in it and then my father scribbled in it too. They lifted me up and put me down again. They did all this without asking me for permission, so I wanted to make a scene but managed to keep quiet when the man in black started mumbling and smiling again, showing some gold teeth. Then they took me home without comment, not answering my questions satisfactorily. But it must have been something important considering all the fuss, followed by 'Hush, go to sleep.' It was many, many years later that I discovered: that had been the day of my baptism. I had become a Christian, a member of the Reformed Church. What was more important, I was not going to have anything to do with Jews, especially at school; I had not been circumcised and my birth certificate had been duly emended. My father, mother and sister had all converted to Protestant Christianity at the same time, seriously but vainly hoping to avoid a tragic destiny.

One day a little old lady dressed in black came to visit. She wandered about the house quietly, came to watch me having a bath, murmured a few words not to be remembered, smiled sadly and vanished. They said she was 'Kleine Omama', the mother of my paternal grandmother (called Stern), and that she was soon going to die. Perhaps I wasn't told that, only assumed it, at the same time wondering if she might not after all start growing again, seeing that she had shrunken to the size of a child. That troubled me.

From an upper window of our house I could watch the world as from a box in the theatre. The main attraction remained the bandstand. The musicians in their khaki uniforms, assembled in the delicate iron pavilion, took up their positions and took their time over tuning their instruments, big and small trumpets, big and small drums. (I didn't know the names of most of the instruments in either Hungarian or German, the language of my mother and the language of Hilda respectively). The crude sounds that reached me before the concert, especially a high-pitched trumpet and the wild drumbeat, were as amusing as the music itself, mostly marches. A little further to the left, in front of a palatial building, a huge black limousine was parked more or less permanently, equipped with a fine spare tyre on the side, a running board and a blue shade above the windscreen. The uniformed chauffeur would wait and wait—and so did I—until a general appeared at last, waving as he got into the back of the car. From time to time soldiers in a different uniform marched past, looking fierce and frightening under their cock-feathered helmets: these were the *csendör*, the dreaded country gendarmerie, quite different from the town police. At that time I was not yet afraid of them but simply observed the men and their uniforms.

Further on, towards the city centre, I heard some sad music that went on and on, sort of moaning, and a large crowd of people stood silently waiting along the streets. 'What a wonderful funeral' someone said. 'Yes, wonderful.' They told me that the old bishop had to be taken to the cemetery to be buried. Why? 'Because he was dead.' What? 'Gone from us. Gone to heaven, God rest his soul'. The great glass carriage was drawn by six black horses. Where is he now? 'In the coffin' they said, but I could see nobody, only a huge heap of flowers. I said: 'I want to see the bishop!' It was rumoured that the priest had fallen from the pulpit when he leaned too far forward while preaching.

Not all stories were fascinating. Some people were boring because they couldn't tell stories properly. Servants and strangers were best at telling stories. In the kindergarten I was often bored, kept my distance from other children and didn't feel like playing with them. They were probably too well brought up, whilst I tended to make scenes—not a good boy at all, they told me. That little operation on my sister's doll was certainly a bad thing to do and also a waste of time for I had found nothing at all inside the skull, no brain, and the hole had to be covered with plaster. Then I had to see the doll with plaster on its forehead every day. My dressing up as a girl, in my sister's Hungarian folk costume with a little head-dress, was not praised either, but at least they took a photo of that event. Cross-dressing was frowned upon but not as much as my spending time in front of the mirror making faces and speaking with other people's voices. And when I went into hiding, so that they couldn't find me at bedtime, mother was anxious and cross. Bad boys had to be punished. Remember *Struwelpeter*, Shock-headed Peter? They chopped off his fingers because he wouldn't stop biting his fingernails. I realised that I was supposed to be frightened but I was not frightened, thinking I could run away or fight if worst came to the worst. And the horrid antics in Max und Moritz, those cautionary tales, always amused me. But I was afraid of burglars who sneaked into our house at nightfall and slipped under your bed. I had heard tales about burglars (in a Hoffmann tale, for instance), and so I would make sure to check and see if anyone was sleeping under my bed. Occasionally I would walk through our apartment from room to room carefully checking every corner for burglars, fighting my own fear, especially when I knew that my parents were out. That was a habit I kept up for many years.

The cinema was a strange place. When you watched a film it was always raining in there, inside the pictures. 'That's not real rain', they said, but something to do with the screen. I insisted that it was rain but not wet rain. Years later the rain simply disappeared from new films. The films shown to small children were not always interesting, but I gave all my attention to a film that showed God turning the pages of his big book where the names of good and bad children were recorded. God was an old man with a long white beard and a soft voice who held that enormous book in his hands scribbling the names of children in it, right and left, good and bad. I was quite troubled by the unfairness of this God—how did he know whether a boy was really good or not, and what if he made a mistake? But members of my family were not keen on discussing God with me at that stage. I also wanted to discuss with my parents the little red stars I could see when I closed my eyes in a dark room. They said 'it's nothing' but I would not let them talk me out of the truth of my experience: there were little red stars under my eyelids and that was that. If nobody else could see them it was because the red stars really belonged to me.

If I had been asked for an opinion, I would have said that the witch in the theatre was a stronger act than God in the film. She dragged herself across the stage bent double, dressed in black and grey rags and a long pointed hat, carrying a large and menacing broom, all the time threatening us in a great big raucous voice which filled the theatre and was truly creepy. But the witch couldn't have been all that frightening either, for after the play I asked to go and see her, somehow guessing that she was hiding behind the scenes.

One day they started behaving strangely at home, sorting and packing things all the time. I could hear mutterings and mumblings but nobody told me anything, they didn't answer my many questions. It was a secret. What secret? The band still played on the bandstand but in our house something went wrong. They were packing up the house, packing boxes, trunks and suitcases—there were shouts and whisperings. I don't remember what happened next, as if I had had a blackout.

3. Childhood in a City of the Plain
Debrecen, Eastern Hungary, 1935

Suddenly I spotted my father looking up at the train from the sunlit platform, waving before the train stopped. He looked well, sun-tanned, his moustache neatly trimmed and his hair smoothed down as usual. He helped me down from the high railway carriage, swung me around gently and gave me a kiss. I was instantly lifted out of my curious blackout and started gazing at the world around me with renewed curiosity.

A horse cab took us from the station to our new home, within walking distance but we travelled with much luggage that could not be sent with the removals. The cab stopped outside a huge grey building with several entrances stretching along one side of Verböczy Street: an apartment block called the Chamber of Commerce (Iparkamara). It was impressive but not lovable. What I liked most in it was the lift, zooming up three floors, the sound of its motor, the doors opening and closing with an impressive clatter and final bang and the mirrors inside inviting me to make faces, grimaces. A couple of years later I also developed a method of high-speed stair racing, my favourite sport, never popular with my mother.

Our large apartment was 'all right' though I thought it could have been larger still, just five rooms plus extra rooms for staff, the new governess, the cook and the maid. My own room was somewhat disappointing probably because I at once spotted my old green-painted cot with the sliding barred sides. I considered that I had grown out of that cage but I didn't protest. I cannot remember my mother coming to my cot at bed-time, perhaps she did come but rarely. The best feature in the apartment was probably one of the drawing rooms that had little daylight as it was windowless, sandwiched between two fully lit rooms. The dimness of this room was a natural place to spend hours thinking about the world or just lying on the Persian carpet tracing its elaborate patterns. I also liked a little sewing room with a Singer sewing machine which I was keen to operate, at first with the help of a visiting seamstress and then, secretly, on my own. In the entrance hall I could watch—past an array of hats and coats and sticks and umbrellas and a cherished stuffed grey squirrel with a bushy tail—the ceremony of a stranger calling and handing over his or her visiting card, to be carried by the maid on a little silver tray to the lady of the house.

The real prize was the balcony from which I could watch the world. In a sense the balcony was an improvement on the upper window in our old home, but instead of the park I looked down on a prison. It was interesting to see so many windows with bars in that dreary long, yellow building. Every day a group of prisoners marched or rather shuffled by in their striped pyjamas, with a guard in front and at the back of the column, each carrying a rifle with a bayonet. I felt sorry for the prisoners but I was told that they were being punished for having done wicked things. Several of my questions on this subject were again not answered. One day I saw a crowd of people gathering outside the prison gate. I naturally asked what they were doing. Ah, those were people waiting for the hanging. Hanging? Later I formed some sort idea of what hanging meant—killing. It was very difficult to think about that. I thought the people in the waiting crowd must be terribly stupid or wicked.

Walking around the district, always with our new and gradually loved governess, Mia, there was much to see. The shiny yellow trams speeding towards the railway station tempted me, so I repeatedly demanded to be allowed to stand near the driver, take over the controls, imitating his hand movements while making all the right noises for speeding and braking. Soon I announced my decision to become a tram driver 'when I grow up'. Within minutes from our home there was also a horse-cab stand where one horse or another would usually present a little spectacle of stamping and whinnying, eating out of a nose-bag or pissing copiously, acts to be watched like a film. One day I overheard somebody say that two coachmen had started a terrible fight, which ended with a murder. I immediately wanted to investigate this incident but my inquiries were met, as usual, with silence while I was pulled away from the site. I began to realise at an early stage that the grown-ups were not interested in the real world and perhaps Mia was paid to keep me out of it. An air of mystery if not menace also surrounded the nearby synagogue, for though it could hardly be concealed as it loomed up facing the street, I was discouraged from lingering outside it, examining its windows with the star of David, or asking questions about it—an early example of the general secrecy hanging over anything connected with the Jews, including the very words Jew or Jewish (just one word in Hungarian). The secrecy grew as I grew up.

A walk to the railway station was always a treat. The blowing and whistling of the steam locomotives, the smells, the smoke and soot in the eyes, the clatter of carriages being shunted, was worth infinitely more than playing with my toy railway, equipped as it was with tunnels and bridges. But I was forbidden to climb up to the locomotive driver—another taboo. Somewhere in the same direction there was a cemetery where I was taken one winter night—I suppose by Mia at Hallowe'en—to see the thousands and thousands of candles burning over the graves. I agreed with my companion that it was very beautiful to look at but wondered if and how the dead could see all that light.

In Spring, Summer and Autumn, our main destination was the so-called Great Forest (*Nagyerdő*), actually just a large park with a forest around it, with a lot of wonderful trees, oak and chestnut—the perfect place for collecting conkers. There was a half-rotten hollowed out old tree there that served as a tram, and rolled forward or stopped as I adjusted the controls. In the same area we regularly visited the nearby swimming pool, the rowing lake (turned into an ice skating rink in winter), the water tower, the clinics around the university and, from a certain distance, the crematorium—subject to the usual hush-hush I was getting used to whenever the dead came into view. (These places only came to matter to me later, when I was a schoolboy.) In those two pre-school years, the reedy streams and muddy ponds held my attention above all, with all sorts of living creatures such as frogs that never stopped croaking, *bre-ke-ke-ke*. It was important to distinguish between frogs and toads, something I *never* quite learned to do, I simply decided that the hideous yellow ones should be avoided. Separating the mushrooms from the toadstools presented a similar task, another skill I never mastered, though I pored over the pictures of fungi I had collected from a certain brand of chocolate.

At the entrance to the Great Forest there was a tall war memorial with stone soldiers who had died in a great world war, they said. I asked a number of questions about that war but again the answers were not satisfactory. I compared the stone soldiers with the coloured picture soldiers carrying rifles (as did the prison guards seen from our balcony) and with my lead soldiers: they looked dead when laid out flat on the floor. I was worried by the news that somewhere a new war had started, somewhere in a country called Spain. Then a young friend of my parents brought me a very nice flag with coloured rings, telling us about the Berlin Olympics, and saying that everywhere in Berlin he had seen German soldiers in brown uniform with hooked black crosses on white on a red armband. Frightening, he said, all those swastikas. I understood that he was talking about dangerous people, dangerous to us. And I soon noticed that those around me, especially my mother, often had a worried look that worried me. And war became another hush-hush word.

On a building site my father had a fine sandbox set up for me to play. I went there once or twice dutifully but somehow the opportunity for play didn't grip me; I would have preferred to go on asking more questions of the kind mentioned. I think my father was at first disappointed by my lack of enthusiasm for the sandbox though I never actually objected to it. Soon he seemed to realise that what I liked most was to watch things happening as we walked about the main street—for example, notice a colonel trying to stride in the high street though he was bent double with a crooked back, his sword dangling and scraping the asphalt; or, after a fire, I gazed at the smouldering beams of a fashionable clothes shop, smelling the remains of charred timber. Such things required explanation. I am not sure exactly when my father began to take me seriously—probably after Mia had left us—but then he started to try and explain questionable things.

*

It was about this time, between ages six and seven, that I experienced my first serious disappointments. The first disappointment destroyed the wonder of Christmas for me when I found out that Father Christmas was a fake. Christmas Eve was the major ritual of the year—far exceeding the lesser, non-secret, fun and games at Easter (when we went around sprinkling girls with scented water, in return for chocolate eggs) or the real Santa Claus (*Mikulás*) on 6th December (when I dressed up as a devil, with a proper mask and horns and managed to frighten a neighbour girl.) Christmas filled a child with awe. Was it my sister or someone outside the family— when I asked too many questions—who pulled down the veil? Perhaps I did not want to be told the truth, I would have settled for a half-truth and remained a doubter. After all, secrecy and suspense were an essential part of the annual ritual, not religious but somehow sacred: the long silence after sending out the wish-list, the threat of no more presents if you behaved badly, and finally the evening when that high-pitched, heavenly bell could be heard at last. Then the doors of the dining room would be flung open to reveal the ceiling-high tree lit up by a host of candles burning and loaded with glittering glass balls, chocolate figures and angels' hair. There was such an abundance of presents that it took an hour or more to unwrap and inspect them, all toys or luxuries, for clothes and other useful things were frowned upon by spoilt children—such things were meant for the cook and the maid who came into the dining room to receive their presents towards the end of the ceremony. Then the five-course dinner would start with fish in aspic (so much fuss went into its preparation that the kitchen was out of bounds for children), followed by pike (seen swimming in our bath tub the day before), oranges and mandarins, figs and dates, assorted cheeses and desserts including the much-desired *beigli* (nut or poppy-seed rolls), and *Dobos torta*, the elaborately layered wafer and chocolate cake topped with burnished caramel. The celebration of Christmas Eve, in the Continental Christian fashion, was doubly rich in our home for it coincided with my sister's birthday—a coincidence that, according to family legend, disturbed my maternal grandmother, Olga, when Eva was born because she didn't know what to do with the carefully prepared Christmas fish meal.

It may now seem that my memories of Christmas were not harmed in the long run yet feeling cheated left a lasting scar. In my first long short story, written when I was 19, I invented a character, a girl, who was so upset by getting the wrong kind of doll at Christmas that she violently tore down the tree; and this episode was the prelude to a lifetime of disappointments that culminated in her remaining a spinster. That was sheer imagination but the association with a Christmas crisis was the story's emotional starting point.

A more serious deception accompanied my operation for hernia. This was preceded by several examinations by Dr Loessl, a distinguished surgeon who was also the medical director of a private hospital. He had reassuring manners and moustaches and a beautiful wife, whose hair had turned snow-white in one night when she heard a rumour that her husband got killed on the front, it was said. I trusted this doctor when he told me that I was perfectly safe in his hands; I did not feel threatened, as once in a dental surgery where I could see the instruments of torture being lifted towards my mouth and I immediately prevented a tooth extraction by the simple expedient of screeching in the dentist's ears for an hour or so. When the second examination for hernia was due, I was told of a dark room where a very bright light would shine through my body, a fun event. Next I would lie down in a very, very bright room, brighter than anything I had ever seen, which would also be fun. All this happened as foretold, except that they put a smelly rag on my face that I couldn't tear off because my hands were tied down, and it lulled me into deep sleep. I remember nothing except the counting over my head, one, two, three, four, five... I awoke screaming, in a strange room, alone, confused and in pain. A nurse came in and started talking to me and stroking me like a child. I resented that and demanded to see the doctor, my mother and my father at once. Dr Loessl appeared soon enough and patiently explained to me what had happened, promising to remove the bandage from my wound soon; meanwhile, it was neatly laced up like a football. This brilliant explanation soothed me but I wanted to know why my tummy was hurting so. There was nothing at all wrong with my tummy, I was told, just a cut above my thigh, a brave soldier's wound. When my mother came to visit I probably asked her why she had not prepared me and not told me the truth. I can't remember what she said. Her way of comforting me included sending to the hospital high quality homemade food brought in daily, in a dish carrier, by a young bank messenger. This was 'nice' but I thought that they were making too much fuss, especially when I was told that my bed was placed in the hospital director's own carpeted study.

The way Mia left us was the worst disappointment of all. Slowly and painfully I accepted that she had to emigrate, though I didn't know why, it was a secret like so many things at the time. (Only years later did I hear that it had something to do with her being an Austrian Jew, and that she had emigrated to England). Mia had been my daily companion for almost three years: she was always there, available in the house or outdoors, when I woke and when I went to sleep. And she was affectionate. It isn't easy to define the relationship: we were very close but not intimate—my mother would have observed and discouraged anything too intense. The phrase 'I love you' was never used between us, in keeping with the scarcity of those words in our family. I knew that I would miss Mia more than anybody else, and as soon as I heard that she might be leaving I promised to be good and pleasant for ever, in case my 'naughty boy' image had been a spur to Mia's threatened departure. I got sadder by the day as the dreaded event approached and on the eve of her last day I could only be consoled by long-prolonged hugging at bedtime (before eight o'clock as usual), accompanied by a clear promise that we would meet again the following morning for a proper farewell. Who made that promise, Mia or my mother? I can't remember, perhaps both of them together in order to cope with my paroxysm of crying. Finally, I went to sleep feeling reassured. But when I woke I found out that Mia had gone. She had left sneakily, without another good-bye. It is a pity, they said, but she just had to go…

This incident had lasting consequences, chiefly in making me quite a cautious boy, sceptical of what people said, especially of promises made. More materially, I banged my head on a screw of the green cot (mentioned before), followed by horrendous bleeding and a scar that remains visible, close to my left eye, to this day. The other consequence was that I would not tolerate any successor to Mia, and my sister joined me in making life more or less intolerable for any governess. Our last German-speaking governess was called Lulu, a name I found unspeakably funny, not least because it meant 'willy' to a Hungarian child (something Lulu could not have known). But there was also something wrong with the way she did things, the way she walked and talked, for example, or the fuss she made about darning a sock, pointing out that in America a sock with a hole would be put in the rubbish bin. So she did not last. The next governess was a tall Hungarian woman. In my opinion there was absolutely no need for me to practice Hungarian and so I more or less stopped talking to her—very unusual for a chatterbox. One day this woman—I can't even remember her name—lifted me up, presumably in a friendly gesture. But it was a mistake, for once I was high enough to look her straight in the eye and study her skin, I decided that she was going to murder me. I may or may not have shared this prophecy with members of my family, all I remember is that the new governess left soon enough, and that she was the last one to try.

The end of the governess era had one good result: my mother and my father were spending much more time with my sister and me. We called them, respectively, Anyuka and Apuka—terms of endearment, with the diminutive 'ka', reinforced by addressing them in the second person familiar (thou), not a universal custom at the time. I suppose that, apart from the new circumstance, we had become more interesting to them as we were growing out of childish ways. At home I made something of a habit of following my mother around, so much so that she would remark: 'you come after me like a little dog' or 'you needn't come with me all the way to the WC'. An attempt at distancing? I particularly enjoyed my mother playing the piano for me, often to accompany my singing simple songs either in Hungarian (*Boci, Boci, tarka*—concerning the dappled calf that had neither ears nor a tail) or in German (*Hänschen klein ging allein...*) I improvised chords and tunes, making vigorous use of all the scales. So my mother wanted me to take piano lessons but I evaded the offer by postponing it: 'later', I said, a word that later became almost fatal to my development in several directions. I roamed around the apartment with my mother, finding opportunities to sit with her and ask questions. Sometimes I sat on her lap, but I don't think she was too keen on that, partly because I was getting quite heavy by the age of six or seven. Once I asked her what was that great gap in her flesh that I could see peering down her pullover below the neck; she said that was nothing—an unsatisfactory answer. I also wanted to know why her bosom was heaving so; she said she was just breathing—not satisfactory. I took great interest in anything done to my mother, for example watching the hairdresser who came to our home to do her hair in front of her dresser and the manicurist who made her nails look pinker with the varnish I could smell long after the job was finished. Once I watched a complete session of pedicure, paying particular attention to the array of scissors employed by the corn-cutter (as we called him) and the ample amount of hard skin removed. But it was an accident that I glimpsed her undressing, naked. I simply opened the door of her bedroom without knocking, and was genuinely surprised by her cry of dismay; it wasn't such a big deal after all, I thought.

I interrogated my mother as often as possible. The porcelain owl with piercing eyes that could be lit up from within fascinated me and I wanted to know why its eyes were not giving light. The electric bulb was missing— again, not a very satisfactory answer, too matter-of-fact. It was about that time that I started asking searching questions like:

If God made the earth, who made God?
What comes after the end of the world?

I think my mother tried to answer such questions valiantly, accompanied by a shrug. After a while I was prepared to drop such questions; my obsession with astronomy or cosmology came later. She also found more time for reading aloud, not necessarily at bedtime, and if a story made a strong impression—like the Grimm Brothers' tale of the greedy fisherman's wife who kept asking the great fish for more and more and more until the time came when she wanted to be God and then the sky went dark and in a great storm and the fish swallowed them all—I would ask for a repeat. The story of Little Red Riding Hood was another favourite; I liked the repetition in her dialogue with the wolf: how big are your eyes, your teeth, and so on to the horrible climax.

Mother let me accompany her on shopping errands. The market, in that market town, was so large that it took the best part of a morning to walk through it looking for a bargain—tasting cheese here, poking a melon there, examining a chicken or a hen as it wriggled and cackled when lifted up for show. The hustle and bustle, the shouting vendors, the pushing and poking crowd of buyers, the pungent smells of food and sweat, the risk of getting trampled on, were deliciously frightening. Then came the shops: the fat grocer's wife, Mrs. Monoki, sat behind the cashier's counter somewhat aggrieved (I could tell by the frown spreading across her enormous forehead) as she conceded another discount; the butcher sliced salami at great speed without slicing off his finger; the man in charge of smoking the ox-tongue handed out 'our' tongue proudly—a row of tongues threatened to start bellowing.

Early on I associated a certain moralising tone with my mother's way of talking: lively yet serious, even earnest, with lots of practical wisdom—do it today, not tomorrow; stop looking in the mirror, what do you see there?, together with quaint reproaches when I behaved badly: 'I'll teach you how to blow into a glove'—sufficiently obscure to amuse me rather than making me feel chastised. It was, in any case, very difficult to chastise me. For I found nearly all the words used to discipline me funny; and any scene that involved my mother losing her temper, to the point of shouting at me, reminded me of the theatre. Even when she put her hand on her heart and said that she might have a heart attack, because I had upset her so, I saw her as a performer. But I did appreciate her colourful use of proverbs like 'even a mother can't understand a dumb child' or 'it's too late for the raincoat after the shower'. She also drew on foreign language references. When I said something self-cheering, she would say 'What's this, the Coué method?', explaining that Coué told people to go on saying 'I'm feeling better and better every day' until they believed it was true. When I was reluctant to do something she had wished me to do, I heard her say *'gezwungene Liebe tut Leid'* or unwilling love is no good. When I brought trouble on myself through my own choice, she treated me to *'tu l'a voulu George Dandin'*, long before I had heard of Molière.

It seems that my father did not play a prominent role in my life until a few years later, just before and after we moved into the elegant new bank building in Spring 1939, right in the centre of the city, in the broad main street officially called Francis Joseph Street but just Market Street by the citizens. As manager of that leading bank branch, with some fifty employees, my father was responsible for the building project and I often accompanied him on tours of inspection. The scaffolding was still up and concrete was still being poured into the foundations when we started our rounds; my father, accompanied by the architect or builder, would explain to me in detail this or that construction process—for example, the method of preparing and perfecting the concrete. At a later stage I was shown how the partitions were erected with panels of asbestos—a new name, a material proudly described as very modern at the time. Later still, I watched the marble slabs being placed around the pillars in the imposing front lobby of the bank and the off-white square stones fixed on the facade. Life-sized bronze statues were raised in a row between the shallow balconies at first floor level, where we were going to live; they were covered in a light green film which my father called patina, predicting that they would change colour in time. So I watched the changes of Mercury over the years that remained to us. All sorts of craftsmen came in a procession: painters and decorators, carpenters, glaziers, experts on wood panelling and flooring, electricians and plumbers—I watched them all at work day by day. Finally I watched the huge safes being installed with enormous effort, in specially constructed strong rooms, which involved my descent into an underworld to be sealed off with a huge steel door—the combination known to very few people apart from my father. Such was my fascination with the rise of that masterly building, in neo-classical style, that I would have liked to be an architect when I grew up—but I forgot all about that when the time came to choose a career.

At the time I took it for granted that my father was my guide to the mystery of building; with hindsight I can see that he really wanted to open the world to me.

When the bank building was complete, in 1939, we moved into a spacious six-room apartment on the first floor, where I had my own room complete with a desk and a washbasin, and with a window opening on a flat roof. Living just one floor above the bank, I inevitably came to regard the bank itself as some kind of extension of my home territory. I visited my father in his beautifully panelled office as often as possible, perhaps too often from his point of view. When he had a little leisure he would show me his rich stamp collection—carefully pointing to stamps from rare states like the Vatican or Memel; soon I followed him as an eager philatelist (both collections were lost after 1944). One day he solemnly showed me our family documents, mostly official copies of birth certificates which he had painstakingly assembled to prove that our family had been living in Hungary for many generations—mostly in the West but also in the South East of the Great Plain—hoping that such proof of our settled and patriotic state might exempt us from the increasingly punitive laws against Jews.

Sometimes I could not resist the temptation of watching my father working in his office from 'my' flat roof—all I had to do was climb through my window. That roof was probably safe enough for someone who walked on it carefully, but I tended to go right up to the edge and leaned over the eaves to get a better view of my father dictating to a secretary or interviewing a client. When my father spotted me, he at once phoned home anxiously ordering my instant removal from that life-threatening outpost. I also took to visiting the main banking hall, admiring the fluted marble columns of the main entrance, where I had heard my father's speech as part of the opening ceremony—a speech that he had carefully rehearsed in my hearing, I was his test audience. (I remember sentences like 'alive we can do little without criticism, dead we shall no doubt be praised or forgotten'). I was on easy terms with several bank clerks who seemed to like chatting to me, perhaps to please my father but perhaps also because they found my oddities of behaviour amusing. One day my father took me down to the cashier and deposited a certain sum—probably five *pengö*-s, worth about half a crown at the time—to open my first bank account. It was in my name and it went with a neat little savings book to show the date, the amount, etc. But that was not enough for me. The following day I went straight back to the cashier and asked to see my deposit. He showed me a register, confirming what was written in my own bankbook. Still not reassured, I demanded to see and hold again the actual 'silver' coin. It was duly produced and shown to me amid general mirth. No doubt the story went round how the manager's son was not satisfied until he could touch his money just one day after depositing it. I never asked to see that coin again.

Still in the bank, I was ushered into secret places: the great steel door of the strong room was slowly opened, by dint of turning the coded lock, supervised by officials who went on to open this or that individual safe. I admired the different colours of the safes, mostly dark green or mottled brown with shiny wheel-shaped locks. Great riches were behind those great steel doors, I was told: silver, and gold, jewellery and art works. Then I would watch the elaborate shutting of the doors at closing time. I was also shown all kinds of business mysteries: the copying of documents including my father's letters just out of a secretary's typewriter, to be filed in the spacious archives; a library of banking signatures kept in a special slotted filing cabinet so that any signature, on a cheque or a letter from any part of the world, could be authenticated; a clerk would help me try out various typewriters before I could write properly in long hand, and before I had properly mastered arithmetic I was shown the workings of a very large adding machine, together with a much smaller desk-top machine to be rotated quite speedily by hand for multiplication and division. I was also allowed to watch the weighing of coins and the counting of banknotes—huge piles of money, which made me wonder why there were so many poor people in the country.

From time to time I went on a walk with my father, really a kind of promenade in the main street, called *corso* as in Italy. I became aware of just how well-known my father was from the sheer number of hats being lifted as we walked around in the city, occasionally stopping to talk to one or another eminent person: a general or a well-known scholar or clergyman, an advocate or a civil servant. He was also on speaking terms with some of the leaders of the community, for instance, the bishop of the Reformed Church (Dr Révész) and the Burgomaster. After an encounter, he would sketch for me the character and status of each dignitary, usually adding, quietly if not in a whisper, some remark concerning the 'decency' of the man (no women in leading positions at that time) where decency meant that someone could be trusted as distinct from a Nazi sympathiser and known anti-Semite, like the Lord Lieutenant of the County (*Föispán*) whom I once heard addressing boys and girls from all the city's schools in the stadium, resounding with the amplified roar of his menacing rhetorical drivel—a style that was becoming widespread among Hungarian Nazis. By contrast, a visit by a Habsburg prince, the powerless survivor of a vanished age, was dignified and low-keyed.

My father was always well dressed, in a new-seeming suit carefully pressed, usually with a white collar, occasionally a starched collar and tie, monogrammed shirts, perfectly polished shoes, sometimes with spats. I took his elegant appearance for granted at the time—later seen as 'the old style', the emblem of a bygone age of peace. Once in a while I would inspect my father's wardrobe and touch a sleeve of one of his many suits; and I helped collecting those starched collars from a special laundry. Among the suits hung a rifle, apparently used, in earlier times, for shooting- wild geese. It was an awesome sight, together with the 'knuckleduster' that he kept by his bedside-table, apparently as a deterrent to bank robbers. (Fortunately, this method of defence was never put to the test). I sometimes watched the early morning ritual of the barber coming to shave my father in the bathroom—with an overdose of lather and a ceremonious wielding of the blade accompanied by a discussion of the latest political crisis; from time to time the tailor came to our home to take measurements for a new suit that had to be tried several times before it was finally approved and the shoemaker came to mark the exact boundary of the sole on cardboard before the leather was cut to measure. Amid all these luxuries, my father worked hard—going down to the bank at eight o'clock in the morning, returning for lunch at precisely 1.45, taking a siesta after he had read a German language Budapest newspaper, the *Pester Lloyd*, and then working on into the evening, sometimes into the night. He found time to read to me—sometimes German poetry—Schiller's 'Die Glocke' or Goethe's 'Erlkönig', that ominous night ride towards the death of a child troubled me. In those early years I got fonder and fonder of my father though not yet so close as in shared travel later, and in the terror of the final forced journey that killed him.

4. Age of Security—Still?

My pre-school and primary school years (1936–41) passed quickly and almost imperceptibly, without marked incidents—before I felt the anxieties of the time that invaded our family. I think I have early on developed a tendency to adapt to a public environment, despite my private liveliness which was often regarded, by my parents and their friends, as naughtiness or rebellious insolence: 'the naughtiest boy in town', along with Tommy Fischer (another banker's son), it was said. I excelled in bad practical jokes like tugging at the legs of guests from under the dining table or placing a frog on the piano in the middle of a house concert. I also conducted perilous scientific experiments—for example, throwing a corkscrew down into the courtyard from a third floor balcony to test gravity like Galileo.

My tendency towards bravado was mixed with shyness at an early stage. I remember suffering acute stage fright when asked to conduct a choir at my musical pre-school—I got confused, despite careful rehearsal and supervision, pointing my baton in the wrong direction with extreme embarrassment. I was better at playing a simple tune on glasses marked with colours corresponding to notes on the diatonic scale, do, re, mi, fa… blue, red, green, yellow, a synaesthetic association that I had lost over the years.

When I started primary school, I was taken there and collected every day by our governess for the first two years, but later I walked the short stretch from our new home to a humble side street, Miklós Utca, and into a humble yellow building. Opposite loomed the yellow Lutheran church, allied to the Reformed Church but significantly different—not just because it had an altar and the priest wore an enormous white fan-shaped collar but because he tended to talk down to children, unlike the learned and eloquent Calvinist preachers. Two things fascinated me from the first day at school: learning to write and watching our teacher, Uncle Elefánti. Writing was sheer fun if one followed the rules, tilting the paper along the line clearly marked in white on the heavily scratched desk, dipping the pen into the little inkpot sunk into the desk, learning not to spill and smudge, and then forming letters, slowly, letter after letter and word after word, then phrases and short sentences, in a dignified calligraphy resembling my grandmother's Victorian handwriting style, though never attaining the balance and beauty of that script. It was a great pity that in the second class a teacher got obsessed with a new type of script called 'string writing', probably imposed by higher authority. Anyway, I resisted that innovation; I think my sister adopted it to an extent that ruined her handwriting for a long time. The act of writing was a kind of physical delight that lasted a lifetime, a gentle pressure and a pulse for which there is no substitute; typing never became a pleasure and the computer never became a friend.

Uncle Elefánti supervised each stage of letter-formation with meticulous care, walking around the classroom, stopping at every desk breathing audibly and occasionally correcting a letter in the process of writing. He was a big, ageing man with a high forehead, so that it was natural to see in him the residual elephant suggested by his name. I paid particular attention to his habit of taking down his steel-rimmed spectacles, breathing on them and cleaning both lenses methodically with a large white handkerchief. I saw this as a circus act more interesting than much of his teaching, which seemed to me, well, elementary. In addition to the usual subjects—arithmetic, natural history, art, etc.—we had weekly lessons in 'living' based on pictures hanging from three walls. One day, the subject was country life—not something I knew much about as a boy kept in town year by year, away from anything muddy. We were shown a picture representing the slaughter of a pig, accompanied by our teacher's commentary. He said something about sharpening the knives. At that a tall, thin town boy jumped up and ran out of the classroom screaming. I had a lot of sympathy for that boy—for it was a scandal to kill a pig like that—at the same time I formed the opinion that 'people shouldn't scream'; it was sufficient to cry to oneself, there was no point in showing one's tears to a class-load of insensitive thickheads.

My father's position seemed to influence the attitude of my teachers towards me. I sensed that, in a subtle way, at least two teachers, in the second and the third class, were giving me special attention. A female teacher sat down beside me for extra time patiently trying to improve my drawing skills, which happened to be my only weak subject; another teacher talked to me after class in an exceptionally friendly and grown-up way. Each teacher had some kind of connection with my father or the bank, I somehow found out. By contrast, the headmaster, who also taught the fourth class, showed an unmistakable aversion to me. At first he probably just saw me as being 'too clever by half', as I dared to point out an error in his calculations on the blackboard in front of the whole class. I also argued with him, something I was in the habit of doing. One day he got really angry when, after my spell as pupil teacher in geography, a backward 'pupil' complained that I had been too strict and rough with her. On that occasion the headmaster roared at me in an abusive way and made me kneel in a corner—the way the naughtiest boy, a poor boy, was punished. The headmaster may have wanted to administer 'classless' justice, but I took his outburst—about spoilt rich children—as a sign of class hatred, possibly anti-Semitic. (I began to practice a type of instant analysis that also remained with me for life). The headmaster was a big, burly man with a ruddy complexion and an unrefined voice, and he really did make mistakes in mathematics; I implicitly classified him as under-educated, and he may have sensed that. When he turned on me, I felt like telling him: 'shout a little louder if you really want to impress me'—but I said nothing, fearing that he might complain to my parents.

As I found all subjects taught at my primary school easy or too easy, I early on developed a tendency to do less than my best—the top grades came regularly in any case and my parents were satisfied. However, I was already conscious that ordinary schooling was less challenging than the world outside, with certain subjects that were not part of the school curriculum. The latter included religious knowledge, taught by a visitor to the school, a friendly and intellectual young Calvinist clergyman, Dr Szenes. I was his only pupil and I responded to his interest in me with enthusiasm, memorised the entire syllabus by heart, with scriptural passages and psalms, and offered interpretations of both the Old and the New Testaments, which I already treated as collections of stories and poems—sacred, yes, but literature. I approached the subject with reverence so that Dr Szenes and an external examiner thought that I must be an unusually pious and religious boy; eventually they asked me, at the end of my fourth year at the primary school, whether I wished to become a priest one day. I answered that I needed time to think seriously about such a vocation. I didn't state that I was currently more interested in astronomy, the cosmos, and what I really wanted to know was what the world looked like when darkness was upon the face of the deep.

Resuming German and starting English became for me important subjects, both taught privately, outside school hours. German was the native language of at least two of my governesses, so I thought going on from speaking to reading and writing grammatically would be child's play. However, at one point I got so bored or lazy that I demonstrated a marked reluctance to aim at excellence. This disappointed my teacher, Magda, an ageing and hunchbacked woman, whom I considered too solemn though I respected her. One day she decided that we might as well go for a walk and converse in German while walking. By the time we reached the road towards the woods, I was much more interested in the scenic view than in the language and started to talk to my teacher's small white dog (a *puli*, seldom seen outside Hungary). When told off about this piece of impertinence, I explained that I just wanted to see if I could teach the dog speak German as Till Eulenspiegel had taught an ass to read. I can't remember how our German lessons proceeded after that incident.

Learning English was fun but again I developed an oppositional attitude, this time supported by my sister. The trouble began when our first teacher, Eva Magyar, young, exuberant and highly competent, had to leave—for England. She left a gap that was not easy to fill, and I soon realized that our next teacher, Mrs. Rényi, a solicitor's wife, was an amateur. I particularly objected to her habit of writing out a very long list of words in a very long divided notebook—English on the left, Hungarian on the right—for every lesson. I realized, perhaps from the example of our previous teacher, that there were more imaginative methods. In any case, I preferred to absorb words gradually through reading and conversation, with as little learning by rote as possible. However, it was impossible to explain this in a direct way. My sister and I therefore conspired to wax the pages of the notebook so thoroughly that the teacher's pencil got stuck the moment she tried to write down a new word for the next lesson. This was, no doubt, a mean trick for our teacher had some inspired ideas for her pupils. For example, she made us perform plays in English: *Snow White* one year and *The Wizard of Oz* the following year; learning while you play. For some reason we then had to change English teachers again and twice a week we trooped out of the city centre to take lessons from an old clergyman, Mr Sebestyén, who had once lived in America. Something in his manner or wheezing irritated my sister but I became fascinated by him, especially by his collection of maps and atlases: we would spend an hour consulting the gazetteer to trace towns and rivers, mostly in the United States. I was also intrigued by his enormous collection of English idioms, his life work that was later published. Thousands of little slips of paper—with one idiom or another written on each in neat handwriting—littered a table covered by a carpet, and from time to time he would jump up excitedly, in the middle of our reading a sentence, to jot down a new idiom—perhaps 'white elephant'. One way or another I must have imbibed, without much effort and without realizing it, quite a lot of English in those early years, thus preparing the ground for my later emigration to England (and my eventual choice of the language as my main subject and first love—against great opposition.) My parents wanted to reinforce my knowledge of English by eventually sending me to the English language college at Sárospatak, in northeast Hungary, only to be frustrated in this wish by a new race law that excluded any boy who did not descend from four Aryan grandparents. I had none.

Over a few years my parents saw to it that I took part in a wide range of physical activities; my father in particular was concerned that I might grow up as a one-sided weakling with puny muscles who would not live up to the principle of *mens sana in corpore sano*. So I was sent to a dancing school, urged to play football and other outdoor games which bored me (unlike chess and Monopoly), go sledging and skating in winter despite my weak ankles and a very feeble love of snow and ice, swimming almost daily in summer, roughing it with boy-scouts, competing in athletics at a holiday camp, and later doing extra gym with an Olympic gold medallist in lightweight wrestling (1936: Károly Kárpáti, our namesake), fencing with a foil under the care of a fairly sadistic teacher and even boxing (my opponent and I agreed to pull our punches). All this was balanced by singing in a choir, attending concerts, visits to the Csokonai theatre (frequent Lehár operettas but also Molière), to the Déri museum (Munkácsy paintings and remarkable skeletons), art and photographic exhibitions (a female nude included—my questions about pubic hair not answered satisfactorily), with little trips to the small airport, the university and its clinics, a model farm or a toothbrush factory affiliated to the bank and, before the outbreak of the war, travel beyond the borders of the country.

Dancing stands out among all these activities as my dismal failure. No sooner had I arrived at the dancing school than I discovered that all the boys and girls there had already mastered the mysterious steps of the dance then being practiced and were confidently shuffling across the floor. One girl, Klári, whom I knew from my primary school, was assigned to me as a partner and I immediately spotted her smirking at my stumbling steps and shaking her head till the pink ribbon in her hair trembled. Then I felt surrounded by supercilious observers of the dance, feasting their eyes on my clumsiness. In short, the dance turned into a punishment with only one escape: quitting quickly in the first break. That one retreat was followed by a life-long series of other retreats.

It is strange that the scorn of one girl, and perhaps it was only mirth, should have so affected me because I had no genuine interest in that girl or in any other girl at the time. I went through the four years of my primary school without close friends, whether boys or girls. Yet I was not lonely, at least I don't remember feeling lonely. In the first year my sister (three years older) went to the same school and I quite often spoke to her, or ate my 'elevenses' with her in a break. I liked to watch her doings, especially when she played a part in a kind of folk play, which had a haunting song running through it to link the adventures of the prince:

once upon a time what did a prince think
hee, hee, hee, ha, ha, ha
what did the prince think to himself?

And then the prince set out on his interminable search for the land of his promised bride. I am still haunted by the tune and can sing it too. Later I did take a certain interest in some of the girls in my class but mostly as an outside observer. On the whole I didn't take them seriously because they were not serious, or so I thought. For example, they did not get distinctions in any major subject. Neither did their faces make a strong impression on me—as they paled beside my love, Judy Garland in *The Wizard of Oz*, and later the face of Eva Lőrinczy, my sister's friend and name-sake. By the time Eva L caught my imagination, to the extent that I proposed to marry her, she had fully developed breasts under her colourful bathing costume; I saw her make a perfect dive into the deep end of the public swimming pool we called the Strand, and she repeated her performance several times without being aware that she had an admiring spectator. Another girl, Jutka, also interested me but for a peculiar reason: her father was an undertaker and I wanted to know how that affected her home life: did she, for example, keep things in a surplus coffin?

At least two girls befriended me outside school through family connection. There was the lovely, rounded, light-haired, permanently good-humoured but somehow elusive daughter of a leather merchant (an old acquaintance of my father)—Marika Vas. She was my age and we kept inviting each other to our homes and discussed the world. It was her father who arranged a great party for a horde of joyfully screaming children on sledges tied together and towed uphill by her father's car. (Cars were relatively scarce at that time; my parents did not possess one, though presumably they could have afforded it). I would have liked to see more of Marika. That is certainly my sad, posthumous wish in the knowledge of her tragic end. For Marika was murdered in Auschwitz in 1944.

Then there was Zsuzsi Balkányi, only slightly older than myself but bigger, almost grown-up in her ways, very friendly, perhaps a rival of Marika. She was a half-orphan living with her grandparents, both distinguished consultants at a lung clinic. Here too the friendship came through our parents—my mother played bridge with her grandmother— and so the girl was inseparable from her family, as was in any case the custom at the time, even for a 'big girl'. Grandfather Dr Geszti was keen on entertaining the children: watching home cinema for hours, Mickey Mouse and—to the sound of unstoppable laughter—Laurel and Hardy. Grandfather Geszti also led expeditions into the wilderness (he had the key to it from the clinic): we hacked our way into the thick undergrowth amid giant trees, stumbling over twisted roots in an ecstasy of fear.

The years at the primary school (up to 1941) belonged, in my world though no longer in the real world outside, to the age of peace. In the years to come we always talked about that 'peace' as something solid and reliable, an actual experience once upon a time... We had been given a chance to be children, untroubled and innocent, with plenty of food and opportunities for maturing and, above all, a certain trust in our environment, in the decency of grown-ups. And there were recurrent moments of joy, despite my mother's increasing anxieties and my own tendency to lose my way, literally or in states of mind. It is not surprising then that I want to dwell a little longer on such a passing golden age, so short, before the catastrophes.

Summer holidays were occasions of joy yet marked by obstacles and taboos that, I had begun to think, were inseparable from joy—in the wider world as at home. Early journeys abroad were circumscribed by the constant vigilance of our governess who forbade us children, no doubt on parental authority, to climb a mountain, swim in a lake, explore a forest or fraternise with strangers: other children, adults and dogs.

The journey to the Tatra mountains, near Mount Lomnice (1936), started with our being held up by the Slovak customs for an incomprehensibly long time. No doubt we were travelling with lots of luggage:: a trunk, neatly labelled and monogrammed leather suitcases for five persons, extra bags and rucksacks, hatboxes, coats, shawls, rainwear, sticks, umbrellas and parasols. It normally required the services of at least two porters to shift all that baggage when changing trains. We might have aroused suspicion or envy, or else the customs officials were practised sadists. They ordered us to unpack everything. My parents obeyed with mild protests while I thought we should resist. The youthful patriot in me considered that the Slovak officials had no business to be there at all, in the Hungarian Highlands, part of our historic kingdom for a thousand years before the unjust Treaty of Trianon (Versailles). I was taught to think like that. After all, every day in every classroom the children had to pray fervently for the resurrection of Hungary.

When we reached our hotel, I felt a lot happier. Observing so many strangers was itself a source of fun, and I wandered about the hotel, the staircases and the corridors as often as I could. My attention was caught by a tall, gaunt man whom I first observed staring for a long time at his own image in the great mirror on top of a staircase. He then began to descend the stairs as slowly as humanly possible, pausing at every step, humming all the way a distinctly repeated syllable: plum, plum, plum, plum, plum, plum. As the sound of 'plum' signified silly, or off his head, to a Hungarian child at the time, the little scene caused great mirth, lasting days and shared with my sister. We were to meet him again on a walk that took us to some stepping-stones laid across a stream. Our man solemnly warned us that those stones were slippery. He was about to take my hand, as a trusted guide to help me cross the river, when he slipped and fell flat on his face. That event coloured my estimation of guides for a long time.

The alpine meadows on the foothills of the mountains (as high as we were allowed to go) were exhilarating: cows with ribbons and tinkling bells, neatly baked shit-cakes scattered all over the grass and acres of wild flowers visited by butterflies. I wanted to be alone with this meadow world and so I lingered and got lost. I think that was deliberate, a reversal of the great panic of getting lost in a field at age three, a lesser anxiety accompanied by a sense of independence. It probably didn't take long to find me and I must have realised at the time that my governess was more worried than I was. I felt fundamentally at peace among beautiful creatures—at peace with the beautiful adder too, on a dusty track in the village, before dozens of people stamped on its head yelling. It seemed to me that the adder was innocent and the killers got angry for no good reason, and if they wanted to get rid of that small serpent, why did they not anaesthetise it and preserve it in a formaldehyde jar—as in a museum. The mad crowd reminded me of another crowd that once stampeded across a field somewhere near the airport of my city, dragging me along. Avoid the crowd then, avoid it always.

The following year we stopped for only a few hours in Vienna on our way to the Tyrolean Alps. I grumbled about that, about not being able to see the cathedral, the Stefanskirche, and the crocodiles in the zoo which, I speculated, must surely be larger than those in the Budapest zoo. My repeated inquiries concerning the exact size of the crocodiles in the Vienna zoo irritated my Viennese aunt-by-marriage, Anni, and years later, surviving in England, she would still mockingly confront me with 'so you are still looking for the biggest crocodile!'—I understood this as her view of my futile searching, like going on a wild goose chase. My curiosity was rewarded with scorn. On our way to the mountains, the express train stopped at Linz long enough for me to drink a glass of cold milk. I was getting sick with thirst and the precious drink, cool and creamy and copious, handed in through the window of the carriage, tasted like nothing else before or since—it was soothing and intoxicating, the elixir of life I had read about. All I wanted was to stay on in Linz for another glass of that precious liquor, wanted more and more. But the train went on. (Years passed before I heard that Linz was near the birthplace of Hitler, the city he wanted to turn into the world capital of art, with looted art from all over Europe—not too far from Mauthausen concentration camp; and I came to see in that glass of milk a foreshadowing of a can of tea handed into our cattle truck on our way to another concentration camp).

I wondered whether something had gone wrong between my parents in our hotel in Zell-am-See, for suddenly father left us, moving to another resort. First I was told that he couldn't stand the smells reaching his room from the hotel kitchen, and then that he couldn't stand the noise; finally, the children—could that be us?—got on his nerves. In the role of Sherlock Holmes I became suspicious but as I had never witnessed my parents quarrel or even disagree, I had nothing to go on in my investigations. It remained just a minor mystery. Meanwhile around us the lake looked wonderful. Once we rowed out into the middle of the lake and I again concentrated on watching the waves and ripples in the water—in the wake of our rowing boat—to compensate for not being allowed to bathe, again. Just watching the water was enough to make me feel at peace, caught up in another world. At other times I would listen to the roar of a waterfall, watching it break against the rocks in a whirl of white foam—to compensate for not being allowed to go to the top of the mountain (Schmittenhöhe), not even on the funicular. Neither did I get a pair of Tyrolean trousers when other boys were wearing a *lederhose* but that did not prevent me from sliding painfully down a pebbly slope in cotton shorts. I was content with a spiked stick upon which were mounted as many silver plaques as possible to mark the places we had visited and to prove my qualifications as an Alpinist. I learned to interpret the colours on the signposts marking the diverging paths into the forest and up into the heights. And I became weather wise on a modest scale: I studied the cloud formations daily to predict the direction of the rainfall. Yet the great storm came unexpectedly, with hours of deafening thunder. I did not allow myself to get frightened but stood on the veranda watching the lightning strike close by, very close. 'It is dangerous to stand out there', someone shouted, not realising that that was the whole point—it was thrilling to think that the lightning might strike. It did strike, and a chalet, perhaps fifteen meters from our place, burned down. The charred remains could be seen and smelt for days.

I overheard adult whisperings about some threatening situation—politics in Austria, Summer 1937—but I did not know what it was all about. It sounded like the warning about the dangers of the thunderstorm, a warning I had ignored.

5. Age of Anxiety—Beginning

The time came, in September 1941, for me to join my secondary school, the Calvinist Gymnasium, a modern component of a famous four hundred year old college. The old building displayed bronze reliefs of former students—poets and other luminaries—and it housed a historic library and oratory as well as dormitories for boarders; the new building was exceptionally well-equipped with labs, art and music rooms and gyms. But the promise and excitement of my entry into that august institution overlapped with the onset of our age of anxiety. I knew, even before my first term started, that I was not supposed to be admitted to that school at all, since all boys admitted were required to be racially pure, with four Aryan grandparents (as in the English language college already mentioned). Nevertheless, my father managed to get me accepted one way or another; I never found out how it was done but he did have some influence in the church, probably through the good offices of the bishop. I was sworn to absolute secrecy concerning anything to do with our Jewish origins, and I kept my vow despite numerous provocations. Anti-Semitism was rife in the school although officially the Reformed Church was in sympathy with Judaism through its reverence for the Old Testament, like Cromwell and the Puritans in England. One of the physical training masters—who happened to be quite friendly to me personally—made us march around the gym singing abusive songs like 'Jews, Jews, what a lot of filthy Jews settled in the Magyar lands.' A number of boys were also given to occasional anti-Semitic outbursts, including a supposed friend of mine, Feri, a boarder in a college annexe in the villa area of the city. When I visited him he did not fail to point out that the elegant villa opposite his lodgings belonged to some stinking rich Jews: the generous Lénárd family, big farmers and our family friends. I did not protest. Later I was told of an ugly fight between boys from my school and a group from the Jewish Gymnasium.

Meanwhile I kept my vow to be perfectly silent or dumb, a discipline that helped me later when the political situation worsened dramatically; after the war years it lingered as a life-long tendency to secretiveness. No doubt my disguise was helped by the fact that I was, at the time, fair-haired and smooth-faced with a moderately sized nose, and I sported a well-known school cap at a somewhat martial angle with a fine enamel badge proclaiming to all the message of our motto: ORANDO ET LABORANDO, praying and working. I took those words very seriously at that time (and later started a school talk on religion by evoking just those words) feeling that work and prayer were indeed inseparable centres of living. And the school cap was my shield. Once I was about to have my face slapped by an angry bystander who had noticed me whispering to a friend—no doubt something irreverent, perhaps a reference to fascists—in the middle of an extravagantly fervent patriotic speech on the market square. But when the angry man spotted my school badge, he contented himself with some tame rebuke like 'I see you are from that college. Well then, next time cheer like a good *Magyar* boy!'

With or without a badge I walked about fearlessly. I lived the good Protestant schoolboy part assigned to me without too much conflict, for a time. But there were some passing crises, as when I was forced to leave my boy-scout team due to a new race law. That was distressing. 'Officially' I quit for reasons of health, my parents having suddenly rediscovered a murmur in my heart, first diagnosed in my infancy. (In fact, the heart trouble was never fully confirmed, but it remained an actual cause of anxiety for my parents; my father went pale with fright once when he had seen me riding my bicycle with reckless speed).

I was quite patriotic in my own way: I honoured the regent Horthy sufficiently to display his photograph on top of my wardrobe, and I shared the irredentist feelings that enthusiastically welcomed the return to Hungary part of the Highlands (scene of the trouble with the Slovak Customs) and of northern Transylvania. Doubts about the Hungarian re-conquest of pre-1920 territories only emerged when Hungary attacked Yugoslavia to reclaim the Bácska district down to the southern bend of the Danube. There were rumours of pogroms; the recent Treaty of Friendship between Hungary and Yugoslavia was violated and the country tied inextricably to the Axis war machine. Personal anxiety about that invasion coincided with the suicide of the scholarly prime minister Count Teleki who refused to accept Hitler's orders.

Teleki—anti-Nazi though anti-Semitic—belonged to a breed of moderate aristocratic politicians that included Count Bethlen, the regent's long-time principal adviser, and Kállay who later attempted separate peace negotiations with the Western Allies, precipitating the Nazi invasion of the country in 1944. My own moderate patriotism, such as it was, did not blind me to the danger of loud-mouthed nationalists around us. I kept overhearing war-mongering talk from my school-mates' parents: one was an army major who showed off his sword to us and was enthusiastic for a German victory; another was a vet who had worked with Nazi Germans in Tehran and was encouraging his son to collect model planes—Messerschmidts and Stukas that were sure to defeat the Spitfires. All that was mild stuff compared with the amplified roar of Hermann Goering broadcast over the vast ice rink while we were skating.

My school, that bastion of high-minded Protestantism, provided a shelter from the increasingly dangerous outer world; I also learned much there, despite interruptions. It had been an excellent school before the war but it suffered considerable decline during the war. Most of the younger teachers had been called up for military service and, just one year after I began my studies, the entire school was requisitioned for a military hospital and evacuated from its spacious and well-equipped main building into mean temporary accommodation—without benefit of good gyms and laboratories. To this day I attribute my lop-sided knowledge of science, especially Physics, which had always interested me, to learning a lot of theory without practice—without experiments shown, let alone carried out by the pupils. Film shows and excursions were also cut to the minimum. Fortunately, the main arts subjects were still being taught very well, or at least adequately, until the government decided to close all the schools for several months in the autumn of 1943 amid a general sense of national insecurity.

I kept getting top grades in all subjects except gym, while taking intense special interest in Geography, History and Literature—in that order. My interest in Geography was noticed at home, for I would spend hours poring over maps that filled my room and I was soon given a globe. I turned and turned that globe with utmost satisfaction. As the war progressed I would illustrate the movement of armies on the fronts (mostly in Russia in 1942–44) to those who cared to watch and listen. Once I demonstrated 'the war situation' to our maid, at some risk, pointing out that Germany could not possibly win, given the Allies' enormous superiority in territory and resources. 'Just look at that globe', I said, tracing the variously coloured areas of the United States, the Soviet Union and the British Empire. 'Compare that with Germany and all its conquests!' At school I was more cautious, producing only safe copies of all kinds of maps—including an atlas-load of islands and peninsulas from Madagascar to Kamchatka. My teacher praised my map-making skills until the day came when I forgot to mark Gibraltar as a naval base. This was unforgivable negligence in the eyes of the teacher who had demanded a red dot on the map of Spain; so my status as 'a very good student' was instantly reduced to the lowest grade possible. But that teacher must have had a grudge against me as a 'city slicker', judging by the quaint questions he kept addressing to me in a class on natural history, his other subject, questions like 'What factory are eggs produced in, eh?' or 'Well, well, boy, have you ever managed to see the sky?' I met such questions with a wry smile, while missing the marvellous biology teacher who had been called up, a genuine scholar whose practical classes in the botanical gardens stimulated my early interest in plant life—making me collect an album of pressed flowers.

History was another subject that I took to with some passion. I instantly connected the past with current events, drawing elaborate lines, for example, from Bismarck to Hitler or from the Jacobins to the Bolsheviks. Some of my 'insights' were too risky to be uttered in class, so I earned my high grades by faithfully re-presenting whatever our master, Mr Pókos, had told us. He was an enthusiastic teacher with an arresting voice and a splendid note-taking system, something I found useful for the rest of my life. At that time I could still effortlessly store in my mind almost everything this teacher said in class, hardly bothering to read my notes or textbooks. My parents noticed my excited interest in history and trundled out old history books—for instance a huge, guillotine-rich volume on the French Revolution—and also gave me a brand new dictionary of world history. However, my developing historical sense also made me aware of terrors past and present, and I started making predictions about the future, amid successive bouts of fear and hope. My underlying view was something like this: yes, victory will be ours but we might not live to see that day.

Another inspired teacher, János Nagy, taught Hungarian language and literature. He was one of the younger teachers (exempt from the army for some reason) who communicated a love of his subject from the start, not only in words but also in his body language, energetically cruising around the classroom, with long strides, brilliant large eyes and a gently resonant voice. He kept order through paying individual attention to every boy in the class. Although my interest in language—my mother tongue—was formed early, from the moment we were taught to read and write, it was this teacher who instilled in me an enthusiasm in two directions: essay-writing and poetry. I think I regarded the weekly essay, at that stage, as just an enjoyable task, without putting much 'soul' into the writing. I developed a knack for choosing words and forming sentences, with a certain taste for rhetoric—probably inherited from my paternal grandfather, a teacher of German. One of my successes was a speech written for Kossuth, as he might have delivered it to a rapt revolutionary audience in 1848, perhaps when declaring independence from the Habsburgs—an event that took place in the oratory of my school. (In fact, I had more sympathy for the inspired but moderate reformer of that age, Count Szécsenyi, whose life ended with virtual insanity and suicide.) My sister later told me that she envied my facility in writing, and she even found it offensive that I should just dash off my written home-work without much work and then spend the rest of the day cycling or reading books that were not homework. Much later I too came to recognise that it might have been better for my character, and for my writing, if I had learned to wrestle with words, experience the difficulties of writing in depth, at an early stage; eventually I had to pay for my early fluency with a painful major writer's block (in English). But there was nothing in the prescribed curriculum at the time to challenge me on a deeper level; nobody has heard of 'creative writing' in that system. It was only after the war that I went in for a year or two of serious writing—still in Hungarian—ironically just a year before I abandoned that language altogether in favour of writing exclusively in English.

The highlight of the week was poetry reading. The syllabus was quite rigorous and included a considerable number of poems, mostly from the nineteenth and early twentieth century, inevitably dominated by Petőfi and Arany who were placed at the centre of a national pantheon. We knew many of their poems by heart. What haunted me, however, were certain lines from other poets, particularly Vörösmarty (d. 1855):

> a few thousand might reach
> happiness on earth
> if only they could use their days
> with divine wisdom and human will...
> ('Thoughts in a Library')

and Ady (d. 1919):

> An angry angel drummed
> alarm at the sorrowful earth
> ....
> Thought went out drunk
> to a blood-drenched feast of terror
> ....
> Some neglected god will rise
> and take me into death
> ('Memories of a Summer Night')
> Written on the outbreak of war, 1914

It is very difficult to translate Hungarian poetry: the sounds are nearly always lost, coming as they do from a peculiar phonetic system intensified in and through poetry, with frequent alliteration and assonance. (The first line of the Ady poem has *dühölt* and *dobolt* separated by just one word). It was just those sounds that kept me spell-bound at times; and later I probably looked in vain for similar sound values in the seven other languages in which I attempted to read poetry.

Meanwhile, 'the meaning' of my favourite reading, for example the poem just quoted, tended to reinforce the pessimism that surrounded me without eating its way into me; on the contrary, the dark vision became part of my normal vision. After all, I lived in a country whose national anthem ended with the words: 'Our people have suffered /enough/ for both the past and the future'. The injustice of our destiny was being recited all the time: the invasions of the Tartars, the Turks, the Habsburgs, the Russians (in 1849), the dismemberment of the country at Trianon (Versailles) in 1920. A whole anthology could be made out of the frightful cruelties recorded: molten lead poured into the ears of Vazul, King Stephen I's cousin; Dózsa, leader in a peasant revolt, forced to sit on a throne of red-hot iron; the wife of a suspected revolutionary after 1848 whipped dead to extract a confession... Why did I have to be born in such a country? I asked rhetorically. My father seemed to go in for similar questioning, reciting a bizarre little verse: 'Oh why was I born a Jew, why not rather a Negro?' (in the original the Jew and the Negro form a rhyme—*Héber/Néger*). In order to prove that our family had been good citizens of Hungary for generations my father collected a large number of birth-certificates and other documents from all over the country, as already mentioned. (Unfortunately these were lost, not in the war but through negligence when passed on from person to person in my family). My mother had a lively pessimistic view about our long-term chances in the country—we could only lose: as Hungarians if the Western allies win; as Jews if the Germans win; as bourgeois if the Russians win.

Latin poetry, when we came to it in the third year, relieved the mind from the burden of the local past and present and was one antidote against gloomy perspectives. Although Latin was fairly mechanically taught—the old system of learning lists of words and paradigms, with chunks of Caesar and Livy and glimpses of Rome (the temples and the baths could not altogether compensate for the cruelty of the emperors, the circuses, the gladiators and the persecution of Jews and Christians)—every now and again a perfect line would emerge and never sink. In the difficult third year, just before the general collapse of our world, a strange young woman was assigned to us to teach Latin—no doubt a wartime substitute. One day she took it in her head to read to us some love poems of Catullus. It was a risky choice (not on the syllabus at all), made riskier by the fact that she read in a somewhat squeaky voice and passionately. When the class heard her utter some words like *mea Lesbia* there was a general uproar of derision. Not that the boys knew much about lesbians, I think, but the whole atmosphere of intimacy and tenderness conjured up by this woman's reading of the poems seemed alien to the down-to-earth and puritan spirit of our school. I found the diversion exhilarating. The poem beginning

Vivamus, mea Lesbia, atque amamus
 Let us live and love, my Lesbia

stayed with me—together with the unforgettable line:

nox est perpetua una dormienda
  sleep in an everlasting night

Sometimes I overheard fragments from the Roman mass: *Dona nobis pacem*—a source of strength in times of trouble, even though the Reformed Church would hardly have welcomed such an influence. It offered its own pain-killers: Luther's famous hymn *Eine feste Burg* and, a local Hungarian hymn, sung to a haunting tune, exhorting the Protestant galley-slaves, with echoes of the Hebrew Bible, to bear their ills with courage: 'Be brave dear Zion.'...

One young teacher, who always took his twelve-year old pupils seriously, tended to say unforgettable things like 'think of God as X—where X stands for the unknown with changing values and definitions.' Far from metaphysics, some teachers indulged in physical violence: the art master (nick-named Gorilla) crashed a drawing board on a boy's head; a P.E. master wielded a fencing foil for discipline.

Mathematics held my attention for a year or two, but not enduringly after that. The master and I did not get on too well: he was irritable and I was irritating; he wanted total silence in the classroom and I wanted to talk to whoever sat next to me. Consequently he kept sending me out of class and I spent at least half the lessons in the corridor or out in the schoolyard, meditating on some mathematical puzzles, perhaps. Yet I remained interested in the subject—especially in Euclidean geometry, unequal angles in the rhombus and the rhomboid, together with three-dimensional solids that could actually be seen and touched when brought into the classroom. Infinite cardinal numbers were also fascinating, dramatised by another master who kept running around the classroom calling out 'on! on!, on!, on!, on!' to illustrate infinity in a finite way. One day I bumped into some intellectual obstacle and had to ask my sister for help in solving an equation. This was quite a rare experience and I soon decided that maths was not 'my' subject. I managed to obtain a top grade in it but without conviction or commitment, something else I had reason to regret later on. I held the subject in awe remembering that Galileo, 'my hero', had said that the world was written in numbers, but I was already developing a rebellious intuition: mathematics was not infallible any more than the Pope or any religion. This thought was not to be advertised—I feared the Inquisition—and eventually I just distanced myself from the subject, philosophically and practically, and lapsed into ordinary laziness.

Music was another subject in which I did well but ended by disappointing myself—seemingly following a certain pattern. We had a very good teacher who kept encouraging me, in particular praising my hand-written copies of musical scores ('you could earn a living by doing that so well'). I duly subscribed to a musical journal and read and summarised a few articles from it; I took part in the analysis of musical forms and instruments in the relatively few records played to us on a radiogram (a resource reduced due to the wartime cut-backs mentioned). I also joined the school choir, linked to the greater choir of the college, which had a nationwide reputation. I enjoyed participating in the choir despite the long rehearsal hours but one day I sang the wrong note. The master could hear that note from the platform and immediately traced it to my mouth. He walked down to my desk specially and asked me, quite abruptly, to sing that musical phrase again. So I did sing it—wrong again. Hearing the false note repeated made the master so angry that he instantly expelled me from the choir. I cannot tell whether my faulty singing on that day was a genuine mistake or a wilful negative response to an authoritarian gesture. Whatever the reason, it ended my active involvement in music-making, as I still had not followed up an earlier promise to my mother to take lessons in piano playing. And my voice was left untrained, though some people said I might end up in the opera. That was blarney, no doubt, but I did have a good treble voice, loved singing, and I later came to see the choir episode as just one more loss, a self-inflicted failure. By way of compensation, I learned to listen to music. My parents took me to concerts in the hall of the Golden Bull hotel—some of these were truly festive occasions. Once I saw the old Dohnányi put his hand on the head of a very promising, barely ten-year old pianist, a handsome, fair-haired boy, Tamás Vásáry. He and I later came to play together: we played not music but electric trains, in the entrance lobby of the bank. Tamás came from a distinguished family in Debrecen (including a former burgomaster and M.P.) and I think it was his older sister who brought us together. The sister's wedding in the Great Church was the first time I attended a wedding; I was preparing to make a celebratory speech but nobody asked me.

These were also the twilight years, moving deeper into the war with frightening changes and rumours. But as twilight has many patches of light, the years before the end were still full of bright events. What is more, everybody—my parents, my teachers, and probably the whole social world around us—contributed to playing 'life goes on' games. After all, the war was far away, physically at least. Every now and again there was an air raid alarm without an air raid; we just trooped down to the well-built concrete shelter of the bank, usually in the middle of the night, and waited for the all clear signal. I can't remember being afraid at the time. One had learned to get dressed with lightning speed and run down the stairs, which had always been something of a sport for me. It was a skill, like learning to put on a gas mask early in the war when there was a mustard gas alert.

Food rationing had started but that did not seem to impoverish our diet—the children's diet—probably because my parents had built up large stores of everything: eggs and apples in the loft, preserves and all things conservable in the pantry, large containers of lard in hidden places, potatoes in a specially constructed bunker, as if preparing for a long siege. We also kept a pig at the back of the bank yard, which was duly slaughtered in December—I refused to watch though I later inspected with disgust the sausage-making process, filling the washed-out guts with freshly chopped-up meat from the pig. Food no longer available in shops was bought on the black market, smuggled in by good country folk in discreet wicker baskets. We missed oranges and bananas, figs and dates and so on but that only encouraged the growth of nostalgia. Meanwhile, the relative luxury of our home life was hardly disrupted in its daily rhythm—the cook still prepared good meals and the maid brought in the dishes for lunch at a quarter to two precisely.

There was extra domestic help for spring cleaning, for washing and ironing, for mending clothes, supplemented by help from two bank servants, Szito (kind, bald and sporting a black moustache, he had taught me to ride a bicycle and rubbed iodine on my open wound after a fall) and Jacko, with occasional help from the concierge, Uncle Harangi. He and Jacko had one thing in common: they both were in the habit of beating their wives, Harangi about once a week, Jacko less frequently. That could not be concealed from a boy with good hearing. It was a very nasty habit but then it was a habit—the working classes were different, everybody seemed to think. And I went on talking to all those helpers, usually about politics. Jacko talked mostly about the first World War, recalling in a trembling voice the horrors of the bloodshed on the Italian front which turned the river Isonso red; Harangi preferred to talk about the ongoing war, convinced that the countries that had most gold would win. I knew that he was referring to the City of London. Sári, our illiterate but shrewd cook, discussed politics with me in the kitchen—between hammering meat for schnitzel or stretching the strudel pastry—just as she would discuss each day's menu with my mother. And still the parquet floors were polished by cleaning women dancing around with brushes strapped to their feet; and still the armchairs were covered in dust sheets in the hot months and the smell of mothballs and naphthalene filled the air in the closed 'Baroque' lounge; and still there was a fuss when I accidentally poured water on the white damask table cloth—for the wetness might seep through and damage the veneer of the table. Tailors and shoemakers still came to our home to take measurements; the barber came to shave my father and a hairdresser attended to my mother, with occasional visits from the foot therapist or corn-cutter (picturesquely called 'hen's eye cutter' in Hungarian).

It was my mother who first alerted me to the gathering dangers. Her anxiety was sharpened by the news that kept reaching us—more often than not bad news from the summer of 1940 on—and passed on to me, probably against her intention. On one occasion she and I were together in the Great Wood, sitting on a bench in a sort of grove, my idea of bliss. Suddenly we heard the news—did a passer-by interrupt us?—Paris had fallen to the Nazis (14 June 1940). My mother got very upset, and no wonder, muttering something like: 'can nobody stop them? It's terrible!' But fear of Nazi Germans did not prevent her from talking to me about German classics, especially *Immensee* and *Buddenbrooks*.

The next crisis was provoked by events in Romania later that year. Hungary had demanded the return of former territories in Transylvania (following the Soviets demanding Bessarabia) with Germany and Italy acting as mediators and eventually enforcing the return of Northern Transylvania to Hungary. Before that, in midsummer, there was a real possibility of a local war within the larger war breaking out. My mother was alarmed by the danger whilst I was trying to enjoy, in my fashion, a boy-scout holiday in North East Hungary, with a base camp placed in a muddy little backwater, the village of Makkoshotyka, where there was only one decent privy; it belonged to the local priest, as I discovered when reconnoitring the area in search of privacy. One day, in the middle of the week when I was supposed to go out with the rest of the team on a trek, my mother came to visit. Alone she walked straight into the mud and horse-dung of the village streets, exquisitely dressed in a summer frock and polished town shoes with fairly high if not high heels. She had come to make sure that I was all right in the middle of the deepening crisis, seeing that the Romanian frontier was not far away. Next, on our way back by train from the camp, I heard my name being called from the station platform at Nyiregyháza, a town only about fifty kilometres north of our city of Debrecen. To my surprise I was asked to step down from the train and I was instantly transported in a buggy to the comfortable home of the local Credit Bank manager where I was given a shower and a good meal, and had my torn trousers mended as well. Then I was escorted back to the station and into a first class carriage on a fast train, instead of the slow freight train I had been rescued from. I was somewhat bewildered by the whole improvised adventure for, unaware of war rumours, I tended to view my mother's intervention with a certain amusement—a scene in my private theatre. But I said not a word.

Things deteriorated fast after Hungary invaded Yugoslavia in Spring 1941, as already mentioned. Atrocities and pogroms were carried out in the 'liberated' Bácska region by the Hungarian soldiery, secretly confirmed. From that year Hungary became a solid military member of the Axis, and there was no escape, if such an escape ever was a realistic hope. Before the outbreak of the war my parents must have discussed (but 'not before the children') emigration either to England, where my uncle Laci and his family had escaped from Vienna in 1938, or to Switzerland where the family had some money but nowhere near enough for settling down. An ex-bank manager aged almost fifty was unemployable in a foreign country. Yet the sense of living in a prison country must have intensified my parents' anxiety. The prison walls surrounded us totally after Hungary had joined Germany in the invasion of Russia (22 June 1941) and had declared war on Britain too, out of sheer stupidity. Soon fresh rumours started circulating concerning the maltreatment of the special Jewish Labour Battalions sent to the Russian front while the Bárdossy regime stiffened the race laws. Jews were being debarred from practicing one profession after another and my father was personally responsible for dismissing each year a quota of his Jewish bank clerks while he himself was still in charge.

We received news about the war not only from local sources but also through the BBC: my father listened regularly to both the Hungarian and the German language broadcasts, and I listened with him frequently. That was always an exciting experience, beginning with the well-known victory signal, and it was also reassuring to hear those balanced and articulate messages delivered by confident-sounding voices. Some of the broadcasts were even amusing like those given by an Oxford historian, C.A. McCartney, with a somewhat halting but still impressive command of Hungarian. We felt encouraged even though the news was getting grimmer most of the time (until late 1942). The radio had to be turned down to minimum volume so that the domestics could not hear that we were listening to the BBC; soon it became illegal to listen and the broadcasts were regularly jammed, but that did not deter us in the least. I fancied myself as a junior war correspondent who had a duty to attend and observe.

6. An Oasis in War

The long summer holidays remain among the zones of light in those twilight years. Our inland travel had many high points but in a sense I no longer 'needed' to travel, for I had discovered how to travel inward. I was quite content to be left alone, especially in the Great Wood and in the Strand (swimming pools). At some point in time I was allowed to cycle out to the forest on my own, along safe paths. Once there, I would re-live my childhood fascination with trees, frogs and insects. I would climb into the hollow of a tree and deepen the hollow. The wood was pulp-like and all that was needed was a little scraping for the damp layers to peel off or else dry sawdust started to run out, like sand in an hourglass.

Throwing stones at an anthill was a little frightening like making a toadstool bleed. For thousands of ants would suddenly emerge and scatter, squirting some sticky substance which was a threat to the eyes. The air was full of summer flies and dragonflies. Someone had told me that the dragonfly only lived for one day. So I let the dragonfly descend on my hand and stay there as long as it wanted to. It was awesome to think that its brightness was for one day only—its iridescence, its large head, long slender body and its strong, translucent wings would perish soon after being looked at. The dragonfly emitted a secret buzz into the silence. Then I saw that its beauty was not perfect for its long black body had a predatory, clawing thrust.

By contrast the rings on the tree stump seemed to go on growing. The rings in the water when a stone was thrown were different again—forming and vanishing, living and dying for the moment. But when a stone was thrown the frogs started to croak, mocking my impressions.

The swimming pools were a source of joy. Pools in the plural, for there was a large cold pool leading to two warm thermal pools, frequented mostly by the elderly. I was taught to swim by a giant, broad-shouldered trainer whose skin had turned Indian brown in constant exposure to the sun; it had a permanent shine, a mixture of oil and sweat. He held me in the water in a sort of cradle made of rope, repeating over and over in a seemingly infinite series of days: 'hands apart one, legs together two, legs drawn forward three', and so on. I marvelled at his patience until one day he suddenly roared at me because I had made some clumsy movement: 'do you want to drown? then drown you fool! Go on, drown yourself!' When I had overcome my initial apprehension, I became quite a confident swimmer and diver and I was soon allowed to go in at the deep end. However, I never enjoyed diving from the high diving board or staying underwater longer than a few seconds; I kept getting fits of atavistic fear—drowning, drowning now. I knew that some of my contemporaries were much more adventurous. I was not above joining other 'naughty boys' in pranks, such as tickling the legs of the old ladies half-asleep in a peaceful alcove of the thermal pool or dive-bombing with precision so as to make a maximal splash around an unsuspecting swimmer. In the middle of a thunderstorm—quite frequent in the heat of midsummer—we dived into the water and waited for the lightning to strike, but it never did. It was delightful to watch the surface of the pool transformed into a lake ruffled with thousands of little spouts or crowns, as we called them. We thought nothing of pissing into the water, when the rain lasted for some time, perhaps believing that a little urine would leave no trace in, or might even enrich, the deep waters of the pool. The total area surrounding the swimming pools was large enough for little expeditional tours: sneakily inspecting other people's cabins when a door was left open; we had a small cabin of our own for morning visits, in the afternoon it was used by the kind, childless Eisler couple—a dermatologist and his wife Anna, distant relations on my father's side. I was fascinated by a drinking fountain and played with it for hours while watching children build sandcastles and tunnels (aged ten, I no longer considered myself a child); I also pretended to be an umpire for water polo or a supervisor of the supervisors as they went about their business of adjusting the water level or draining the pool down to the slimy concrete floor, exposing its debris of swimmers' belongings—ribbons, shower caps, belts and keys. Sometimes I listened to adult conversation while comparing the size and styling of female bathing costumes and the quality of male body hair on a scale from ape to child-like furlessness. On one occasion I strayed onto a secluded sunbathing terrace inhabited by a colony of nude men who did not welcome me. I tried to make myself leave invisibly but, just then, a row of those big men became more visible—sporting huge purplish balls; they looked grotesque, so I could only hope that mine would never grow into such an outsize appendage.

My sister and I went swimming almost every morning, taking the tram to the pool, using our season ticket. I liked riding on that shiny yellow tram, the sound of its brakes, its whine, its speeding and slowing, and the calling out of the stops by the conductor. Everybody travelled on the tram, democratically. On an average day dozens of interesting faces could be scrutinised, eyes returning your discreet gaze as if wanting to say something that could not be said. Every day you might see the same tall, long-faced, bespectacled young man hanging on to a strap on the tram, babbling and moaning—a pitiful sight. The retarded son of a local physician, he was free to spend all day travelling, trying to talk to anyone around, incomprehensibly. Later we heard that he and his parents committed suicide together when the Nazis invaded the country.

7. Sister Eva

I keep mentioning my sister, so it is time to present her. Clearly Eva and I shared a lot of experiences, especially journeys and outings as well as tastes, and we were friends and allies without being all that close. Eva was three years older than I and by the time I was eight we had separate rooms, soon to be followed by separate secondary schools and friendships, and we also began to show different orientations, as in her talent for math and mine for arts. Generally our family 'style' of loving tended to be a little reticent: there was not much demonstrative hugging or kissing going on. There was no need for a taboo on incest for a certain distance to be kept between us. There was, however, a strong sense of belonging, caring for each other, and a growing awareness that we had a shared destiny. Despite a few sister-brother quarrels, accompanied by nothing worse than screaming, pinching and kicking, there was no deep-seated or emotionally enduring rivalry between us—so that I cannot remember what our fights were about. By contrast, as we were growing up, we tended to experience real concern when one of us got into trouble. Thus my sister became truly worried when I was marked as a virtual delinquent: accused of having tripped up a boy of my age on the skating rink. The boy had a fall and hurt himself badly: a sprained ankle or something worse. The boy's father threatened litigation unless we offered compensation—his telephone call came at lunchtime when any interruption was supposed to be banned. My sister was so upset by this incident that she kept making anxious entries about it in her diary. Meanwhile I took refuge in detachment mixed with defensiveness, something I arrived at instinctively (as later in much tougher challenges). I denied that I had tripped up the boy deliberately—it must have been an accidental collision. As for the boy, I considered him a clumsy idiot, and the father a blackmailer. None of this would have helped me if there had been witnesses to prove me guilty but there were none. However, my sister remained convinced that I had done something wicked; that made her more anxious but it also gave her a sense of solidarity.

In turn I became worried about Eva one day. At the main entrance to our building—a large gate—the concierge informed me that my sister was seriously ill. My first response was to treat this as a routine event, for my sister did get tonsillitis all too frequently and I thought it was a 'mere' recurrence of that malady. 'There are three doctors looking after her', the concierge told me, and I was forbidden to go upstairs to see her until the consultation was over. That went on forever. So I ran around in circles in the backyard of the bank building until they summoned me at long last. There was to be no operation, the tonsils were to stay—an anticlimax. Alarming symptoms had been diagnosed even so, with a risk of complications, perhaps diphtheria; the family doctor and the specialist could not agree about the treatment so they called in a second consultant to our home for the final decision. (I must add in brackets that later generations do not realise how dangerous infectious diseases were in our time—diphtheria, scarlet fever, polio, even measles.) I had an image of my sister as strong and robust yet, apart from those bouts of tonsillitis, she kept suffering from various minor afflictions—car sickness, train sickness or just being sick (especially after consuming an overdose of apricots in our uncle's orchard); she was regularly bitten all over her body by mosquitoes and other insects (whereas insects abhorred my blood, probably finding it too acid), and later she also developed hay-fever. Meanwhile I seemed to escape illnesses and allergies, though I was still regarded as a fragile boy by my parents, partly because I was so thin that people would pinch my arm and complain that I had no muscles, and partly because of that early alarm concerning a murmur in my heart.

The death of my sister's canary, Hansi, was an occasion for mourning. I think we regarded that death as a symbol of our darkening times. Long before the little bird died—aged over ten—she stopped singing, stopped quite suddenly one morning, without notice. I found that abrupt end disturbing and I wanted some kind of an explanation. 'She was old and no longer felt like singing', some such words did not satisfy me at all. Eva and I did a few things together quite spontaneously. The backyard of the bank building was also our playground and there we improvised games and little adventures. In winter we had a snowball fight which was exciting and hilarious, surprisingly so because it was not 'our style' and I never liked the smell and taste of snow. In summer we went hunting maybugs: picking them off the fruit trees one by one in great numbers and dipping them into buckets. This was not an activity I approved of, despite being lectured on the damage these insects could cause to the fruit. I considered my sister too enthusiastic in her campaign against the maybugs, perhaps because she was so fond of apricots. It seemed a pity to disturb the paired maybugs as they clung to each other peacefully—perhaps they should have been spared until they completed their decorous mating.

With the onset of puberty came sex-consciousness. I will come to this later but here I should mention that the more I knew the less I wanted to discuss the serious business of copulation with my sister—or with anyone else. I had little or no respect for either party: the softies who kept babbling about birds and bees and the toughies at school who talked smut without, I considered, any detailed knowledge of biology, whilst I would have got a

51

distinction in any exam concerning procreation, I thought—as interesting as the study of the brain. It seemed to me curious that 'everybody' should be so confused about this activity which I simplified by deciding that a) it was a natural function to keep the general population going if necessary and b) a proper gentleman and lady would probably NOT do it unless absolutely unavoidable. In any case there would not be enough time for it if one devoted oneself to higher things like learning and constructing things. I was in some such frame of mind when somehow, I don't know why, my sister brought up the subject. I then rapidly put a finger from my right hand through the oval created by my left thumb and finger; my sister nodded and repeated the gesture—it took up less than half a minute, more than enough time spent.

8. Györ—Grandmother Olga

I seldom saw members of our extended family because they all lived, by the standards of the time, quite far away: my paternal grandmother, an uncle and two aunts in Budapest (220 kilometres) and my maternal grandmother in Györ, (another 100 kilometres), my unknown birthplace that I left when six months old. (It is an elegant small Baroque city halfway between Budapest and Vienna.) The logistics of travelling to Györ involved changing trains in the capital, accompanied by intense excitement and fuss: shouts of 'Porter, porter! Taxi! taxi!', the burden of luggage, anxiety about time-tables and delays, unreliable information, the scramble for seats whether reserved or not: usually second class, for the first class was too expensive for a family accompanied by the governess and the third class was over-crowded, smelly and slummy; there uncouth fellow travellers produced leaking juice, huge tomatoes that split open and crumbling biscuits. There was further fuss about the right clothes for rapidly changing temperatures, sudden fits of tiredness and train sickness (Eva), dirty lavatories not fit for children, soot in the eyes when the window was opened and suffocation when the window was closed. The ordinary exigencies of the old railway age were exaggerated by travel fever (given expression especially by my mother) as if to prove that travelling was an actual or threatening ordeal.

The aftermath of the journey added to the excitement: for example, hunting for the children's hats left behind on the train. A day could be spent telephoning and telegraphing Austrian Railways and waiting for those objects, no doubt indispensable, to travel back to their owners all the way from Vienna. Arrival at my grandmother's house was always accompanied by a lot of hustle and bustle: an excited welcome, then a resonant shout for hot baths and towels: 'Vilma! Vilma! Hurry up!' (Vilma was a chamber maid). After the bedtime ceremonies, we slept in huge Victorian beds in a room that had a little wooden box fixed to the doorpost; I no sooner spotted this strange object than I started asking questions, and got unsatisfactory, embarrassed answers. After all, I was not supposed to probe our Jewish connection. And I never found out what the scripture said on the parchment called *mezuza*.

All that commotion of travelling and arriving was followed by precious peace: the dialogue of barking dogs and the sound of trains being shunted to and fro on the nearby marshalling yards all through the night—a cradling rhythm I came to love.

Later, after the war, we always thought of grandmother Olga's way of life as representing a vanished world—privileged and protected, tiny discomforts accompanied by cries and complaints. But before 1944 nobody seemed to foresee the total destruction to come. It all seemed 'natural': the predictable daily rituals, the elaborate domestic arrangements with two servants looking after one old lady, only telephones and telegrams disturbed an otherwise 'Edwardian' order. That order survived World War I and grandfather Ödön's death (1926?), though he had personally lost a large fortune in war loans (never repaid) and in the great inflation that annihilated money. Grandmother Olga still lived in a fine two-storey family house; part of it was let, together with the moderate-sized apartment block next door, also owned by her. She was then in her sixties, a *grande dame* with an oval face and a long neck—a precious necklace dangling always—tall, well-dressed and perfumed (usually with *eau de cologne* 4711), attended by a hairdresser daily. She was a little remote from children with her formal manners and hyper-correct language, carefully enunciating refined words: 'so you are going to your summer resort' (üdülö) instead of 'on holiday', for example. She had to be constantly reassured that everything was in order as she thought that something was bound to go wrong. She carried all the keys of the household—keys to the pantry, to the cupboards and locked rooms in her large apartment—in a little silver casket with a handle. In summer time most of the rooms were dark, the Venetian blinds drawn, the sofas and armchairs sleeping under dust covers, the smell of naphthalene abounding. Whenever I wandered around the dusky rooms I could catch glimpses of almost hidden treasures: a *vitrine* with Meissen porcelain figurines or silver candlesticks on large old-fashioned sideboards. Apart from such curiosities the place would have been boring. There was not a lot to do except play with grandmother's dachshund, amusing enough but not as amusing as the wildly untrained dachshunds in a story we read where the dogs were constantly up to tricks like tripping up their lady owner by twisting the lead around her. Occasionally we, the children, were allowed to roam around the well-kept park facing grandmother's house, in a strictly limited way, as usual. Once or twice a week, we were invited to a patisserie for a special treat of high quality water ices served in silvery cups with little silver spoons by a waiter as we were sitting around a marble table like perfect children. Or we would walk down to the Danube arm, lingering through the beautiful Baroque streets of the inner city, to watch the swimmers and the rowers—without ever practicing those skills. Or we would be taken to the ' kiosk', where grandmother played bridge, to be shown off to the assembled old ladies who would ask embarrassingly personal questions that were supposed to be answered politely—an immense effort of self-discipline was required to perform such a 'good boy' act without grinning or grimacing impertinently. Then the day came to drive out to the Jewish cemetery on the island in a one-horse cab, a fiacre. My mother stood in long silence above the great white marble grave where her father, Ödön Szántó, lay buried; the other half of the grave was waiting for grandmother. After some searching we found, close by, the black marble grave of grandfather Emmanuel Kárpáti—teacher, just the one word; there too one side of the large grave was set aside for my other grandmother. Neither grandmother had a proper burial: Olga was murdered in Auschwitz in 1944 and Serena died in the terrible siege of Budapest early in 1945.

9. Budapest—Grandmother Serena and Uncle Miklós

While staying with grandmother Olga, a telephone call announced the sudden death of her son-in-law and my uncle, Andor. Travel fever turned into an emergency forcing us as all to re-pack at speed and take the next fast train to Budapest. My mother and Olga were dressed in black—our whole world turned black, the children imitating the grown-ups. We were to comfort Aunt Agnes, my mother's elder sister, now a widow not much over forty years old. I only glimpsed her as a tall veiled figure dressed in black from head to foot, her face barely visible under the long black veil. It was out of the question for us to stay in her splendid apartment overlooking a corner of the parliament by the Danube, for Aunt Agnes, childless herself, could not cope with children. Nor were we allowed to attend the funeral of our uncle and everything concerning this death remained hushed up. I remembered my uncle vaguely as a pale-faced, bulky man with a big dog and a big chauffeur-driven Buick; he had been an absent landlord for years, staying in one sanatorium after another suffering from heart disease that required rest (so they thought at the time), a very expensive but wrong treatment. He must have been the richest living member of our extended family, competently managing a large tenant farm and other assets. Now that he was dead I overheard a buzz of anxious questions between long silences: what if… what was going to happen, how will Agnes manage at all, the estate, the will, the confusion, the lawyers, the heirs, what if those vultures from uncle's clan descended to pick his bones and possessions.

So we went to stay with my other grandmother, in a modest flat in the unfashionable part of Buda—quite a contrast. There all was serene. She lived up to her name, Serena, in every way: welcoming us warmly but quietly and somehow accommodating two children comfortably in narrow space, helped by just one maid—unlike Olga and Agnes who could afford two domestics. She was round both in face and figure, silver hair neatly tied in a bun, dressed in black or in black-and-grey or black with little white polka dots, or dark blue for lightness, and she sailed around the house like a boat. She tried to entertain us, while mother was out to tend on Agnes, in all sorts of ways: showing family photographs, telling and reading stories, reciting stale yet somehow charming proverbs and doggerel verses like 'winter too cold, summer too bold, autumn too wet, good weather never', spoken with the usual serene smile. I tried to find out about my dead grandfather but Serena was very discreet and said little—just that he had been a very good German teacher and terribly disappointed when pensioned off early instead of becoming headmaster, a position he had hopes for. He was considered to be something of a 'lady's man' and an irrepressible talker: everybody had to hang on his lips. And yes, he was about to be hanged by some revolutionaries during the dictatorship of the proletariat in 1919—due to a mistaken identity. He was fond of staying in Vienna where he once fell asleep at the Opera in the midst of listening to Wagner's *Parsifal*. And he died in Vienna of a sudden heart attack. An all too elliptical life story.

I started reading some of grandmother's books, a novel by Jókai, with a hero called Kárpáty (our family name chosen by grandfather to replace an un-Hungarian name) and a lurid magazine story which the maid was reading—about a French baker and his adulterous wife, which I was not allowed to go on relishing for it was 'not fit for small boys', said my grandmother serenely. I appreciated some of my grandmother's possessions: a superb paper-weight with a whorl of coloured threads shimmering under the glass; a silver-topped cane which I wanted to borrow; and a strange pack of playing cards laid out in patterns by grandmother hour after hour on her own—a game of patience. Despite her serenity, a certain amount of apprehension hung in the air here too, for grandmother was pessimistic about Hungarian politics, speaking with dread about extreme right wing prime ministers from Gömbös to Imrédy. She warned me not to talk about serious things (i.e. the family and politics) with the maid who might be anti-Semitic, at least the girl had hurled insults at a rag-and-bone man probably because she thought he was a Jew. And, in general, people could no longer be trusted. However, she was lucky to have decent neighbours like the old lady next door who had travelled as far as Egypt to see the tomb of Tutankhamun—rare in those days. It was easier to talk about the long ago past than about the present.

I strongly associate Budapest with Uncle Miklós. He was considered eccentric by the family: relatively unsuccessful, a middle-ranking bank clerk, who had married 'beneath' him (according to Serena who was otherwise not particularly snobbish), with no children and no house or grand apartment in the city, only a country cottage—where the apricot orchard tempted my sister to eating an overdose of the fruit. He had a tendency to sudden outbursts of anger with little tolerance for fools. Both his temperament and his relative under-achievement were attributed to his war experiences in World War I., when he was taken prisoner on the Russian front and, after many misadventures, was eventually shipped back on a long sea voyage from Vladivostok, in a damaged state. 'A little wild' was my mother's expression for my uncle. For a boy of my age Uncle Miklós was fascinating just because he was less conventional than other members of the family. You could literally smell his presence—a mixture of cigar smoke and brilliantine—and he walked with a kind of swaggering sway, probably a balancing act as he was over-weight. He drank a lot of beer—*Pils*—another habit not cultivated by my parents; I loved to watch the beer being poured into his tall glass forming a big foaming white head. I don't think he ever shouted at me, on the contrary he smiled a lot, especially when listening to me singing a funny song I learned somewhere—based on an interminable cumulative story with amusing refrains—which I had to sing with several encores before getting on a train that I nearly missed thanks to his enchantment with the song. He also took us on sight-seeing trips: to the circus where he laughed at the tumbling clowns more heartily than his brooding nephew; to the zoo where the scrawny wolves were disappointing but where I could re-live my old obsession with the jaws of the crocodile; to the high wooded hills above Buda; and to Margit island, the long island on the Danube with its acres of flowers and vast swimming pools. He added to the excitements of Budapest by letting us actually see it: taxis roaring past traffic lights, beautiful theatres and museums, palaces and bridges, the tunnel under Castle Hill where the stone lions of the Scot-built Chain Bridge were supposed to sleep through the night (I pretended to believe that to please uncle), the elegant cafes with crowds of idle cake-eaters and the abundance of flashing neon lights. These were sights not seen in a provincial town and it was a thrill to discover a throbbing metropolis with a million inhabitants; and a sense of danger from a pro-Nazi government.

Uncle Miklós was also good company when my sister and I came to Budapest to join a holiday camp up in the so-called Swabian hills—for three summers in succession. We would travel with him on the funicular railway that moved slowly enough to allow one to see the rich foliage and the birds in the trees. The motors of the little train hummed soothingly, quite distinct from the roar or splutter of other motorised transport. And the gradual ascent or descent combined the pleasures of a lift with a desire for flying (not yet experienced).

I would have preferred to spend more time with my uncle roaming the busy streets of Budapest but that was out of the question, for a 'change of air', beyond the zone of city dust, was the principal stated goal of our being at the camp at all. The rules of the camp were quite strict, as discipline had to be kept among all those lively, somewhat show-offish children, mostly from the capital's upper middle class, mostly Jewish or of Jewish origin for conversion was wide-spread; I recall a group session when each of us in turn volunteered to declare his or her religion, quite a range from Roman Catholic to all the varieties of Protestantism including a Unitarian. When not taking part in organised games or excursions, the children indulged in endless chattering and gossip—much more so than their contemporaries in the provinces—with a tendency to boast about their achievements. I made no friends. In any case I was too busy practicing for our own Olympic games, entering for the hundred-metre run and the high jump and the long distance jump competitions. I kept winning a series of first prizes—always chocolate, heaps of chocolate. I had got used to coming out top in school subjects but never before in sports (I have already mentioned my father's anxiety about my poor performance in the school gym). My brief fame as a gold medallist must have been due to the relatively feeble fitness of my metropolitan competitors and my innate tendency to be good at almost everything for a short span, like sprinting as distinct from long-distance running which bored me to tears.

We played a war game that was quite original. Each team was equipped with random numbers on distinctly coloured cardboard shields, which were tied to every player's head. These numbers were visible at a close range but hard to read from a distance or when the player had found a good hiding place. It was forbidden to cover up the number with one's hands or in any other way. Reading out the numbers of the enemy, the rival team, was the goal of the war game: when your number has been correctly called you were dead, and the team that had killed the largest number of numbers was the winner. Part of the excitement came from the challenge of moving across fairly difficult terrain: climbing and sliding up and down rough hill country for hours, perhaps for half a day. I quickly learned the art of reading numbers at a distance and was tolerably successful in avoiding detection but I had a weakness: a tendency to be caught out when I lapsed into contemplation, thinking about the horrors of the real war going on—out there, far away but frightening.

The best place for contemplation was from on high, for example looking down on the vast panorama of Budapest spread out under you from the viewing tower on Mount János or Mount Szécsényi. These were my favourite excursion points and it may have been there that I developed a life-long addiction to views: the world seen from towers, steeples, rooftops, hilltops and mountain peaks. Fortunately I have never suffered from vertigo, merely from a morbid tendency to wonder what it would be like to be pushed or to jump from one of those dizzying heights. I would recall the legend of St Gellert, pushed, a victim of violence, hurtling down the high Budapest hill named after him; and I would even think of the temptation of Jesus, urged to take a leap into the air by Satan.

10. Inland Journeys

In addition to those holiday camps, attended through three summers, I also took part in a fairly adventurous scout camp near the backward north-eastern village of Makkoshotyka in 1940 (mentioned earlier). I will return to that place briefly only to record the still puzzling responses my mere presence in the camp (for I cannot recall any good deeds or bad ones either) provoked. One day when the whole team was gathered for some function—some public discussion—I was suddenly called by the Scout Chief (a schoolmaster) to come forward and stand at ease. He then embarked on a somewhat solemn speech in which he held me up as some kind of role model for other boys, saying something like 'this boy is clear-headed, he knows what he wants, with genuine ideals that will guide him through life', and so on. I had no idea how I had earned this praise and I was naturally embarrassed, even more than at the time of my over-dressed mother's visit (p.46 above). The punishment came soon enough. One night, in the middle of a night, I woke to a bright light—a torch shone straight into my eyes—and an order: 'Stand up at once!' I tried to obey but could not stand up for the simple reason that my feet were tightly tied with rope. Then somebody, an older boy, brought a mirror so that I could study my own interesting face blackened from forehead to mouth with thick black boot polish. There was some guffawing but I was eventually freed and cleaned up, probably because the perpetrators were afraid of being caught in the act. I did not protest at the time or after, merely remarking, to myself, that there were too many idiots in this world. A few days later, when we went bathing in a lake, it seemed to me that my bathing trunks were unusually wet and heavy at the back. I reached down to see what it was and pulled out a toad—speckled yellow and slimy and fully alive. I simply went on with my planned swimming. What I liked best in the camp was the singing by the open fire, traditional but new to me. Some of the songs were based on age-old pentatonic Hungarian tunes, melancholy and haunting, urging us to celebrate the camp fire for

> God knows when we shall see it again
> God knows when we shall see it again.

In 1941 it was my good fortune to visit the estate of my Aunt Agnes in the county of Fejér (Transdanubia) in my father's company. That journey offered me a chance to get a last glimpse of the old agricultural world, not yet fully modernised and still recognisably feudal in character. Already on arrival at the nearest country railway station we were greeted by signs of bounty together with backwardness: an elegant cane-framed carriage drawn by two fine brown horses, with a liveried driver seated on his box, waited for us. The chief steward bowed and joined us on a tour of inspection which was to last several days. He spoke to my father with respect, even a degree of deference (addressing him as 'honoured Sir', a standard greeting) and he was very friendly towards me but quietly shut me up when I started asking questions about the farm, making a gesture of lips sealed and remarking that 'the walls have ears'. I could see (or feel) no walls, only rolling fields of golden rye as far as the edge of the horizon—freedom from fear. Soon we reached a modest country house, more modest than it need have been if my late uncle and my aunt had chosen to stay there more often but they had little taste for country living. I was given a spacious enough bedroom with a large double bed and a huge wardrobe. At nightfall an older woman servant came in to wish me good night, painstakingly lighting a well-designed paraffin lamp that gave a flame at once bright and mellow. The ceramic and copper of the lamp-holder reflected the soft light, and then the whole room was suffused with a dark light, excelling in beauty any other light, I thought, even the light of chandeliers.

During the next few days I saw many facets of life and work on the farm. I delighted in those large cornfields (mostly rye) and fingered the ears of corn, separating the chaff from the seeds in a private act of threshing. I watched sun-browned muscular men straining to lift and cart heavy sacks of corn to a barn hour by hour. Cutting across the broad acres huge steam harvesters moved to the rhythm of a strong pumping beat—one of the few machines allowed by a law designed to protect agricultural labourers from over-rapid modernisation. Then came the feeding time for animals, especially hundreds of pigs and their litter, the piglets all striped as if wearing handsome pyjamas; geese being force-fed (a horror more strongly felt later than at the time); women labourers singing as they worked in a field; dozens of poor children gazing at us speeding past them in our carriage. Wherever we went we were still accompanied by the chief steward but the coachman had shed his livery for an ordinary working day.

Left alone I kept walking around the house exploring the orchards—maturing apples and pears—the kitchen gardens, the plots of red paprika and the extensive vineyards. The green and red grapes were not yet ripe but already too tempting not to be tasted, a little hard and sour but 'real'. The sun was shining all the time but it was never too hot, or I did not feel the heat since I was, after all, a mere idle spectator not required to lift a sack of corn (I tried to and failed even to budge one). So it was like a local paradise until something disturbing happened. My father stood beside me in a vineyard one evening, when I suddenly heard him groan and, looking up, I could see that he had gone very pale. 'What's the matter?' I asked, having never seen him like that before. 'I am... just a little dizzy', he said and leaned against a post. He stood there for several long minutes, motionless and silent. I had no idea what to say or do. At long last he straightened himself and together we walked back silently to the house for early bedtime. Next day and later I heard no mention whatever of this mysterious 'attack', which remained for me just a moment of fear. (Many years later my sister claimed that it was a heart attack; I think a cardiologist would call it a spasm). Afterwards, or perhaps even before that event, my father showed repeated signs of nervousness. One day we had a visit from a high-class landowner (there were plenty of lesser gentry around, and three thousand acres were tenanted from the Counts Zicsy). I could see that my father was ill-at-ease with our visitor and after he had left I gathered, from a chance remark of his, that our aristocratic visitor was not to be trusted, a 'smiling villain'. It was somehow implied that we were dealing with another anti-Semitic patriot who was just waiting for his chance to take over a Jewish property, waiting for another race law from the government. By that time I was getting used to such signals of menace and secrecy and I was determined not to let the dark cloud get larger while exploring a local paradise.

But my father remained tense for the rest of the journey. We stayed a night in Székesfehérvár (the ancient city and the place where I began this story) and I could see that my father was not in a mood to wander about, as I would have liked; he did not even enjoy the delicious, steaming hot broth poured into a silvery bowl, an act and a taste I savoured with delight. By the time we got to Budapest, my father had developed eczema on the back of his neck and kept scratching it; I could not tell him to stop it because that kind of father-son relationship was not our social style. Most of the time he was busy—probably doing things for my widowed Aunt Agnes—and there were few if any fun outings. All I can remember is going up and down, up and down, on a sort of perpetual lift called 'paternoster' in the imposing headquarters of the Credit Bank where I was presented to admiring strangers making the usual ridiculous remarks: how tall, how blond, how thin, how bright, etc. Sitting in a cafe along the Danube embankment, I wanted to act as a grown-up: I asked for coffee and reached out for a newspaper held in a cane frame. Unfortunately, a strange gentleman claimed prior right to the paper and growled at me; my father seemed to side with the stranger and rebuked me. I considered that an injustice; I expected my father to stick up for his son's obvious need to be educated in current affairs and rebuke the stranger, not me. For days I asked myself a few anxious questions about my father's health, his nerves, but when we got back home life seemed to go on as before. Only three years later, when our ordeal began, did I fully realise that my father had been less robust than I had imagined him to be—by age fifty or so the political anxieties of the time, the threat from Nazi Germany and local laws, had taken their toll.

We had other summer holidays, all inland, before the fatal year of 1944. Some of these summers were marked by incidents characteristic of the time. At Lilafüred, a splendid hill resort in the north of the country, I thought I had found a friend: a beautiful girl of my age dressed in white, who philosophized about the meaning of life and talked about her musical ambitions. We sat facing each other from two separate rocks, keeping distant while we talked. We agreed to meet again the following day at the same spot, but she never turned up either that day or the next. Perhaps my philosophy didn't appeal to her, I worried, or she looked down on me—a proud creature from Budapest—because I was staying at a humble pension, a hut compared with her luxurious hotel, with neo-Gothic stained glass and historical Hungarian paintings in imposing lounges and a grand piano in a sumptuous music room. I imagined her practicing on that piano before the gong sounded for dinner, perhaps expecting me to break in, listen and applaud discreetly. But I resolved not think of her any more, ever, and consoled myself by attending an old lady who sat on the terrace typing away day by day: letters to her lawyer most of the time. The act of typing itself fascinated me; I had never seen such a small portable typewriter before and it seemed more precious than a grand piano.

On fair days father took my sister and me rock-climbing (that is clambering up moderate outcrops) then hill-walking and into the woods. My mother did not feel like coming on the more adventurous excursions and tended to worry about us. One day we were caught by a tremendous thunderstorm and hid under the canopy of the thick foliage. Naturally, we were back late only to find my mother very anxious by then and instantly prescribing hot towels and a glass of brandy to prevent our catching a feverish cold. Yet I seldom felt better. After that event I should have been extra kind to my mother but instead I seemed to have taken to teasing her. Travelling home by bus I suddenly burst into strange speeches—making up streams of disconnected words and nonsense words, something along the lines of 'On top of the bottomless mountain the devil swallowed me with my Mohican scalp and gave me a splitting headache...' 'What's the matter with you? Do you want an aspirin?' asked my mother desperately while the passengers looked on.

11. War, Literature and Early Sex

In the last half-year before the tragic turning point in our lives (September 1943–March 1944, just before and after my thirteenth birthday) my attention to war and the other sex became intense, which would have been judged precocious in another time. When our education was interrupted by the government's decision to close down all schools for two months, late in 1943—we were supposed to continue studying through radio broadcasts—it became virtually impossible to concentrate. Even a boy keen on learning was left with lots of leisure: an opportunity to keep cycling around the outskirts of the town, brooding but also reading. Though I was not yet obsessed by literature (that came three years later), I discovered the 'great books' for juniors one after another: *Don Quixote, Robinson Crusoe, Gulliver's Travels*, Dickens and Walter Scott (but only one title from each author), Jules Verne, Fennimore Cooper, a number of Hungarian novels (Jókai, mentioned before, and Gárdonyi's historical novel about the Turkish siege of Eger) together with a fair amount of poetry and plays and, sustaining my earlier interests, history and science books, especially psychology (more precisely a book on psycho-neurosis 'borrowed' from my father without his knowledge) and astronomy. But I was still restless and I became more adventurous. When my mother noticed that I was sleeping badly she—in her usual anxious response—called in Dr Orbán, the family doctor, who wanted to know what sort of things I was thinking about before going to bed. I answered, without hesitation, 'the universe'. 'Interesting', said the doctor who asked me a few more penetrating questions and then prescribed a nightly hot bran bath to be soaked in for half an hour or more. The bran stank, the soaking bored me, but it gave me time for further reflections—about the universe, the war and later about the body of our buxom maid.

Cutting across all other preoccupations, there was the constant, obsessive war news. The official news, supplemented by listening to the BBC together with frequent rumours, fed fresh hopes and fears week by week. The Red Army's advance deep into Ukraine together with the Anglo-American landing in Sicily and the dramatic collapse of Italy in 1943 (half-cancelled by the rapid and tragic German occupation of Northern and Central Italy and the rescue of Mussolini) created a climate of great excitement, with rising waves of optimism, seemingly justified. I made a model map of Italy, for example, on which I carefully marked the advancing front-line before it unfortunately froze around Monte Cassino. At the same time I 'planned' a major landing by the Western Allies on the Dalmatian coast (from Italy), a lightning advance through Yugoslavia and then up, across the river Drava into the Danube basin, liberating Hungary. Meanwhile the Red Army would advance to the Carpathians and beyond, possibly joining the other Allies pushing up from the South, meeting in the great Hungarian plain. (I could not know that landing in the Balkans was an actual plan advocated by Churchill and that 'my plan' for the Russian forces would become reality, too late for us). In this way I became absorbed in playing war games or *Kriegspiele*, daily if not hourly poring over large maps laid out on the floor and marked with coloured pins at crisis points. I went on making decisions about the conduct of the war like some half-demented retired general. I also made up and sang some triumphant songs, one about Montgomery marching on, with new English words to the familiar old tune of 'John Brown's soul goes marching on'. It was getting difficult to keep my mouth shut concerning the Allied victories when talking to my (not to be fully trusted) friends but I managed it somehow. Around me people in my parents' circle were all the time eagerly discussing the war, adding benign scenarios and Hitler jokes—from the fall of Stalingrad and El Alamein on.

One day, I think it was a warm day in late Summer 1943, we were sitting in the garden with friends when somebody in our party alarmingly disrupted the hopeful mood. It was reported that a train had passed through Debrecen station—it had sealed wagons—hands were stretched out from the wagons—people screaming—voices crying 'Water, water!' In what language? Probably in German but it was understood that they were all Jews from another country. The train was heading for Poland, a railwayman said, and there were unspecific but frightening rumours connected with Poland by that time.

Nothing more was said, nothing definite was known. After a long silence our friends took their leave, visibly subdued. It proved impossible to erase the memory of that moment of fear.

Our maid Rozsi (the name corresponds to Rosie) was the sort of girl whom everybody would have liked, or so I imagine. She had not been in our household long before her friendly ways, her sense of humour and a cheerful kind of helpfulness, became manifest. She was a little plump, brown-haired and brown-eyed and walked about the rooms of our apartment very quietly but with her head held high. I got used to talking to her, as in the compact geography lesson about the war (already related). I don't think I found her physically attractive to begin with: I was too young at twelve, just before puberty, to think along those lines and it was not my style to get too friendly with a chambermaid. Not that I shared my mother's social snobbery—I had always tended to see something strong and authentic in 'good country people' from the peasantry—but I had already developed a preference for intellectual or ethereal types, as in glimpsing that strange musical girl in white at Lilafüred (or Eva L, my sister's clever near-contemporary, to whom I was going to propose.) So I hardly noticed Rozsi as a young woman (about nineteen) even when she was standing beside me turning the globe with me to discover the vast expanses of the Soviet Union that could not be defeated. What happened between us, about a year later, was pure chance. One day, I saw her busily brushing the parquet floor in one of our rooms with the square brushes tied to her bare feet. She was moving backward and forward energetically as in a dance. But it was hard work too and the girl was sweating. A strange new pungent smell reached me—not all that pleasant but somehow exciting. Rozsi turned round, caught sight of me and laughed out loud without a word. I left the room at once and afterwards still paid little attention to her until the day I accidentally saw her washing her breasts. It was early Spring and I was coming back from my private promenade on the flat roof outside my room—and there she was. I could see her through the open window standing over a wash-basin alone in her room, soaping one full round breast, with the nipple clearly visible, the other breast wet and covered in soap lather. My inexpert eyes immediately responded to those perfect shapes. Suddenly she saw me and called out something in protest so that I hastily retreated, fearing that she might think I was spying on her—whilst I told myself that I was above spying, I just could not resist a vision. It was then that I began to think about Rozsi often, not surprisingly as my discovery of her coincided with unmistakable signs of puberty, under the powerful water jets of the handheld shower in the bath. And it was in the bath tub that Rozsi first touched me, uninvited but undoubtedly responding to my Peeping Tom act. On that occasion it was she who came to me sneakily, looked, reached out and left within ten seconds. After that we just passed each other in the corridor smiling.

The morning ritual included Rozsi's wake-up call—drawing the Venetian blinds—at a quarter to seven precisely. One day she took the opportunity to slip her hand under my blanket and pretend surprise at what she found. After that she repeated the act once or twice, each time with lightning speed—quite enough to excite a boy just entering adolescence with occasional wet dreams. She noticed my eagerness and one day she grabbed my erect penis and drew it to her genitals. With lightning speed she moved away, muttering something about getting hurt, it would hurt her to go on. And it was time for me to go to school! She repeated this game several times and I somehow accepted it as 'natural', grateful for the initiation and uncomplaining about the rest. One day she carried things a little further by lying down on my bed, or rather leaning back from the edge of the bed so that she could easily jump up again, and making me repeat the act that stopped a few seconds after play began—just as she had devised it. On these occasions we hardly talked and there was no kissing or caressing. Neither of us mentioned the imminent possibility of one of my parents entering, my room happening to be next to their bedroom and some of my father's suits were hanging in a large wardrobe in my room. Rozsi said very little about her private life. Once she muttered something about a country boyfriend (in Hajdu county) but I think she wanted me to think that she was a virgin. Meanwhile it occurred to me—though I was not particularly anxious—that if our games developed in intensity I would have to marry her. But I knew that I didn't have enough money to buy her a ring.

That episode, left over from an almost feudal age, may seem questionable from a social point of view. At the time it had a lightness about it, yet the experience left a deep and punishing division between body and spirit in my approach to women—something that dogged me throughout my boyhood and youth, at least until my marriage at age 27. On one side came the friendly Rozsi figure suddenly appearing out of nowhere, cheerful and sexually forthcoming on her own initiative and then withdrawing as quickly as she had come. On the other side loomed the distant princess, untouchable and unattainable, cultured and puritanical, preferably dressed in white, to be loved for years, in pain and solitude, until she too vanished without trace. At age 13 I entered the world of love's tragicomedy. The comedy resembled that of the gentleman who, visiting a mansion (mistaken for an inn) in *She Stoops to Conquer*[1], can only make love to the barmaid (or the young lady dressed as a barmaid) whilst the young lady in her proper state reduces him to trembling awkwardness. That would be followed by unsatisfied desire and intense longing for The Lady, checked by high-minded self-control—passion converted into monkish adoration.

---

[1] William Goldsmith *She Stoops to Conquer* (1773)

12. Year of Terror Begins

The wheel of fortune turned for my family suddenly but quietly at first, one Sunday afternoon, on 19th March 1944. The phone rang and my mother, answering the call, was visibly upset but not much more so than she might have been on hearing any unpleasant news. She said in a disciplined voice: 'The Germans have occupied Budapest, your father has just told me.' Father happened to be in the capital, and for a short time our main concern was only for his safe return home. After all, the situation in our city seemed completely normal, we assumed it was safer there than in the capital (the opposite turned out to be the case). At the same time, we felt a strong urge to keep the family together, an instinctive feeling accompanied by a fear of getting separated. So we took the risk of staying where we were, unable to imagine the long-term consequences of that decision.

Within an hour after that phone call I decided to go on a surveillance patrol, prompted by curiosity. I went with my school-friend Feri, whom I managed to lead to various centres of possible action without revealing to him my secret agenda. That was exciting, for I alone knew that we were facing a historic emergency. We passed a cinema that was just then announcing closure, without giving any reason; we noted an unusual number of policemen on the main street; we walked to the station where we saw notices of cancelled trains. These signs confirmed the black news of occupation, but I still said nothing to my friend and I returned home to report my findings in the manner of an objective observer.

Father returned safely and resumed his work in the bank; the city remained unchanged and there was no sign of the invading German army the following day. School went on for some time: reading Julius Caesar in Latin, studying the French revolution, reciting poetry, solving equations, copying music. I avoided conversation on the subject of the Nazi invasion. I had plenty of practice in keeping silent concerning my Jewish origins, and my silence had become second nature and was not felt as concealment or disguise. Fully integrated in the life of that bastion of Protestantism, the Debrecen *Collegium*, I went on with my daily round, studying and talking to friends as if nothing had happened. I mentally dismissed a few triumphantly Hitler-loving schoolfellows as idiots. I wanted to remain an ordinary boy in that extraordinary context. For example, as a member of the junior cadets (*Levente*) I followed an order to go on a training exercise; one day I cycled at breakneck speed towards our meeting place, the stadium, with a government-issue gun dangling from my shoulder—a model patriotic boy soldier.

Soon we heard of a regime change on the radio: the appointment of a pro-Nazi prime minister, Sztójay. But the Regent, Horthy, remained in place and it was hoped that he would prevent a total Nazi takeover of the country, especially as the victory of the Allies was approaching.[2] I returned to my war maps with obsessive agility and decided that the Red Army would reach us within a few months, in rapid advance through the not too distant Carpathian mountains. Leaning on those maps I prepared the final collapse of the Third Reich. In short, I was not afraid, not yet.

When the schools were closed down, by order of the new government, I felt relieved: so I would not have to explain my absence or else expose my compulsory yellow star—the new decrees made no distinction between practicing Jews and those brought up as Christians. I walked about in a split state of mind: consciously acting a part in a theatre, the theatre of war, gripped by a strange new solidarity with all the others branded as I was; at the same time, feeling that it was all wrong, quite inappropriate, and I was tempted to tear off my 'badge' and walk away or at least hide that yellow star as if it had accidentally slipped under my lapel.

Then the pace of change accelerated, and our situation deteriorated day by day. Long columns of German soldiers could be seen marching up and down the high street in their grey uniforms and jackboots. We could watch them from our balcony as from a box, in fear and trembling, yet I still pretended to be a kind of protected observer; their cars and motor cycles were parked all over the town, often surrounded by small crowds of people who wanted to fraternise with the occupiers. There was no resistance as the national propaganda had succeeded in presenting the occupation as 'legal', since it took place with the Regent's consent (a forced consent but hardly anybody knew that at the time). The new extreme right government speedily launched a barrage of severe racial laws, which affected every aspect of our life: everything was forbidden or restricted. I came home one day to find that both the cook and the maid had left quite abruptly; so I never had the chance to say good-bye to Rozsi—what was she thinking, how would she remember me, was she sad at all? Then our living space began to shrink as if rolled back or folded up. One day the furniture was moved around in our apartment to create accommodation for a German lieutenant-colonel billeted in our place, a friendly enough officer from Bavaria, who probably knew nothing about our circumstances and who managed to convey a degree of war fatigue. Soon his place was taken by a high-ranking officer (a general?) from the *Kommandatur*, stiff but polite. Three rooms were requisitioned for him, including our best drawing room, and when he

---

[2] Facts of Hungarian history checked, here and elsewhere, in Miklós Molnár (transl. Anna Magyar), *A Concise History of Hungary* (Cambridge 2001).

arrived he peremptorily demanded extra pieces of furniture including a sofa. I was puzzled by this request as he already had a fair-sized bed, but one night, as I rashly indulged in my habit of night watch, wandering around the apartment, I could hear female sighs and groans from the room with the extra sofa. I guessed what they were up to although I have never heard that sound before. The officer next demanded a deckchair to be placed on our terrace for his comfort; so I brought him one only to see the canvas snap instantly under his weight. He went red in the face but did not punish me. (He too probably did not know that he had been billeted with Jews.) Meanwhile I managed to talk with the general's orderly who quite outspokenly lamented the war and the way it was going: *Dass ist ein Jammer*, 'it's just misery', he said. Such normal encounters contributed to the illusion that we were in no great danger.

Our living space got narrower and narrower but we managed to hang on to three bedrooms, including my own room. One of the bedrooms was converted into a makeshift sitting room—with some of the old Biedermeier furniture—and there we received our guests, for people were still coming to visit and share anxieties. One visitor, a middle-aged man from the neighbourhood, kept making pessimistic forecasts but that was not surprising as bad news kept pouring in. Next day we heard that he had jumped from the fifth floor of an apartment block next to our house. This was the first in a series of suicides. The impact was horrible but already dampened by the instinctive need to build emotional defences against disasters. I don't know how other members of the family reacted but it was about this time that I began to develop a kind of immunity, mixing detachment and curiosity. Or rather it was not 'I' who developed such a state of mind; a new 'I' was developing unbidden and stayed with me for a long time, for a good portion of my war experiences. These would have been much more traumatic if I had not succeeded in pretending that I was only an onlooker.

I even observed my father's increasingly agitated behaviour calmly though I felt truly sorry for him at heart. One day father stopped going down to the bank—before he had been officially dismissed and without his giving an explanation or notice—and disappeared. I think he crossed the former Romanian border to the city of Nagyvárad (Oradea) and then kept travelling to other places. This seemed a rational reaction to the fear of being taken hostage, for a number of distinguished citizens, mostly Jews, had indeed been rounded up. On the other hand, the fact that my father had not been included in this haul of hostages suggested that he was not on any black list, probably because he was a relatively recent citizen in Debrecen and known to the authorities only as a leading bank manager and a respected elder of the Reformed Church. He could have safely stayed with us or else gone into hiding permanently. But under the pressure of events he did not seem to know what to do, and kept changing his mind: going away, returning, going away. When he was with us for a short time he prepared an escape route across the flat roof under my window, with a kind of rope ladder fixed to the far end of the roof. And when he was away he was mostly out of reach. Meanwhile telegrams and urgent telephone calls kept coming from the bank's head office in Budapest, possibly because they had some kind of rescue plan for him, perhaps to send him on an errand to Izmir in Turkey (a neutral country), or to summon him to the capital. (The directors of the bank may or may not have known that the Regent was going to intervene to stop the deportation of Jews from Budapest). But all that is speculation, a painful kind of speculation involving a life or death choice.

As our future became more and more threatening, father attempted to find safe havens for my sister and myself. He asked the bishop, Dr Révész, to place my sister as a novice deaconess. The bishop was only prepared to act on this proposal if a solemn undertaking was given that my sister's choice would remain irrevocable—after the war. As my father refused to accept such a condition, the plan came to nothing. Similarly, the attempt to place me in the house of my school friend, Feri, failed when his father, a country parson, made excuses: he argued that a spoilt town boy like me, used to all modern comforts, could neither fit into a household with modest facilities nor escape becoming conspicuous. After that we made no further escape attempts even though there must have been opportunities. None of us looked recognisably Jewish and I was fair-haired and not circumcised. I was also equipped with a 'safe' identity card that stated my Christian religion but left the relevant slot on race blank—a benign clerical error, no doubt arranged by my father. My parents also had safe (false) documents but my sister had none, which increased the risk not only for her but for all of us. It was once more decided that we must keep together.

Why did we not try harder? Was it out of despair or some residual hope that our troubles would soon come to an end? I shall never know. Instead my parents started distributing a whole range of valuables to trusted friends. I witnessed several acts of such property transfer. I saw my father handing over a tube, filled with gold coins, to an honest bank servant, Szito, who refused to accept any reward for his pains. On another occasion, a whole pile of high quality clothes—including shirts and ties— was handed over to a junior colleague who was in tears when my father told him why he was being entrusted with those personal possessions; the colleague tried to convince us (that is, himself) that we were not in

71

imminent danger. Porcelain vases, silver candlesticks, fur coats, even linen were likewise passed into trusted hands or else given away as presents. My father also showed me the family documents—nothing of commercial value—left in a small safe in his office; these included all the birth and residence certificates he had painstakingly collected over the years to prove that our family had been citizens of Hungary since the eighteenth century at least. As mentioned earlier, my father had pinned some of his hopes of exemption from the race laws on just such a proof of long-standing patriotic loyalty (quite rationally for in Vichy France, for example, settled citizens of the country were not deported). Meanwhile every member of the family was allocated a sum of cash for emergencies; my share was ten hundred *pengö* banknotes in a little canvas bag suspended from my neck with a string. A thousand *pengö*-s represented roughly a senior manager's monthly salary, or five hundred times my weekly pocket money. I was instructed to carry this moneybag on me all the time, hanging from my neck. A few days later, on a cycle ride, I felt the place—the bag was missing. I re-traced my cycle route inch by inch; I looked for it in every corner of my room, in vain. I had no idea how the money had vanished; perhaps the string got loosened and the bag dropped out, but how and where remained a mystery. I felt guilty but I could hardly report this incident—the police was unthinkable, and how could I tell my parents? I thought: we are losing everything, so why not this? In the confusion of the times I said nothing until greater losses overshadowed this act of carelessness.

13. The Ghetto

In the middle of May we moved into the ghetto, into the house of a family friend within walking distance of the city centre. At first it might have looked like an ordinary move: we went 'voluntarily', obeying orders, of course, but without very conspicuous police escort. With hindsight both the voluntary move and the lack of physical force seem extraordinary; but we were still acting as law-abiding citizens of our country and the authorities were not supposed to exceed—their authority. I know that such a timid, even defeatist, attitude is scarcely credible to the generations born after the war.

In reality the move was far from ordinary and was accompanied by evil omens from the start. As our minimal possessions were piled on a horse-drawn cart behind the entrance gate of the bank building, I saw a group of secretaries (not working for the bank) amusing themselves at our expense, with mocking gestures and shouts of jubilation. Others started to pull down accessible objects, anything sticking out from our baggage like an umbrella and, absurdly enough, my fishing rod. As soon as we arrived we immediately realised how limited was the living space waiting for the four of us: less than half the size of one of our bedrooms with practically no space left between four mattresses in four corners of the room. Hardly had we started sorting out our things when a frightful hammering and cursing began outside the single window as it was boarded up from top to bottom until little daylight reached us. When I left our tiny room I could see that the whole house was overcrowded, every room occupied by families with their bundles and an overflow of people sleeping in the corridors. Outside the house the narrow streets were full of careworn people carrying bags, poor quality suitcases and useless-seeming possessions; the entire area of our contrived enclosure could be traversed in a very short time. All the streets leading back to the city had been sealed off with a tall fence, turning them into blind alleys. This then was the ghetto—a word hardly heard by me before, though I had seen it in a history book referring to some ancient Jewish settlements, in Venice or Prague.

I again felt that I was not really part of this masquerade. I had been dropped into an alien world by some kind of parachute and it was my job, for the time being, to keep my eyes open and watch the strange goings-on. I could see that there were a large number of orthodox Jews around—some imposing old Rembrandt faces, bearded, with side-locks, in traditional long black caftans, in the heat of early summer. They seemed to be at ease there, relatively speaking, disputing and bargaining or praying. In a sense they were on home ground as many of them had lived in this area under normal circumstances, in the vicinity of one of the synagogues, a world apart from the thoroughly assimilated middle-class Jews, not to mention the 'Christian Jews'. I must have been invisible as I walked through those streets for nobody ever stopped me or greeted me; perhaps with my blond hair and school-trained marching steps they thought I had come from the enemy.

As if to underline the difference, a small group of people who were members of the Reformed Church were visited one Sunday by our own parson, Dr Urai, the bishop's deputy and a man of some influence but regarded by my parents as unable or unwilling to do anything for our safety. He came and conducted a formal service with an eloquent sermon; I can no longer remember his text. (In 'Back to Normal'—one of my stories, first published in Stand magazine in 1981—the boy Peter hears the words 'suffer the little children to come onto me', feels sick, and can see the sealed freight wagons of a train reflected in a silver chalice—hallucination or pre-vision). Unlike Peter, I did not feel sick. But the whole ceremony was disturbing, at once significant and futile. As I accompanied Dr Urai to the gates of the ghetto I wondered whether he could take me with him, back into the real world. And when I witnessed his perhaps compassionate but certainly final good-bye wave I felt abandoned as never before.

I wonder what I did in those forty days of transit. Not much, for there was precious little to do. Our parents joined the other adults in the labour of keeping up standards of cleanliness and order under difficult circumstances. My mother cooked and did housework, probably for the first time in her life; my father was asked to join a Food Distribution Committee, handing out the meagre rations brought in from the outside world. But people still had accumulated stocks of food, not yet confiscated. The children played, or tried to play perfunctorily, but I no longer regarded myself as a child and had no inclination to join any group. I had no friend in the ghetto and if there was someone somewhere I had no means of finding him or her. Communication was minimal and my desire to communicate was also minimal. There was nothing to read for we brought no books with us and I did not feel like going in search of reading matter. It was about that time that it occurred to me that, whatever else happened to us, I would end up as an ignorant fool—with no school, no reading, no radio, no intelligent occupation of any kind except avidly devouring any newspaper that found its way into our walled-in world and, as before, footing around the inner perimeter of those walls.

Hygiene was kept up though water was rationed, and people had shared baths. Walking around the house one day, I was alerted by the sound of two young women laughing loudly—shrieks of lusty, escalating, non-stop laughter. It turned out that those women were in a bath together and found the experience hilarious. Others amused themselves with card games, dominoes and patience, and half-hidden lovemaking: I observed a middle-aged man courting a giggling young woman in the same corner of the house day after day. Much time was taken up with packing—unpacking, re-packing and pre-packing—as rumours of our pending deportation intensified. Some people became visibly gloomy but the majority seemed to carry on the daily round with dogged determination.

One day I saw my mother dig a hole in the garden; I went up to find out what she was doing—she was burying her wedding ring so that it would not be taken away from her. One night, towards the end, we heard a tremendous crash, hammering and breaking glass, followed by piercing shrieks. The frightening noise came from the house next door—another suicide. The man who hanged himself, the lawyer Markovics, had been a close colleague of my father on the Committee for Food Distribution, a perilously close connection. However, it was only years later that I came to realise that Markovics, together with the rabbi who disappeared at the same time, knew something my father must also have known: our destiny—something the rest of us did not know. So my father must have faced the immediate future with a burden of frightening information while we benefited from the relative bliss of ignorance.

Towards the end of May conditions got much tougher. It was announced that the entire population of the ghetto would be evacuated (the word deportation was never used). House-to-house searches started almost at once: police agents were looking for valuables. The inhabitants of our house were frisked one by one, brusquely but not violently, as far as I could see. When it was my sister's turn to walk into a makeshift booth to be 'examined' by a young officer, my father suddenly stepped into the booth with her—no doubt to prevent any indecency. Surprisingly, the young policeman finished the inspection in minutes. Nor was the search as intensive as we feared; my mother managed to hang on to some gold coins sewn into the shoulder pads of a jacket, quite a risk. Our policemen were relatively moderate, just 'doing their duty'; it was policy to act so as to avoid panic among the condemned and conceal the truth—that they were condemned.

14. Worse There Is None?

We were marched towards the outskirts of the city by the feared country gendarmes (*csendör*). With their cock-feather helmets these men were well-known oppressors of the Gypsies and the rural poor, though they themselves were recruited from the peasantry. They were not often seen in the towns and a law-abiding citizen might go through life without coming into the clutches of such paramilitary thugs. Their mere presence was therefore enough to create alarm, confirming that we had just been further degraded, as criminals, and were about to be exposed to rough measures. The gendarmes excelled in shouting at us as we marched through streets flanked by the local population: ordinary men and women mostly just standing and staring, some clearly sympathetic, others indulging in malignant laughter. 'You won't need an umbrella where you are going, Jew!' someone called out with evident satisfaction. Unfortunately my father stumbled at one point and must have heard a gloating insult—painful, as he was getting visibly weaker. I remember nothing else from the march because my attention was concentrated on keeping pace and not letting go of my rucksack and haversack—an early example of that 'look after number one' and 'don't think or feel' mentality which our forced exodus was breeding.

Nothing prepared us for being turned into animals within an hour. We were herded across a field to a primitive wooden structure: ordered to climb up some rickety wooden steps, with our remaining baggage, into a complex of dark wooden chambers, the barn-like loft of a crude brick-works (*téglagyár*). We found ourselves squatting in a cramped corner— sitting on our rucksacks, all four of us in a huddle—as more and more people were being pushed relentlessly into the shrinking space until it was impossible to move in any direction. As darkness fell it was also impossible to know what was happening and what might happen next. Fire? Shooting? Why else should they have brought us here, penned us in? The screams of children mingled with the groans of the sick and the elderly and the dying (a man not far from us). There was no silence. The roar of gendarmes broke moments of relative calm and—for the first time—a very young SS man joined them, cursing in German as he roughly stepped over the heads of squatting people, kicking and brandishing a whip. But soon every sight and sound came from far, far away, as the mind was dulled by half sleep. I was no longer present. I was somewhere else, sliding into a deep hole but prevented from falling through the floor by a crowd of arms that kept pushing me back into some hollow.

At dawn the compact crowd became visible stretching over the vast loft and we became conscious of having survived the night. Some people were sick, others dying, but all that seemed far away though quite near. Some kind of order was established, enough to urinate and defecate in a disciplined way, using pots and pans and somehow disposing of the soil through holes in the floor. I cannot remember eating anything or doing anything at all until, towards noon, news came that we would be allowed to move down to ground level, still within the terrain of the fenced-in brick-works. By that time I had reached a kind of inner indifference, muttering to myself 'ah, yes, I can see now, open air, no immediate danger, no suffocation, oh yes.'

Down there, there was certainly more space but there was also a lot of dust—a powdery, whitish dust on the ground, in the air, settling on hair and skin and on all objects. Nevertheless we decided—it was my father's decision—to move down there and take shelter, such as it was, in one of the many drying sheds of the brick-works. It was far more primitive than the simplest tent, just a few upright poles holding up horizontal ones without any roof. It was too hot by day and too cold by night, open to the rain. The entire area was about three-and-a-half square metres for a large number of people, mostly people known to us, spilling out onto the surrounding open ground. We slept in our clothes and on our packs, always ready for a sudden order to march; exhaustion insists on a portion of sleep even in discomfort. I was reaping the benefits of the camping experience that had counterbalanced my spoilt home life; and despite my slender build, my constitution proved tougher than expected. My mother and sister also seemed to cope, relieved to be out of the nightmare of the loft prison.

It was my father who was weakening, something I probably did not realise until towards the end of our ten days in the brick-works camp. At first it looked as if he had regained his old energy and spirit of enterprise. In the morning of our move down, I watched him talk to an SS officer, an older man with tired eyes, curled-up lips, hollow cheeks and a grey complexion. The SS skull badge was plainly visible. Yet my father confronted this frightening figure, in his good German, apparently asking for information. What the question was, and whether the SS man had answered at all, I never found out. But thinking about that fateful day later, I imagined that my father was told—perhaps by that officer or by someone else in the know—that it was safer for us 'down there'. Something had already been decided, some kind of sorting of the prisoners had been envisaged, with long-term consequences. But my father could hardly have known that his decision to 'move down' would save us: we were herded onto the one train that was not for transport to Auschwitz. (Records show that an

SS transport officer had made a mistake in not sending our transport to Auschwitz.[3])

We did not realise the extent of father's growing apathy and his illness, dysentery. No wonder, for sanitary conditions were appalling: just a latrine ditch to be reached from a slippery and filthy slope to be squatted on, requiring athletic skill in holding on and relieving oneself, together with a total suppression of disgust. But we had enough water, drawn from a pump, to allow some washing of bodies and clothes. I could see a middle-aged woman washing herself semi-nude, over a rough metal basin, splashing her breasts with evident delight. Others were washing the accumulated white dust from shirts and blouses. There was also just enough food to keep going, food sent from the town and distributed by our own improvised leaders (my father no longer among them) and supplemented by our scant food reserves. We took a risk in starting to eat our last reserves for nobody knew when they might be needed in another extreme situation.

For a boy like me there was nothing to do all day except wander about and about the large camp observing the scene; the word may sound callous but that is what I was doing, automatically. One day I saw an old-world, simple black horse-drawn hearse enter the camp, driven by the father of Clara, my one-time classmate in the primary school; we stared at each other without blinking but I felt sure that he had recognised me and would go home to tell Clara that he had seen me—in abject circumstances. The hearse probably came to take away the body of Zsóka, the owner of the house we had lived in the ghetto. We heard that she had taken poison before we were marched into the unknown, and she was carried out still alive. I saw her lie on the ground: purplish face, eyes staring fixedly, tongue hanging out, her tormented body tossing about. The next day the father of another friend of mine appeared in the full uniform of an army major; I saw him hold his son's hand as they left the camp together, walking into freedom. Only the boy's mother was Jewish, so somehow his rescue was arranged in the last moment. It was an incident that again set me thinking about 'destiny': why was this happening, why now, why him, why not somebody else, why not me? And why not walk out even now, escape invisibly, as nobody could prove who I was.

There were incessant rumours. We would be transported the next day or one or two days later or not for another week. We would be taken to Poland where the camps were horrible (unspecified). Or we would be taken to Germany and work in factories or on farms; we were needed—a repeated assertion—our work was needed by the Reich.

---

[3] Rudolph L. Braham, *The Politics of Genocide: The Holocaust in Hungary* (New York: Columbia University Press 1981) Vol. 2, p.651.

One day a group of people was selected—names called out one by one—separated from the multitude, and taken to another part of the camp. It was said that these men and women were known Zionists on an international list and that they would be taken to Switzerland and eventually to Palestine. It was also rumoured that further groups would be selected, for one reason or another. All these rumours made us more restless and anxious while fatalism became the dominant mood. I myself pinned my hopes of survival, again and still, on items found in scattered newspapers about what later came to be known as D-Day and other Allied successes. I tried to ignore the agitated buzz of speculation about what might happen to us, where and when.

Meanwhile, people were still being taken for interrogation—which meant torture. Detectives accompanied by gendarmes combed the camp to find the rich or those reputed rich (our family, as I said earlier, had not been on the 'Jew list' at all). The unfortunate ones were roughed up and if they did not reveal where they had hidden valuables—perhaps because they had none—were beaten again. This went on from the day of our arrival until our deportation. I watched one detective at work and heard him mockingly greet a middle-aged man he had recognised: 'Ah, Blau, so you have decided to join this nice holiday camp. I do hope you are having a good time. Would you mind coming with me for a little chat?'

In the midst of growing tension, the camp was drenched by torrential rain. Nobody seemed to mind that—the rain had reduced the heat and had offered an extra washing facility; women let their garments be soaked in rain. All possessions were piled up in the sheds, which were not in the least waterproof. But struggling with nature was infinitely preferable to facing men bent on evil. The rain was followed by a perfect summer day—fresh air, no stench. Somehow I came to join a small group of prisoners in a field, still within the camp but free from the crowd and their belongings. There I sat among two or three young women and a gendarme, quietly conversing as if on a day out in the country. We talked about something completely neutral—something like what to do on weekends—and I remember thinking that, after all, there was no reason why we should not all become friends, gendarme and prisoner. And once again I wondered what would happen if I explained that I had been brought here by mistake—then I might be escorted out of the camp, like my friend the major's son, and settled in a safe place before it was too late.

From the field, in that unreal hour, I could see a very long freight train being shunted on the line nearest to the camp, like an international express. It was a sight that brought on my first fear.

15. The Deportation Train

Reprinted from my article in *The Observer*, Sunday, July 16, 1961.

The Observer, commenting recently on the Eichmann trial, wrote.
'What did it feel like to be packed in cattle trucks and sent slowly
across the length of Europe? We don't know; we read the trial reports
with the detachment of the railway workers who transported these
millions.' Today we publish this account by one who does know...
who, as a boy of 13, was himself one of the millions to endure that
terrible journey.
By Andrew Karpati

The day before we were deported I went down to the tracks by
our camp to take a close look at the cattle trucks—we called them
simply wagons—then being assembled into a long train. I was not
much more than thirteen, not particularly brave, but I had always
taken risks to satisfy my curiosity.

In the event, the few SS men and Hungarian gendarmes who
were around paid no attention to me, and I kept walking up and
down along the train with the excitement anything connected
with a journey always aroused in me. What fear I had seemed
to come from the metalwork and the rails; but the wooden part
fascinated me. For many of the wagons were painted in colours
different from the usual brick red of Hungarian goods trains. I
started deciphering letters and names I had never seen before.
"Italia" was easy, so was the German "D.R.B."; but "S.N.C.F."
and "B" took longer because I knew very little French; in the end,
I even guessed some of the Slavonic names—and I was pleased
with this discovery.

Sudden fear

"Where did they come from?"—this question set my imagination
working and passed the time. "Where is the train going?" This
meant a sudden fear that I tried to avoid, looking at the rails
that ran through dry grass in a directionless place, apparently
unconnected with any main line. Again, the fear was in the rails
and the metalwork: the wheels, the black grooves of the heavy
sliding doors and the bolts.

When we knew that families were not going to be separated,
being put into the wagons frightened us less than we expected.
Our turn came in the evening. There was even a certain relief in
this, after having stood all day in lined-up groups of about ninety
in the oppressive heat, after the improvised latrines of the over-

crowded camp, the shouting and the whip-cracking, the beatings by Hungarian fascists in search of valuables, the uncertainty about our immediate fate. Now something definite was happening at last, perhaps the worst was over—and did not the very fact that they bothered to get all this transport organised, that they counted us, show that the pessimists may be, must be, wrong? Mrs. E. need not have poisoned herself. Mrs. E. was a close friend of my parents, and I kept thinking of her: the livid face, the lolling tongue, the hair falling back as she lay dying in pain.

Before climbing up into the trucks, I looked at the SS officer who counted us, half-muttering. Again the same double feeling: terror in the thick protruding lower lip, pouches under bored eyes, riding boots, holster, death's-head cap, but some reassurance in being checked in the required quantity on a sort of bill of lading, in the smooth way things were ordered. At least he stopped people from pushing—to be crushed to death was a recurrent fear—if people don't panic there's no cause for panic: instead of a stampede, a silent procession.

Inside the truck there was still a little light from the small air-holes. My parents, my sister and I succeeded in getting quite near to one of these "windows," near one of the corners: a privileged position, I at once realised. As the others kept pressing in—about ninety of them—we somehow still had some space left: I sat on top of my rucksack with my legs drawn up, facing an old man, who sat propped up against the side of the wagon. I soon learned to loathe this man as no one before: he was far too big and he took up far too much room, he shouted in a raucous voice when in distress, his bony giant's fingers shaking with palsy only an inch away; between his trembling legs a half-full demijohn that held not a drop of water for others—except his wife.

My family was somewhere to my right, but increasingly distant, partitioned by bundles of things and limbs, the distinction between these two finally obscured by the darkness. (The late nightfall of summer solstice. Our watches had been taken away; the light through the air-holes was our timekeeper.) And if in the dark this huge old man dominated the narrow space before me, I had at first no notion of what went on behind me and to my left: that was outer space whose events I tried to guess by the sounds that came from it. Somewhere, very far, a child started to cry, then someone called for light, several people, one after the other, called for a doctor. All was vague and unreal, deadened by futile attempts at sleep and by my boyish determination to detach myself from it all. But one of the cries was answered, and I recognised with a certain joy the voice of a doctor I knew: "Be patient, I am coming, I still have some opium," or something like that—the word opium stuck in my mind.

Obsessive thirst

It was the same loud, confident voice I had often heard from my room at home when a party in distant rooms had kept me awake. So now I had to think of the immense space in our flat and as, at the same time, quite unaccountably, I managed to stretch my legs a little, my sense of unreality increased—making each infinitesimal gain in space seem infinite. There was a great expanse between my head and feet; I thought of it then as a bumpy field covered in thick undergrowth. Perhaps I was only camping; I was a Boy Scout again.

Meanwhile, the train had started, and I must have slept a little because when it stopped again somewhere, no one knew where— there were guards shouting outside and some people shouting in the dark within—I woke up to a dry numbness and to my first bad thirst. In the two-and-a-half-day journey that followed, the outline in the wagons became clearer—there was even a sense of settling down, of organization—but the numbness and the thirst grew all the time. The need for water was the hardest to bear; then there was the need to dispose of refuse, urine and faeces, and the need to know where we were. Our thirst was so bad that I at least could not take any food at all throughout the journey despite the fact that we still had some reserves. But we had no water left in the heat known as "dog days," and thirst became both chronic and obsessive: in paying attention to this particular condition one forgot the general condition. I don't remember anything else of these long hours! I didn't even realise how ill my father was (so ill that he was to die soon after arrival).

The dryness in the mouth gradually absorbed the rising stench; only saliva, getting rarer, offered some refreshment. But once, when the train halted in the middle of some fields, a peasant woman ran to our wagon and, with astonishing speed and skill, handed in a big jug of water; there was enough to be shared out with considerable fairness among those near the air-hole. Again, when we reached the Austrian frontier, we stopped in line with a military train; a German soldier leant across and pushed up his billy-can full of cold tea. That was enough for some of us; I think I must have had an unfairly large share, thanks to my age. These unknown helpers restored one's sense of humanity; the experience is now linked in my mind—perhaps arbitrarily—with the Samaritan woman at Jacob's well and the promise of living water; I am certain that such people are the wellspring of hope in a time of troubles.

Dread of north

The second need, the disposal of excrement, was organised by the most active members of our congested community. Saucepans and all sorts of other cooking utensils were produced from the luggage, and these were relayed from person to person till they reached the air-hole where their contents were emptied with some difficulty. Of course, they could not be washed out, and the fact that many people were suffering badly from diarrhoea made things worse. But although all this spread squalor, it also seemed to rouse people from their torpor—it called for energy and even humour.

Finally, the mind's greatest need: the need to know where we were. Soon after the dawn of the first day we found out that we were heading west; later in the day we realised that we were passing Budapest, and even houses were recognised with a strange excitement; the first day had passed and we were still heading west. This was generally interpreted as a good sign. Although nobody at the time knew about the death camps—if people had known many would have escaped—there was a dread connected with the north and north-east: the way to Poland. There had been rumours of previous deportations. certainly, people felt the west could not be so bad. I think this was partly based on a general—unfounded—belief that people could not be killed in the Budapest area, or—as the train rumbled on towards Vienna—in such a "civilised" place as Greater Germany; and somebody had seen a postcard sent by a deportee from Thuringia saying "We are safe." Someone else had heard that an important bridge to the north had been blown up; someone else that there might be prisoner exchanges.

On such rumours and speculations our whole structure of hope was founded -mingling with the knowledge that the allies were advancing towards Northern Italy, that they had landed in Normandy, that the Russians had broken through the front west of Vitebsk, and might soon be advancing through the Carpathians; the Yugoslav partisans were also said to he doing well. And the slowness of the Eighth Army in Italy was thought of with impatience even as we suffered from the slowness of the train. Yet every glimpse through the air-holes, every recognised station, helped to make the worst part of the journey—when some became hysterical and many wholly apathetic—more bearable.

By the time the doors were opened, at a camp that turned out to be in Lower Austria, most of us were so lifeless that the sun and the air were welcomed only in theory, because one knew, from memory, that they were beneficent; but exposure to this change, after clambering down and trying to stand on one's feet, weakened the body and confused the mind.

Like a parcel

I remember staring, for a long time, at the filth of the wagon we had left behind, with a renewed and sickly sense of unreality: waiting to be moved like a parcel and prepared to be thrown back, to stay in the train for good. In the wagon next to ours there was a corpse. I looked at it with indifference: big yellow feet, a woman, not very old—what did it matter? This lack of feeling, and not wanting anything, was also a new experience. I think it was the thirst that helped me to recover. I saw a man from the camp carrying a bucket of water, ran up to him and, without asking or warning, dipped my mug into the bucket. An SS man roared at me, but by then I had drunk. Then only did I feel it was better to be out of the cattle truck.

16. Strasshof Transit Camp

After I had slaked my thirst I began to feel almost human again, and I was not suffering from an underlying illness. But my father was.

Almost re-assured by the seemingly tidy rows of barracks seen from the railway line, stretching between fields and woodland, I tried to guess what lay in wait for us. I saw a vast concentration camp resembling a makeshift prison town for thousands of inmates. It was called Strasshof, not far from Vienna. The name of that city was legendary in our family, often invoked in conversation; my grandfather died there, my father studied Economics and banking there, an uncle practiced as a paediatrician there until 1938; I had been taken on a little tour of the city myself (aged six, as related earlier) and I had formed a mixed image of its culture and frivolity through numerous anecdotes and jokes, photographs, music and songs, and the imitation of its peculiar dialect. That kind of familiarity stirred a provisional hope—like that postcard from Germany—and counteracted the dread of the unknown. Meanwhile, all around me people were dying—my father among them, though I did not know it. Hundreds were sick or totally exhausted, and cries of panic could be heard as one or another person felt threatened by the conditions, by the chaos. The Ukrainian guards, both men and women, wielded big sticks and gave contradictory orders in incomprehensibly accented German, cursed the prisoners and treated them like a herd of cattle. The barracks were overcrowded, unclean, dark and cold at night, food was promised but not delivered on the first day, information nil. Then countless rumours sprung up again concerning our next destination, with every kind of threat and promise from extermination to work for the fit.

Within two days some kind of order was established accompanied by an excess of orders. Men and women were forced to stand in separate long queues: waiting to be selected or disinfected or processed… The waiting and the uncertainty was enough to create acute anxiety but splitting up the family was the worst trial, for that was what we had always feared most. My mother and sister vanished from view. I was left with my father who, I could see, was dragging his weary body with increasing difficulty. I was afraid that one of the guards would harm him, as they had attacked other invalids, choosing the weak to be victims in the service of 'the survival of the fittest'.

After a long wait in the heat, we were finally admitted to some super-barracks with huge spaces and long corridors. In groups we were taken into a large room where a male doctor or medical orderly in a white coat thoroughly examined us one by one; he scrutinised my pubic hair with obsessive attention. Then they shaved our heads, took away our clothes and took us into a mass shower room—the lukewarm water felt good on sweaty skin and it was a sign, I thought, that we were needed as workers, the recurrent hope. We were then herded into another enormous room where a battery of tough-looking women sat behind desks and large typewriters ready to 'process' us; they had bored, blank faces and uncaring voices. Names and other data were recorded and we were photographed. At the end of it all, I was given a printed identity card with a number stamped on it and ordered to return to our barracks.

It was a great relief to leave that people-sorting office. Although we did not know about the danger in full (did not know about the death-bringing shower rooms), there was something inherently sinister about the procedure we had endured: cool and clinical and yet uncanny, all the time being pushed around without any information, without a word being spoken to us, other than curt questions and orders. But fear was subdued. In keeping with the mental tricks I had recently learned, I just concentrated on each and every event in turn, as if taking part in a training exercise or watching a puzzling film that I had not chosen to see.

For a time I was left alone in our barrack with my father. He lay on top of his bunk bed, fully dressed and hardly moving all day. I brought him some food but he refused it with a single dismissive hand gesture and then he refused a drink too. When I tried to tell him the 'good news'—for I was beginning to believe that we had come through—he used a similar sad, defeated gesture. He rarely spoke at all and when he did his remarks were always pessimistic, as if he felt compelled to reject the few signs that pointed towards possible survival. He looked grey and apathetic. I have never seen him, or anyone else, in such a diminished state and yet I could not accept as a reality that he was seriously ill. I also felt completely helpless, as we had no medicine and no medical advice. Soon there was no communication between my father and me. In the end, I just took possession of the bunk bed nearest to him and waited for his recovery, which I instinctively expected.

Another, simpler, instinct aimed at survival: eating as much food as possible, even though the main diet consisted of a ghastly soup with slices of turnip and some crunchy dirt-like bits mixed in, drinking water whenever possible, and getting as much sleep as possible—against the constant coming and going of restless sleepers who had diarrhoea, like my father. These deliberately willed acts of 'looking after myself' were accompanied, again, by reduced consciousness. Just as in my early teens every day seemed to bring a greater intensity of thought and feeling, so now the days passed with reduced brain activity, like half-sleep suddenly broken by strange events: seeing the sky lit up by criss-crossing searchlights during an air raid. I watched that as if mesmerised; in the midst of so much anxiety, here was a spectacle of sheer beauty, recalling the fireworks on St Stephen's Day (20 August) in Budapest—though the colour was missing, it was all silver.

Somehow, I know not how, my mother and my sister found us and we were reunited. That should have been an occasion for joy but it was overshadowed by my father's deteriorating condition.

Early one morning I was woken by a chorus of shouts: 'get going', 'we are going', or some such words—the German shouts echoed by Hungarian shouts. Then in the chill and half-light of that early hour a large grey crowd, ordered about by armed guards, was on the move again towards the railway line—the source of fear—until we noticed that the train, towards which we were being herded, was made up of ordinary passenger carriages. It was a sight that, for the moment, lifted the ever-present anxiety about 'what next?' because those dilapidated, old carriages were the kind normally used to transport human beings.

We arrived at one of the smaller stations of Vienna. We tried to tell father about this, hoping to lift his spirits, but he was too far gone for any encouragement. In any case, the authorities decided that he must be separated from us—perhaps sent to the Robert Koch hospital. But how could one trust anything said to us?—after the deportation train and the Strasshof camp, and against the rumours of worse to come. I last saw my father lying on a stretcher almost motionless. I waved to him and he waved back with a sad, faint gesture of his hand.

We rejoined the column being marched through the outskirts of the city, grasping any sign of hope. We kept going from hour to hour. (My story, 'Two Occasions', *Double Vision*, pp. 42–45, attempted an imaginative recreation of the experience here recorded.[4])

Our next transit camp turned out to be a run-down doss-house (*Obdachlosenheim*) where disorder ruled. Was anybody in charge at all? Probably a few Nazi civilians, not the police or the SS. Thousands of people roamed around aimlessly all day; the walls were covered in crude or pornographic graffiti accompanied by un-witty words in several languages; there was a lot of shoving, shouting, arguing and barter trading among the inmates (cigarettes for food, for example) and the rumour-mongering about our next destination had started afresh. All this might have been

---

[4] Andrew K. Kennedy *Double Vision* (Cambridge: Meadows Press 1999) pp42-45

interpreted as 'good signs', in a benign regime, inducing an almost optimistic mood for a time. So when I realised that the gates of the place were hardly guarded, I simply walked out of the messy building into the neighbourhood—into an ordinary street in suburban Vienna. For quite a while I wandered up and down as if on a promenade, gazed at the window of a pastry shop, eavesdropped on a conversation and read the headlines of a newspaper. Suddenly the urge to escape—the dizzying urge I had earlier experienced in the ghetto and in the brickworks camp—reasserted itself. It seemed so easy to vanish: take a few steps and walk into freedom. But what then? Where would I go? And how could I possibly leave my mother and sister behind?—with my father so ill, perhaps never to return. The thought of 'freeing myself' then turned into a threat. Everything was possible and nothing was possible: I might... I could... but every thought of escape was accompanied by an enormous 'but'. Again the idea of destiny shaping my life totally beyond my control—or any control—troubled me deeply. The seeming loopholes in my situation created anxiety—with random opportunities, potentialities and unforeseeable consequences. It was safer, after all, to be properly locked up and guarded. I chose to surrender.

Back in the 'doss-house' I kept walking around the dormitories and the courtyard, as did many others, with nothing to do. In the narrow courtyard we all circled around an unmarked centre as prisoners do. At one point I found myself surrounded by a small group of strangers, middle-aged male deportees who started questioning me, I knew not why. A burly man with an unattractively patchy scalp—little lumps of black hair sticking out of his baldness—started cross-examining me in a bass voice:

'Where is your father?' 'In hospital?' 'How do you know?' 'What's the matter with him?' 'Do you think he will get out alive?'

I tried to answer all questions quite meekly though I could see in this stranger a self-appointed torturer.

17. Working for the Reich

Within a few days we were marched through several anonymous streets in southern Vienna. Just to be in this city was barely credible and a gift to those optimists who had been building hopes on the old argument that in 'a civilised place' we would not be killed.

We came to a sprawling network of factories, an industrial area so vast that it was impossible to gain an overall impression. Once inside, it became obvious that the place was teeming with prisoners—the sound of Russian and French words reached us. Trucks loaded with ominous guns and other armour crossed our path. Those marshalling us looked different from any soldiers or police we had seen before, they must have been the factory's uniformed security guards. And the men in grey suits, with grey faces and conspicuous swastikas on their lapels, were presumably in charge of Ostmark-Werke, the name of the place, we soon discovered, rumoured to be part of the Todt organisation, a huge Nazi enterprise employing slave labour. So we were about to be forced to produce destructive weapons for the Third Reich—an unacceptable situation quietly accepted without protest by all of us, as a way of survival. Soon after our arrival, top officials from the factory inspected us coolly, without any visible or audible contact, and left abruptly. We did not see them again until there was an emergency.

We were taken to the third floor of a multi-storey warehouse and into an enormous empty storage space. It had an uncovered concrete floor and secured narrow windows. Electric bulbs hung from the ceiling. Tiered bunk beds were being assembled and allocated to names read from a long list; as we were a family of four—so we kept saying, still with conviction—we were given a double unit of two-tier bunk-beds with a small wooden cupboard at the head of each bed. That left very little personal space but it counted as luxury accommodation after the extreme confinement of the deportation train and our transit camps. That small corner of the warehouse floor could be thought of as a lair or a den, certainly a refuge, though wide open to other prisoners on three sides. On the right side there was a space of about a yard before the next pile of bunk-beds where a family we knew had settled, while on the left we looked on to a space that was shared territory with its own window letting in precious beams of light. In front of us there was empty space—nothing but the vast concrete floor stretching from one end of the warehouse to the other; only along the opposite wall, which seemed quite far away, could one see other people moving about jerkily like marionettes in front of another row of bunk-beds. At that time there were probably only about a hundred people sleeping in this room—

again a great improvement after being squeezed into minimal space with a multitude of worn-out bodies.

Soon we unpacked our remaining belongings, taking care to put father's things—everything he was not allowed to take with him—on the carefully prepared fourth bed, under my bed, in our complex of four beds. We expected him daily, I certainly did. Yet as the time of his absence lengthened, an unspoken dread visited us daily.

For a time we all worked twelve hours on a night shift tending noisy machine lathes. But whether it soon became obvious that child labour was virtually useless under extreme conditions or whether there was a benign director in the factory management, my workload, as well as that of my sister but not of mother, was reduced by half—to six hours a day. Most of our work consisted of fetching and carrying everything required for the assembly of anti-aircraft guns, especially for the anti-rust painted steel plates that were to form the two sides of the guns. This was carefully explained to us by the foreman, a Viennese craftsman of the old sort in whom we intuitively recognised a humane person, though he would rage and roar like a wounded beast if anybody did anything wrong. These conditions were bearable, at least in the early months of the remaining summer and the long autumn. In that early phase we were not yet very hungry and the children—up to sixteen—even got occasional fun out of their daily round, entertaining each other with stories and memories as they were allowed to talk quietly while carrying armoured plates from site to site. It was actually at the workplace that a certain cabaret spirit began to develop, with satirical mimicry of the foreman and his bossy underling, Mr. Weiss, a corpulent and ageing Jewish deportee. And already escape plans were being hatched, for a quick exit when the day of Germany's defeat came, to keep our spirits up.

My mother, however, had to pay the full penalty of slave labour—twelve hours through every night, from seven to seven. She had to operate a drilling machine that required great concentration; it is a wonder that she managed to do that at all, never having done manual work before. Already in the early months she was visibly exhausted every morning, and it was difficult for her to get decent sleep during the day in the general noise of the concrete barracks. The food rations were getting more and more insufficient for a working adult, especially as my mother would go short of food so that we, the children, could eat some of her portions—a sacrifice not realised by me until much later.

One day, at least a month after our arrival in the factory, my mother, sister and myself were called into a sinister little room serving as surgery, run by the doctor couple Geszti (known to us from Debrecen). They had been placed in a privileged position by the Nazi authorities: given power not only in all matters of hygiene and health but also in the internal oversight of the prisoners. We were solemnly asked to sit down. I sat on a bed wondering why Dr Geszti looked so gloomy and why we had to sit in silence. Eventually, in a low voice, as if officiating at a ceremony, he told us that father was dead.

He went on to give us some details that I cannot recall because I had lapsed into a state of 'not being there'. I listened and I could not listen. I questioned the reality of the place, relapsing into the state I had earlier experienced in the deportation train. I remember thinking—in so far as I had coherent thoughts—that they were telling us something that could not be proved: I wanted to be taken to see my father's body or at least to be told precisely what had happened, information about his illness, his treatment, his state of mind, his messages, his burial. Perhaps they were giving us false news, to conceal something—perhaps he had been taken to another camp, a much worse camp where his life was in real danger. But he would survive to be reunited with us when the time came. Meanwhile, I wished Dr Geszti would shut up. When I tried to listen for a few minutes, he was in the middle of a sort of funeral oration: 'a great financial expert, full of ambition and promise, cruelly cut off. His untimely death marks the end of a career that might have led to a high position, perhaps in the finance ministry of a new government after the war…'

I walked out quickly. At the earliest opportunity I went for a long walk around the territory of several factory buildings—crying but still in the company of my father. I did not talk to him, but I felt sure he was with me.

My sister had been informed of our father's death before my mother and I were told. This was a pity because, though the Drs.Geszti meant well (assuming that Eva, at age sixteen, would bear the news more bravely than my mother and me) they placed a terrible double burden on her: the loss compounded by the enforced secrecy to be sustained for several weeks. And my sister had been very close to father for many years. As far as I remember we never talked about what happened at the time, and not for a very long time.

My feeling of unreality was deepened by my father's death and created a recurrent feeling of all-embracing unreality. Days or weeks passed in a dream-like state, and news from the outside world was met with incredulity or it was material to be spun into fantasies of deliverance. One day (just after 20th July, the attempted assassination of Hitler) I saw a newspaper headline in big black type:

Es lebe der Führer! (Long live Hitler!)

I spontaneously interpreted this as meaning that Hitler might not live: why would they say 'long live' if he was alive and well? He must have been badly wounded by the assassination bomb or crazier than ever or dying, only they dared not announce it... Later, when the siren sounded in the factory, I took it as a signal of general alarm, perhaps the beginning of the end for the Reich. Everywhere around me I looked out for signs of a final collapse: in the troubled faces of the factory police, the huddled groups of workers whispering, the peculiar slowness of the working day, the oppressive silence.

For months nothing seemed to happen, time stretched without contours. After the traumas, I went about my new daily routine—of work, eating, sleeping—as a sleepwalker. The bereaved family held together: we were close but not particularly communicative. And contact with other people tended to be minimal, apart from the occasional argument about the distribution of food—a daily rush to the huge food containers to make sure one got there in time for a fair portion and not just the dregs. The theatre of observation had also contracted, with a daily viewing of the same people doing the same things. For instance, immediately to my right the good-looking, grown-up daughter of the Lukács family, Marica, could be seen going to bed every day with the same over-cautious modesty, making sure that not an inch of flesh became visible as she furtively pulled down her stockings. On the left side, an old woman invariably grumbled at the start of each day about something that mattered only to herself; at a time when many prisoners still feared the worst for the whole community, it was odd to hear that woman complain about her corns or some such thing.

One day a whole new transport of people arrived, unexpectedly, to be accommodated in the middle of that enormous warehouse floor. So the population of the camp (we called it the lager) had virtually doubled and the open space was now going to be fully occupied by an intrusive row of wardrobes and bunk beds from which strange new faces stared back at us, the primary settlers. These people had been deported from southern and central Hungary—cities like Szeged and Szolnok—and were inevitably viewed with some apprehension: would they not reduce our scant resources as they had already reduced our space? But the newcomers were eager to present themselves as friendly, even amiable, people who had come to bring succour and entertainment, so to speak. And soon, out of that anonymous but suspect group, there emerged a bright and beautiful girl, another Eva (Weser), my mature contemporary. I am not sure how soon, but before winter set in and conditions in the camp started to deteriorate rapidly, the two of us struck up a friendship. It was warm and spontaneous and it practically ended my long-drawn-out lethargy. We met frequently for hours of animated talk, usually after everybody else had gone to bed, in or near a public place like the communal bathroom. We talked and talked just about everything in our short lives—past and present, under the shadow of our threatening future—but I cannot remember a word of what we said to each other. When in a short story—'Surviving' (late 2003)—I tried to re-create a version of these encounters, I found I could recall nothing at all; I had to invent the entire dialogue, together with the feelings, the implicit love or friendship that kept up our spirits. We must have looked forward to seeing each other after the war, if we survived; but we never saw each other again.

As winter and the air raids disrupted our brief period of calm, we compensated ourselves with certain cheering distractions. A group of talented children—led by a girl called Agnes—directed a group performing a whole set of cabaret acts and lyrics. Satirical verses on individual members of the 'company' were sung to well-known tunes; I was targeted with a jingle about the boy who didn't know how to steal potatoes. Storytelling, juggling and singing also formed part of our performance. A tall young soprano from Szeged repeatedly sang the pearl-fisher's aria from the Bizet opera of that name with finely controlled passion. The audience of prisoners was stilled and for a short time we forgot the horrors lived through and our troubled situation—in itself a wonder.

The life of the forced labour camp was getting bleaker. The air raids started in early winter and went on and on for months, night and day. The raids gained in intensity until one day it really felt like the end, the expected end, in an unexpected form. We had been cowering in the air raid shelter for a long time when it started to sway, the roof and the walls seemed to move as if we were suspended in a concrete hammock in the wind. Simultaneously the light and the ventilation went out. We could hear shrieks from the next shelter. There was a tremendous explosion somewhere very near and what sounded like a massive building collapsing above us. All one could do in that dark was to wrap one's head tightly in an overcoat and think of nothing. But it was impossible not to think darkly as the raid went on and on, with the sound of explosions from several directions. I thought I would never see my mother and sister again, for they had been ordered out on extra duty to clear up the rubble from previous raids. What if they were ordered to clear up our shelter after it had been hit? And what if we were killed by a bomb from a British bomber? Apart from thinking up such bitter ironies, I took refuge in repeating some mantra or other, some simple words, probably 'deliver us from evil'—'deliver us from evil'.

The shelter was not hit but when we finally crept out it became clear that the building above us had been totally destroyed. Hardly any factory structure in the entire area was left standing, in whatever direction one looked, except for the multi-storey building where we were housed. There it stood, intact in the midst of the general ruin of the vast factory.

My mother was still in a distraught state when we were re-united for, coming back from her rubble-clearing work in the city, she and my sister were greeted at one of the ruined gates by people calling out:

Ostmark-Werke kaputt. Alles Kaputt!

They could see nothing but heaps of rubble and human confusion; they could not have known that I was safe in the concrete shelter under the massive ruins.

In the remaining buildings, and among the ruins, work resumed right through the severe winter. It must have been decided not to evacuate the prisoners, and I think we all welcomed the continuity despite the worsening conditions. Fear for our future increased: we sensed the nervousness of the factory guards, of the foremen and of the factory managers who suddenly re-appeared like gods out of a machine. They came, a small party of men still wearing elegant overcoats with swastikas, hats and scarves and gloves and polished shoes—utterly incongruous against a landscape of devastation dotted with emaciated prisoners. I could see those mighty men staring at one of the ruined workshops, gesticulating helplessly. I stood quite near to the group and stared straight into a clean-shaven face above his perfectly cut winter coat. He noticed my stare and stared back at me, our eyes met. The director and the slave, I thought. My mind's eye brought back the image of my father inspecting a factory building in just such a well-cut winter coat and I envisaged the present Herr Direktor as a future prisoner or a war criminal—I did not wish this on him, I just foresaw his fall.

In the next major air raid a large number of incendiary bombs were dropped on the factory. A firestorm raged, engulfing previously undamaged parts of the built-up area. I managed to walk around, not too far from the conflagration, watching the roofs fall in and the walls crumble. The spectacle of tall red flames all around us was frighteningly beautiful; it warmed the air as if spring had come; the dark smoke and the acrid stench lingered for days. Apocalypse. Surely the end was coming. We had heard, from our own rubble clearers, that the inner city was mostly in ruins, the famous Vienna Opera had received a direct hit soon after a performance of Wagner's *Götterdämmerung*, it was rumoured. But it was impossible to suppress the nagging question: how could we possibly survive the general collapse of the Reich?

Again I observed the nervousness of those in charge of us, rushing up and down, giving futile orders. Then came a great frost that froze the charred remains of all kinds of material, an unreal scenery. I wandered about 'inspecting the damage', feeling less and less real myself. One day a resourceful boy called Gábor, about my age, discovered that there were stacks of burnt sugar lying under the snow and ice in one of the destroyed store-rooms. He excitedly invited me to join in digging up this food treasure—by that time anything that could be eaten was a priceless windfall. So I went with him and started digging—with my nails—and managed to unearth a few grains of sugar. Minutes later I stopped, sickened: what was the point of all that? Who cared? It was futile; everything was futile. Soon we would starve anyway. Gábor acted as the essential practical man whilst I was moving further inward amid fits of passivity and a kind of nihilism.

By midwinter we were always hungry. Even low-grade hunger is a sensation that cannot be forgotten: it is felt in the morning, during the day, especially after a meal, and again at bedtime and on waking at night. It was about this time that I had developed the art of cutting off miniscule slices of rind from cheese and from the salami that constituted my mother's ultimate emergency food reserve. It was like sneakily raiding the pantry, a thoroughly antisocial act that would sooner or later be discovered. Less guiltily but unsatisfactorily, one could get hold of a tiny portion of left-over cream cheese or mustard and spread it thin on a dry chunk of bread—just to have something in the mouth. Another source of food supply could be found in the large containers: if you volunteered to carry these heavy metal tanks, you could be rewarded with an extra portion. Failing that, you could wait until the container was empty and see if a few drops of nourishment could be scraped from the mess at the bottom. Sometimes the man in charge of the food distribution—a Jew appointed by the camp command—would take pity on a hungry-looking boy and dish out a little extra portion. That act of mercy was quite unpredictable, depending on the giver's mood; if he happened to be in a bad mood he would send you away with a shout. Rarely, food gifts came my way: a sandwich from a Frenchman, a privileged prisoner, and some small green tomatoes from an Austrian workman who saw me struggling in the wintry cold with the usual metal load to be carted to another block.

At the same time we were always cold—except in the workshop itself. Our winter clothes were not sufficient to protect the body, especially fingers and toes; my damaged toenails were framed in pus. At bedtime I would curl up into a kind of ball under the blanket and wait until my body generated a certain amount of heat by itself. Outside, the best way of fighting the cold was to creep into one of the remaining workshops in another part of the factory and stay in a warm corner as long as possible, pretending to be invisible. Once I hid near a giant steam hammer, watching the molten metal being pounded and storing its fire and heat under my skin.

One day, weeks into the new year of 1945, I woke with a high fever. I may have caught it after I had fallen into a contaminated pond when the ice broke under me during a clumsy walk. Soon the fever got worse—about 40 degrees Celsius or even higher—and it turned into undulating fever; it may have been typhoid but it was never properly diagnosed. I was exempted from forced labour and allowed to stay in my bunk-bed through the good offices of the influential Drs. Geszti who also procured some medicine for me—I don't know what. Without such help I would not have survived. In any case I felt repeatedly that I would not survive. Most of the time I was sleeping or dozing, roused only by the air raid sirens; it was obligatory to go down into the shelter even when very ill. From my bed I watched the life of the camp as a kind of phantasmagoria. From time to time a half-familiar face would bend over me—my mother? my sister?—and ask me something incomprehensible. Strange faces appeared, one after another, staring at me with protruding eyes. 'Drink this', I heard, 'drink it!' One day a round-faced, strongly built man came right up to my bed—was it the 'food-man'?—and threw some object towards me like a dart. As it landed on my bed I heard him shout an order: 'eat it!' and he vanished. On examination, the object turned out to be a piece of bread: I ate it and then I ate some more.

Winter was nearly over by the time I recovered, but the feeling of unreality outlasted my illness. Not much was left of Ostmark-Werke by the time I was well enough to return to my daily stint but we were kept working, still, under increasingly futile conditions. One day I observed that a freight train, loaded with completed anti-aircraft guns only a few days earlier, had been re-shunted to a railway siding with its damaged cargo—undelivered. Also, there seemed to be fewer swastikas around, the local workmen no longer sported them on their lapels and the management had retreated into final invisibility. Our arch-Viennese foreman had become exceptionally friendly and kept reminding us daily how well he had treated us all along. He, Herr Kuplein, was organizing a secret rescue plan: he would drive us out in a lorry straight to the Hungarian frontier, when the time was ripe, in return for a specified sum to be paid mostly in gold (out of the reserve coins sewn into my mother's shoulder pads). The conspirators seemed to be cheerfully confident concerning this secret escape route, though I remained quietly sceptical about the scheme's chances of success. I was equally sceptical about the efficacy of the orthodox Jews' prayers—they seemed to pray ever more fervently several times a day in a corner of the large lager room, in carefully preserved prayer shawls and phylacteries fastened to their foreheads with leather thongs. Instead I put my trust in the little maps culled from newspapers where I carefully marked the forward movements of the Russian front, relentlessly advancing in our direction—trying to estimate the time it would take for the Red Army to occupy 'our' territory and wondering whether they would use bombs (as the British and the Americans had done) or heavy artillery. Doing what I had always liked doing, concentrating on Geography and strategy, kept me sane and tempered that recurrent feeling: nothing was happening, nothing real.

18. The Lottery Again

A nerve-racking period of transition came to a climax one day in late March when we were suddenly ordered to pack our belongings and start marching again, to the nearest railway station. Our walk took us across parts of 'civilised' Vienna near the Danube: we crossed the famous amusement park of the Prater. There was something uncanny and disturbing about passing those boarded-up fairground booths and the giant Ferris wheel, once more in complete ignorance about our ultimate destination and in a run-down state. Even a relatively short march was too long for many after nine months on diminishing food rations, and in my case after a serious illness. We were physically feeble. My mother had lost some twenty kilos in weight and was looking emaciated. We were hardly fit to march and the old fear, of being punished by our guards if we dragged our feet, returned. (My story, 'Surviving', is an imaginative reconstruction from minimal memory).

A slow train—dilapidated carriages but not cattle trucks—took us back to the sinister but supposedly survivable place we instantly recognised as Strasshof transit camp. There was a curious sense of relief in that familiarity, though fresh rumours started almost at once: we would soon be taken somewhere else. But where? I overheard but tended to dismiss such rumours and took refuge once more in lowering my state of being alive. I was aware that people all around me were complaining anxiously— about the general chaos and uncertainty, the permanent dust in the air, the dirty barracks, the thinnest soup and coffee, near-starvation rations, the screaming Ukrainian women guards with their sticks or whips supervising the food handout—but I saw all these things as transitory. Whether or not we came out alive was another matter, unforeseeable, mere chance, I thought. Did it matter? Not in the perspective of history or nature. In any case, we/I could do nothing. 'They' were playing roulette with us. Was the lottery divine or diabolical or totally accidental? No answer came to such questions. There was no need for people to indulge in futile preparations for they knew not what. Preserve your energy, I instructed myself, and wait for the Red Army—my small maps told me that the Russians had reached Austria.

Yet the rumour-mongers were proved right, there were new developments and threats. Within a few days we were rushed back to the railway line and pushed into another train—this time into sinister cattle trucks. We were not even counted, as far as I can remember. The old fear returned. But there was more space inside the wagon than in our deportation train the previous year and you could actually survey the crowd of people sitting on their luggage and recognise a few faces. Before climbing on that train, I had discovered something that was presumably meant to be a secret: I had noticed a word, a place-name, a destination, scrawled in chalk on the outside of a wagon: Theresienstadt. Didn't someone say that was a 'good camp', visited by the International Red Cross? Wasn't that the place that had a Jewish orchestra? The 'good camp' rumour was false. Had the truth been known, the prisoners (thrown together from many different camps) would have been maximally anxious.

That train never left for the destined camp. The sirens sounded and soon we could hear a series of tremendous explosions coming from very near. The wagon was shaking, luggage suspended from the roof crashed to the floor. You could see the fear in people's eyes but there was no panic. I had time to consider: there was a good chance that we would be hit—no shelter this time—and there would be no meaning (or something like it) in perishing then, so near to our rescue. Then further explosions stopped all thinking.

19. Doomsday to Liberation

Before darkness we were led back into the transit camp: into our former barracks, now in great disorder; and disorder generated further anxiety, after the brief spell of relief when the bombs failed to hit us in the train. All the known negative features of the camp—scant food, overcrowding, the dust, the stink, and the screaming Ukrainian guards—revisited us in a more intense form. At the same time the uncertainty increased daily. What were the Nazis going to do to us? What were they up to? Where were they anyway? Their presence seemed to be getting less and less conspicuous.

One day I saw a group of soldiers carry a body singing *Ich hatt' einen Kamaraden, einen bessern findst du nicht*—marching slowly to bury a fallen comrade. They marched towards the woods outside the camp and did not return. I had the feeling that—probably corresponding to fact—our armed jailers were invisibly drifting away from the camp. Shots were being fired frequently somewhere or other but who was shooting and who was being shot? What was happening? Where did those threatening noises come from? Then we woke to a subdued but alarming boom that sounded like distant thunder, in the wrong season. It went on and on, boom, boom, boom for days and nights, at first in spurts and then continuously. One morning I looked up and saw that the sky had turned red.

As the distant noise approached, the camp lapsed into an ominous silence, at least I can remember nothing except that constant, heavy artillery bombardment accompanied by earth tremor as the noise grew. By the time we were certain that the boom came from the heavy guns of the Red Army, there were no more German uniforms of any kind to be seen in the camp. The officers and the guards had vanished without any signal and there was nobody in charge—the kitchens and storerooms, the barracks of command and administration had all been abandoned. Days passed: we were caught in an eerie no-man's land.

I don't think anybody felt jubilant at that time; if anything, I felt apprehensive. However, the most adventurous prisoners—led by Mrs Lénárt, an old friend of ours who retained full health and a commanding confidence—started to organise our exit or escape. It was decided, very sensibly, to stay put while the battle was still raging not too far from our camp but in an uncertain direction. The food problem was settled by looting: as soon as it was generally realised that we were 'free', all the storerooms were ransacked. The looters were not content to take any food they could lay their hands on, they also took objects of value, destroyed files and broke up the furniture. I saw a man smash a picture of Hitler with joyous abandon. It was a revolution. That was satisfactory in itself, but I could not help fearing that they might come back, any minute, and take revenge; the broken Hitler picture would rise up and inflict some terrible revenge.

Then I lapsed into my unreal, sleepwalking state again and could barely believe that it was I—the surviving I—who was somehow chosen to wander about that desolate camp, still alive.

I was reluctant to join the looters. But then I was ordered to go and bring back a bucketful of jam from containers abandoned in the bombed train on one of the railway tracks. So I took on the role of the courageous burglar and walked up to the damaged tracks, clambered up one of the wagons and began to ladle the sticky red liquid jam into a bucket. Out of nowhere a man in a worn German uniform rose up and pointed his rifle straight at me. I instantly jumped off the wagon, taking a large quantity of jam with me—not in my bucket but on my trousers. No shots were fired. As for those trousers—the knickerbockers I had been wearing throughout our deportation—they later got badly scorched when hung out to dry by a wood-fired stove in our barracks. Clearly I had become a danger to myself in a dangerous environment—not in full control of my movements or my possessions. That worried my mother and angered her practical fiends: in one episode they turned on me when I revealed that I had seen a pig's head somewhere outside a storeroom. 'What?', someone shouted, 'and why didn't you bring it back at once?'—'Well, I might have done, but, but...' What's the point anyhow, I speculated. I became aware that most people around me were much more determined to survive than I was. I had my doubts about the point of surviving as I resumed wandering about the camp half-asleep.

I had only just woken one morning when I went out to collect some firewood from a shed. Suddenly a fierce-looking soldier in an unusual uniform confronted me. He looked me up and down, took off his strange rifle and started firing—above my head and with a broad grin. 'Russky Russky!' he roared and lifted me up high. He put me down, shook my hand and we had a kind of conversation: I interpreted his meaning through his tone and gestures. He wished to celebrate our freedom; and I, in turn, thanked him, for what?—for freedom? After a few minutes the Russian soldier left as suddenly as he had come and I returned to the barracks bringing the good news; apparently I was the first person in our part of the camp to have seen someone from the Red Army live. Later that day, towards nightfall, I was befriended by a Russian officer. We walked together for at least a quarter of an hour, communicating somehow, about the camp, the battle, the end of the war; he spoke a little German and I guessed his drift from his body language. Suddenly he stopped and called my attention to the buzz of an insect just above our heads; '*Maikäfer!*' (maybug), he said and then we just stood there listening together with rapt attention to the prolonged buzzing, as if to a concert. Before leaving he pointed to the decorations on his uniform and said simply: '*Kommandant*'.

That encounter turned out to be very helpful when, the following night, a far from sober Russian soldier stumbled into our barracks and spotted my sister lying in her bunk bed. As he lurched towards her, I felt as if inspired: I walked straight up to the soldier and indicated that I was a friend of the *Kommandant*. Somehow the soldier understood the information I was trying to convey to him: he turned round and left peacefully.

That day it became generally known that being liberated (a new word to us) by the Russians had at least two major disadvantages: 1) they raped women without distinguishing between friend and foe; nor was it necessarily an advantage to admit being Jewish for there was anti-Semitism among the Russian soldiery, we were told, though I had experienced nothing but the moving friendliness I had related; 2) they were not making the slightest attempt to organise either a rescue or provisions, so the abandoned camp became a source of new danger—disease and further malnourishment if not starvation. We were still in the middle of a battlefield—somewhere between the camp and the city of Vienna heavy guns were raging incessantly and war planes kept flying over us. The disorder and the sanitation got worse daily. Scraping for food, my mother exchanged a fine pair of black shoes, left over from my father, for a small loaf of bread. As conditions deteriorated, our group—led by the strong-willed Mrs. Lénárt—decided to leave immediately, walking roughly in the direction of Bratislava. And so, when night fell, we set out on a strange 'voluntary' forced march.

20. On the Battlefield

For almost three days we walked through an often nightmarish landscape: through abandoned villages, fields strewn with the debris of war, scattered personal belongings, the rotting carcass of a horse, a dead German soldier lying across our path. In broad daylight we were targeted by a German fighter plane: bullets from its machine gun landed all around us churning up the earth only inches away from where I was taking cover in a ditch. Pieces of earth fell on my back, a bullet came very close. (That was my fifth escape from death.) Later that day a lorry passed us and, travelling on it, we recognised the only surviving young couple from our camp, the wife fatally wounded in one of those final machine-gun attacks; that beautiful woman died within a day, we heard afterwards. On every road vast convoys of the Red Army were moving westward; after the motorised units came a long procession of horse-drawn carriages filled with every kind of loot, from clocks to wardrobes, guarded by women soldiers (*barishnya*). It was hard to believe that this was the army that had defeated the Nazi forces all the way from Stalingrad and was now marching on Vienna; in reality what we saw was the dishevelled rear guard, which might as well have come from the First World War or even earlier times. These troops took not the slightest notice of us; we were left entirely to our own resources—a kind of freedom we were not used to.

At night we had to go on marching without rest because the empty house with its tempting beds, where we had hoped to get some sleep, was judged unsafe; Russian soldiers were said to be on the rampage in the village and the women panicked. Walking through the night was a new hardship that threw me back into a state of half-conscious detachment. This was not just my response to a new crisis. Deprived of sleep and suffering from chronic diarrhoea—after the first good meal, all that fat on top of hunger— I was totally exhausted. In the end, the group decided that we must split up: the sturdy ones marched ahead while our family and a small group of weaklings were left behind. But by that time the craving for safety was secondary to the craving for sleep, sleep! Finally, a haystack offered a resting place. It had clearly been slept on by refugees and abandoned in great haste with heaps of possessions, kitchen utensils, clothes and sheets. No object, however useful, could possibly tempt us, as we were ourselves forced to jettison one thing after another when carrying our few remaining possessions became an intolerable burden.

It was hard enough to carry our own bodies along those interminable roads in our weakened state. In one of the villages we somehow acquired a small horse-cart, without a horse, and, having loaded it with our collected rucksacks and bags, moved eastward, pushing and pulling that modest vehicle with our remaining strength through the long hours of the night. Or was the cart pulling me of its own will? Was the earth under us a moving platform? Was it happening at all? Once more the whole experience felt unreal. I was walking like a sleepwalker, barely conscious for long hours of darkness. Towards dawn a horse-drawn carriage came to our rescue. The driver was a strange, wild-looking, member of the Red Army, almost certainly a Tartar, with big turned-down black moustaches—we remembered and feared the type, from illustrations in history books showing the devastating Tartar invasion of Hungary in the Middle Ages. Our rescuer expressed himself in short, staccato monosyllables, incomprehensible as words but supported by ample body language: he pointed his whip to his carriage, then to us and our baggage, and then eastward in the direction of the Austro-Slovak border, or so we guessed. We climbed atop his carriage and enjoyed the luxury of moving effortlessly in a slow, shaky trot, as the Tartar vainly urged his horse to speed up, with shouts and cracks of his whip. The hilly scenery slowly unrolled around us, unknown territory with not a village or a human being in sight in the half-light of early morning. I began to wonder whether we were being kidnapped. Where was he taking us, to the Crimea, or to Hades? 'Bratislava', I shouted. '*Da da*', he shouted back. After a long while the carriage stopped, the driver signalled that he had another errand, dropped us in the middle of nowhere, and pointed his whip once more to the East, which we took to be our promised land. We waved him off and he waved back with a stiff grin.

21. Unreal Survival

Finally we arrived in Bratislava (once a leading Hungarian city, Pozsony) with help from another lift. Our energy was beginning to return after some rest—our long journey's end in sight. But I was unable to shake off my dazed and confused state, which lasted a week or longer, so that everything I here relate was seen through a veil—nothing was clear at the time.

A lot of information reached us in a short time. We were still walking through the city streets when a group of local people surrounded us and kept questioning us—they were curious and incredulous that Jews could survive. (They did not survive in Slovakia). Suddenly a woman said: 'Roosevelt is dead!' That was moving and upsetting. To be given this news just when we were all waiting to hear something good—the end of the war? the death of Hitler?—intensified one's feeling of insecurity: the world we were entering was still insecure and all life was fragile.

Better news could be read out of rough posters in the streets: a map with red arrows pointing towards Berlin, a huge hammer and sickle over Hitler's head, and the pincer movement of the Allies closing in on the entire Third Reich. I also managed to decipher certain headlines in Czech or Slovak, for example: The Red Army is approaching the Oder. That was just what I needed to restore my spirits, maps and more maps showing the advancing front lines, just as I had imagined it a year earlier.

The reception centre turned out to be an unfinished block of flats run by some unspecified and distinctly bureaucratic local authority (supposedly under international control, probably by UNRRA for the benefit of displaced persons). On arrival we were immediately screened, bombarded with instructions that were far from reassuring for frightened and exhausted people. The chief measures concerned disinfection and interviews to determine our identity prior to the eventual issue of individual repatriation papers. (That was the first time I have heard of 'repatriation' and I pondered the meaning of the word and its root—*patria... pro patria morir*). Those who were eager to leave for Hungary at once were detained. Nothing could be done, it was proclaimed, until all documents were in order; in any case, there were no trains running yet and no other transport either. There was quite a lot of tension, with squabbles due to poor communication, with translation snags. In effect we were still prisoners, with armed guards standing sentinel at the entrance to the block. And the new uncertainties revived the old ones, so that 'liberation' came to be felt as the continuation of our captivity by other means.

At some point I decided to sneak out of the building on my own and went on a long exploratory walk around the city which, not seriously damaged, was already showing signs of revival. In my poor state—chronic stomach trouble still coupled with a kind of sleepwalking—ordinary sights everywhere looked extraordinary. People were actually walking about the streets with a sense of purpose in their eyes, children were running around freely, shop-windows were filled with goods not seen for a year and extravagant heaps of food (our own food at the reception centre was barely adequate), diners were sitting around the bright white table-cloth of a restaurant eating and drinking at peace, and the flags of nations fluttered from a row of silvery masts: U.S., Britain, the Soviet Union, Czechoslovakia and others—with the swastika nowhere to be seen or seen only being smashed with a hammer on one of those lurid victory cartoons already mentioned. I stopped to stare at the sad framed photographs of dead Russian soldiers on staves in a city park. Then I watched a bunch of tipsy revellers knocking about a barrel of red wine—the wine spilling all over the street. Blood flowing under the feet of all those soldiers and civilians alike—the horror of war, I thought. At the same time there was something life-affirming in the abundance of that spilt wine.

(This episode concludes my short story, 'Wine',
Stand 1992, reprinted in *Double Vision,* 1999).

One day we had lunch with a 'normal' family who had survived the war intact. There they were, safe in their old bourgeois apartment, husband and wife and children, somewhat younger than my sister and I, behaving and talking as if nothing had happened. Lunch was served by a maid—wearing a white apron and a little white head-dress—and the murmur of our conversation resembled the pre-war murmur of citizens not yet damaged. No doubt they could see that we were in a poor condition, they understood that we were accidental survivors after a year of extreme danger, that father had died and that our future was a blank. But the only way they could respond was by asking polite questions and making polite noises, as they might have done if we had just returned from our old planned tour of the Tatra mountains. All that normality and surface smoothness only accentuated my feeling of apartness—I became the alien observer who wondered how these strange humans could go on living among the ruins. Yet the visit in itself must be considered a 'success', an achievement of my mother who had remained practical and inventive despite her being physically weakened. It was she who remembered that my father's old colleague, Mr Farkas, had been appointed manager of the Credit Bank in Bratislava, and it was she who tracked down his address and got permission for a brief exit from our guarded block. And despite my own feelings of estrangement, the visit must have been a significant step on the road back to rehabilitation, to a degree of—that word again—normality.

A few more days of confused waiting followed. What did we do all that time in that overcrowded block of flats? Nothing? Uniformed guards still stood sentinel at the entrance gate. I probably spent my best hours with war maps again, meditating on history—connecting the general story of the war with the story of my family, asking whether it had all been mere chance, or God's will, or a destiny that could be thought about but not explained.

My next definite memory is travelling very slowly by rail on top of an open freight car—through a cold night. The train stopped, nobody knew why, for a long time amid cornfields somewhere in north-west Hungary—I got off and enjoyed pissing in a bush. I enjoyed that more than anything for a long time, for there were no fences and guards, not a human being in sight, only spring corn and a line of trees in the distance.

Again I felt the old temptation to escape, to move away—but what from? Back on the flat-topped freight car for another cold night, waking from restless sleep, it was again difficult to know what was real and what hallucination. The laughter of peasant girls gossiping in Hungarian—that was real. But why was the train moving as slowly as a horse cab and where and when would it arrive? Why did nobody know where we were heading? But, somebody said, the train was moving eastward, perhaps towards Budapest, perhaps. In broad daylight a great dome loomed up quite suddenly on the north side of the Danube: the basilica of Esztergom (the seat of the Roman Catholic primate). So we were on the right route, approaching our destination; but still the train kept stopping jerkily at all kinds of arbitrary places as if it did not have the capacity to continue. Then somebody told us we were near Gödöllö, site of an old royal palace, not far from Budapest. As we clambered off the train my mother had a fall, her weakened body pulled down by her rucksack. I caught her in my arms, suddenly feeling very sorry for her but simultaneously very angry that such a thing could happen now—so near to our journey's end—and I was afraid of the future for her, and for all of us.

At last we reached Budapest where a large crowd, pushing and shouting, immediately surrounded us. On a main road excited people were marching with banners and red flags, roaring incomprehensible slogans. Eventually I could make out 'Long Live Rákosi!' 'Who is Rákosi? I wondered. Why not Rákoczy? (a famous eighteenth century hero with a march named after him). 'Comrade Rákosi is the great leader of the party.' 'What party?' I wanted to ask but the general mood was not encouraging questions. 'It is the First of May', somebody said solemnly. Sure, that's the date—but what was all that hullabaloo about? Another revolution? A Communist take-over?

22. Budapest—Ruins and Relatives

Somehow we found our way back to the city centre, to the splendid Parliament building still standing by the Danube. I looked out over the Danube and instantly saw that the beautiful Chain Bridge (designed by two Scottish engineers, both called Clark) lay broken in the water and high up on the Buda hillside the Royal Palace was a ruin. It was a sight that haunted me for decades.

We tracked down Aunt Agnes's nearby apartment—also in ruins, though parts of the building were still standing. 'Destroyed in the siege', we kept hearing—it was uncanny to hear a word familiar from the history books (the Turkish Siege of Eger, for example) thus applied to a great modern city. So Agnes had become homeless too. Eventually we found her in her refuge, in one small rented room in the same district. She had been reduced to poverty, after losing not only her once sumptuous home but also almost all her worldly possessions both in the city and in the country. Our quiet reunion was solemn rather than emotional, for Agnes responded to our return with polite disbelief. It soon became clear that she could do nothing for us. Having been used to servants, a chauffeur-driven car, advice from lawyers, accountants and other unreliable consultants, she hardly knew how to cope with virtual destitution—another survivor and another victim of the final year of the war.

Uncle Miklós had survived too. Contacted by Agnes, he hastened to meet us, out of breath and sobbing. He did not know until that moment that his younger brother was dead, and he was overcome by the strange fact of our survival—totally unexpected. We spent hours telling each other sad stories, and this time there was a lot of emotion, for the grief felt by Miklós revived our own grief. He told us that grandmother Serena had died during the winter siege—bare, stark news without detail. She died of exhaustion and undernourishment amid anxiety about our fate (after news of the deportations had reached the capital) and amid immediate daily danger: Arrow Cross fascists shooting more and more Jewish victims and throwing the bodies into the river during the prolonged siege and sending others on death marches towards the Austrian frontier. I wanted to know where Serena was buried, remembering that it was some comfort to know where we might one day find father's grave. Nobody knew the answer and Janka, the wife of Miklós, found it necessary to say, rather harshly: 'what does it matter where those bones lie!' Then I realised that my relatives had also been suffering—and have suffered a change.

Miklós and Janka had moved into a dilapidated little flat in a siege-damaged building near one of the Ring boulevards. From the entrance we walked across planks and then up some half-ruined stairways. Somehow beds or sleeping places were found for all three of us; I was given part of a larger room occupied, behind a screen, by an amorous middle-aged couple who, I gathered, had to be cajoled into accepting someone just returned from a Nazi concentration camp. I remained awake for the greater part of the night, mixing excitement and sadness, trying to absorb what had happened that day and in hundreds of days stretching back over that over-long year.

It was at a reception centre set up to help the survivors that we first heard of the death camps and of the vast number of people who had perished there—over four hundred thousand, all of them deported from Hungary at the same time as we had been, in early Summer 1944. What we heard was far more atrocious than any of the rumours and fears over the last year—rumours that we had disbelieved, fears that we had repressed, for the sake of survival. We met people who had returned from a death camp and we met others who were still anxiously searching, 'hoping against hope', waiting for the return of their loved ones. We quietly accepted the death of grandmother Olga, judging it impossible that she might still return, for all the deportees from Győr had been sent immediately to Auschwitz—another name heard for the first time in those days. It was later discovered that a senior SS officer had muddled the transports: our train should have been sent to the extermination camp and not the train from Győr. In a sense, grandmother Olga had taken my place, though it is dangerous to think like that for more than a second.

We also visited the headquarters of the Credit Bank (we were not told that it had been ransacked by Soviet soldiers). Mother was received with helpful sympathy. Father was given a posthumous promotion to Class 2, presumably the second highest grade in the bank entailing a higher widow's pension, if there was to be a private pension at all in the unsettled political future. For the time being, mother was assured, we could count on being given the use of two rooms in the bank building in Debrecen, since our old home had been requisitioned by the new Hungarian army. A senior director, Ullmann, had visited the bank building and recognised one of our Persian rugs still lying around after heavy looting—he praised the beauty of that rug as there was nothing else left to praise.

I walked to Buda on my own across a pontoon bridge and saw again the ruins of the old city under the Royal Palace. I spent hours walking around among those ruins. There was hardly a single undamaged house to be seen and everywhere the streets were covered in rubble, often impassable.

Burned-out tanks and artillery pieces had not yet been removed. The risk of unexploded bombs made people stare at their feet as they walked. Dead trees commemorated the dead. I remembered the biblical Lamentations over the ruins of Jerusalem and kept asking: can this city be lived in? can it be re-built? how long will it take, twenty years or more, how long?

23. Home = No Home—Just Another Transit?

A week later we set out on a snail-paced train journey back to Debrecen—our childhood home. But how could we call it home still or again? What was the point of taking that train at all? The old third-class carriages were so overcrowded that for many hours I stood in the corridor sandwiched among other weary travellers and large articles of luggage—memories of the deportation train with full awareness of our new freedom added. At one point somebody lifted me up to enable me to pee from the window, to general mirth, but that too reminded me of the horrible makeshift disposal of urine and faeces in the cattle truck.

Ruins were the first thing that met the eye on arrival at the station, more ruins. But the city centre, the main street, was surprisingly intact (unlike Budapest, this city had escaped becoming a battlefield). We entered the bank building amid tension and a peculiar, almost sick curiosity, surprised to find it standing there, rock-like and indifferent. Our old six-room apartment was occupied by the new Hungarian army—we knew then that our home was lost forever. I certainly expected something like that. Our first-floor apartment had been thoroughly looted: some blamed the escaping Germans, others the marauding Russians. It was probably the combined effort of the two invading armies, helped, it soon became clear, by some of our good neighbours and other trusted persons. My mother, who had astonishingly regained her energy, started to organise our new life with relentless effort and set in motion a search for stolen property. She kept discovering missing objects all over the place: a porcelain vase in the concierge's window, a broken Biedermeier armchair in a house across the street, linen and other goods in the house of our former cook (after her home was searched by an aggressive detective). She travelled to Budapest where she tracked down one of her Persian rugs at an auction; she also reclaimed a porcelain dinner set from grandmother Olga's home in Györ, only to have it immediately stolen in transport. A few valuable articles were returned voluntarily: my father's clothes and my mother's fur-coat, worse for the wear as the person looking after it had used it as a blanket nightly in an air-raid shelter for months. Most memorably, Mr Szito, the faithful bank servant (whom I have mentioned before) returned a complete collection of gold coins in a tube and again refused to accept a reward. His honesty counterbalanced the obvious greed of others who, no doubt convinced that our exit was for all time, helped themselves to generous portions of loot. Meanwhile, the bronze chandeliers still hung in one of our sitting rooms (re-visited with permission from the army)—a single object out of all the furniture and belongings my parents had collected in a life-time.

I took note of these goings on with bemused detachment—a version of the 'unreal' feelings I had stored up in the lager. I was still asking silently: does all this matter? If my mother and my sister emerged from the deportation strengthened—or hardened or just more practical and purposeful—I think I was softened up in several respects. I kept participating in events without—I felt—being there, or else I saw everything through the prism of the experiences of the past, the deportation year. I attended the funeral of a classmate's father seeing it as a substitute funeral for my father, carefully observing every moment of the ritual: the open grave, the lowering of the coffin, the casting of lumps of earth and flowers ... mourning or watching mournfully. Another time I visited, with my mother, the son of a bank official in the hospital where he lay, still partially conscious, with severe brain damage—at age seventeen he had shot himself in the head for unrequited love. He died within days. Mixed feelings and questionings followed: how could he throw his life away so lightly?—life that we found so precarious yet precious, preserved through chance, an unexpected gift; but then, again, what does it matter when a man dies? seventeen or seventy—does it matter how or where or when?

I walked around the ruins in the city almost daily—the railway station area—as if in search of something, I knew not what, composing fragments of speech addressed to an invisible audience, mostly on the subject of war. I laboured carrying bricks on a building site—to earn some money, since we were now poor—but gave it up within a few days; sheer laziness complicated by the brickyard reminding me of the brick-works where we were cruelly rounded up in 1944. And then I saw no point in re-building that house. Why can't they leave the ruins alone, I wondered, contradicting my need to imagine the ruined cities restored. Such feelings went with fits of depression and death-consciousness which, later on, recurred with growing intensity.

(I have tried to reconstruct this post-war state of mind in a short story: 'Returning to Normal', *Stand,* Spring 1981, reprinted in *Double Vision,* 1999).

I must have been emotionally disturbed for several months after our supposedly wonderful return. But intellectually my brain seemed to function, in so far as schoolwork can be called intellectual. I immediately resumed studying and found I could learn, usually by heart and without much effort, just about everything on offer: Hungarian poetry, Ovidian pentameters in *Fasti* (why not the *Metamorphoses?*), and the heavy

Calvinist catechism in preparation for my confirmation; I also followed three science courses and mathematics. After two months I was given a grade of 'distinction' in every subject. Of course I wondered whether these grades were not offered to me as a kind of compensation for what I had been through, but as I managed to keep up my progress in the following two years, I had to conclude that the learning compartment of my mind had not been damaged after all.

At the same time I became more solitary than I had ever been before. I could not renew my friendship with the two boys who had been my constant companions in the first three years of the Gymnasium (Feri included) and my new friendships tended to be casual or occasional. I spent some time with the tall fair-haired boy whose father had died; then I just walked around the city centre with another boy who was the son of a senior civil servant, 'the enemy', returned from Austria where his family had escaped from the Russians; later I came to like a boy because he was seriously interested in ideas whilst I could not take seriously another boy whose special interest was his penis and mine (I drew back from a planned act of dual measurement). Meanwhile, there was scant sign of girls. The segregation of the sexes in the school system was, no doubt, the main reason why 'when I was a boy there were no girls'. However, my new attitude of detachment or even indifference—so unlike my sexual keenness at the onset of puberty a year earlier—meant that I wouldn't go out of my way merely to meet or please a girl. For example, a class-mate and I together met, by chance at the swimming pool, a stunningly beautiful fifteen-year old girl who claimed to be Jewish: he pursued her—tracked down her home address and chatted up her mother, a market vendor, whilst I dropped her after one conversation. As she seemed to show little interest in my deportation, which I had mentioned, I decided that the girl was a fake, not a fellow sufferer—probably only interested in chitchat, flirting and dancing. So I left all the courting to my classmate and went swimming on my own. While I missed Eva W., from the Ostmark-Werke camp, I made no effort at all to contact her though she had probably returned safely to her home.

My passivity was relative as I remained alert to the world around me and cherished ideas—concerning religion, the war and post-war politics—and kept reading. Religion was an almost inescapable aspect of my life since I had returned to my old Calvinist school and it was taken for granted—I was not consulted—that I would present myself for confirmation with other boys in my age group. So I duly swatted up countless chapters of a catechism I hardly believed in and then one day walked up to the Table of the Lord to receive the bread and the wine for the first (and last) time. I saw the confirmation ritual as another step in my rehabilitation and I voted for that rather than the questionable theology of Calvin (predestination, etc...) More importantly, I was trying to find an essential religious core I could live with—beyond or under the dogmas we were supposed to parrot. That essential core turned on certain fully significant books of the Bible, especially the Hebrew bible/The Old Testament—the Psalms, the Book of Job and the major prophets—together with the parables and the eight beatitudes of Jesus. I still thought that the Christian ethical ideal—'love thy enemy'—was to be followed, if possible, while I remained acutely conscious of how many Christians had betrayed their faith utterly in helping the Nazis. I also thought that I had to cope with a Nazi type in one of my religious teachers—the one who had cross-examined me on some tedious points of the catechism with pedantic zeal; the word fundamentalist was not yet in vogue. He was satisfied with my knowledge and let me pass on that occasion, though his body language communicated distaste. But we clashed soon enough in another place. I played into the hands of my willing persecutor by smiling broadly while he was preaching one Sunday morning in the historic Oratory of my college (where the provisional National Assembly had met in December 1944 as did the revolutionary government of Kossuth in 1848). For no good reason, I kept smiling until and after the reverend preacher noticed me; he instantly raised the pitch of his voice and pointed his finger at me from the pulpit: 'even here in the house of God we find intruders who desecrate our faith.' The following day he came into my classroom and made a more explicit speech in front of the class, addressing me by name and calling me a 'brigand who deserved to be expelled from the school'. That did not happen but my conduct grade was reduced in the term report for the first time. The incident did not perturb me, mainly because I thought I had seen through that clergyman's animosity: he felt personally offended by my survival. My mother did not seem to be very perturbed either, even though she was worried, from time to time, about the development of 'this fatherless and unruly boy'.

I was helped in maintaining a good conscience by two other clergymen who approved of me: in town Dr Szenes (the man who had once asked me if I wanted to train for the priesthood) and in the school a benign teacher of religion who liked the fervent speech I made to our debating society. In florid rhetoric I claimed (with some reason) that our school had been a pillar of Protestantism, the Hungarian Geneva (not, as some said, the Calvinist Rome, a misnomer); nourished by our school we were to become grounded and mature human beings, not just scholars but moved by faith. For when faith is lost, man becomes a reduced, maimed, aimless, lost creature... waited on by death.

24. Another Transit

When the war finally ended, with the defeat of Japan, there was little rejoicing, as far as I remember. Too much had been lost, and the dead outnumbered the living. And there was another shadow. One day, on 7th August, I leaned over the printing room of a local newspaper, which happened to be visible from the bank's backyard. I peered down through the press window and saw a banner headline being printed on the spot announcing that a powerful bomb had destroyed Hiroshima. Amid instant mixed feelings, the enormity of the occasion could not be fully realised— partly because there was not yet enough information. So I went home bringing the good news of the war's imminent end, without giving the bomb much thought until later.

Meanwhile it was impossible to ignore the slow, strategically slow, political revolution that was taking place in the country. With the approach of the first democratic election, in November 1945, all the parties were engaged in massive propaganda campaigns. I intuitively feared the totalitarian aims of the Communists though they were still a minority (they gained only 17% in that election); yet it was already common knowledge that—with Soviet troops continuing the occupation of the country—the Party was manoeuvring for full power behind the scenes, especially in the police. However, our family had friends among the Communists: Dr Géza Eisler, my father's cousin twice removed, and his wife Anna, emerged as gentle card-carrying party members, after many years of concealment. The son of one of my mother's best friends, Ivan Jakobovich, had become a state prosecutor in the newly set up people's court. And another friendly young man, István Rado, who had returned from the Jewish Labour units sent to occupied Soviet territory, became the editor of the local Communist newspaper. I had a private discussion with him about 'the present situation' and the future, but our talk was so bland that we hardly disagreed. With such good people in middle rank positions in the Party, why should we worry unduly?

On an ideal level, I had a lot of sympathy for radical social change—for eliminating the injustice of class differences. As a small boy I experienced compassion—mixed with a kind of curiosity—towards the victims of the class system: the boy at the primary school who came barefoot into the class and kept being punished by teachers for bad behaviour and being teased by class-mates; the peasant sweating in his thick black suit in a third class railway carriage (I was stopped from talking to him); our illiterate middle-aged cook soaking her sore feet in a bowl of lukewarm water; the squalor and smell of certain houses where the poor lived (as I discovered when I went collecting for a charity with the boy-scouts.) At the same time, at the other end of the class scale, I tended to shake my head at signs of unhappy luxury (including my rich aunt in Budapest) and thought that my mother paid excessive attention to money, custom and material goods: underpaying the servants; making a big fuss over objects broken or water spilt on the white table-cloth and repeating the little phrase 'it's not the done thing' while looking down on the lower orders, including poor Jews. Yes, it was time for change but the Communists were heading for dictatorship and violence.

The Marseillaise captivated me, blaring from the loudspeakers of the Social Democratic headquarters day after day. Such a stirring tune! I felt like marching to its beat, until I recalled the guillotine. In the end, I was drawn to the left wing of the Smallholders who soon gained an absolute majority, forming a government under Ferenc Nagy—namesake of the later tragic victim, Imre Nagy—and nominated the President, Tildy. I started going to the Smallholders' party rooms, not motivated by a desire to be on the winning side (an unpredictable winner and very soon a loser) but more by a sense of being welcome there. The local member of parliament designate, Dr. István Vásáry—a former liberal mayor and uncle of Tamás, my friend, the child prodigy concert pianist—actually discussed politics with me, aged fourteen. I have no idea how he found the time for this; perhaps it amused him, perhaps he was looking for future recruits. I may have mentioned my interest in politics as a career, for I did harbour such thoughts in that time of illusions. After tasting the political climate, I mistakenly 'diagnosed' a relatively hopeful situation for the country—it seemed to be governed more benignly than anything I had experienced before. It was known by that time that the Communists had taken control in Poland, Romania, Bulgaria and in Tito's Yugoslavia, with the connivance of Churchill and Truman. But why should Hungary succumb in the same way? We were surrounded but remained a firm inland island. In this respect I joined the countless other people who repeated the deadly mistake my parents had made before the outbreak of the Second World War: counting on being an exception, for no good reason but perhaps out of desperate optimism.

The day came when the returning Soviet army, led by Marshall Tolbukhin, marched through the main street in a long and impressive procession. Watching from the flat roof of the three-storey bank building, we had a perfect view of the Red Army displaying itself at peace— formidable battalions of infantry with a huge array of heavy armour. It was a historic occasion but it did not evoke the awe-struck fear I had experienced when Nazi German soldiers marched through the same street in lethal steps less than two years earlier. But neither could I revive the spontaneous spirit of celebration found in the encounter with 'my' Russian soldier and commanding officer on the day of liberation. The Soviet forces had committed a lot of atrocities and were increasingly seen as a threat: Moscow would become the new capital of Hungary as another colonial satellite. For the time being the country had a democratically elected government; and now and then a few British or American soldiers from the Allied Commission could be seen driving through the streets in their jeeps, especially in Budapest.

Still in Debrecen, I kept wandering about the town, collecting local experiences. One day I strayed into the people's court temporarily set up in the great hall of the Golden Bull hotel. A large crowd had gathered there howling abuse at the accused enemy of the people, stamping feet on the sawdust-covered floor. It was barely possible to hear the prosecutor's questions or the answers of the accused. The latter was probably a former police officer who had attacked striking workers—I heard something about drawn sabres. Whether the crowd could hear the proceedings or not, it, a collective it, had made up its mind that the accused must hang.

In the Déry Museum I stopped for a long time to gaze at Munkácsy's famous 'Ecce Homo', a huge canvas, a dark-and-light vision of the drama preceding the Crucifixion. In the same museum I also stared at the skeletons displayed—probably from prehistoric times—skeletons and skulls that seemed to follow me. They joined the recent dead in my private procession of the dead. On the square outside a brass band played well-rehearsed marches, including the march from *Aida*, with encores; so the skeletons marched in my head to Verdi's resuscitating music.

Sometimes I would meet people from 'old times' in the street. Walking towards the Great Forest, as of old, I ran into our one-time maid Böske (Bessy): I gave her a friendly greeting but she just passed me without as much as a nod of recognition, with a sullen look. I concluded that she must have carried some hatred or resentment towards us. A former female bank clerk also gave me a distinctly unfriendly look as though I had hit her; I later realised that she, a Jew, must have been among those unfortunate employees whom my father was compelled to dismiss from her position following a quota system in the race law imposed on the bank. More disturbingly, I met the mother of my friend Marika Vas (mentioned before), whose hollow cheeks and staring eyes confirmed that she had been to Auschwitz, from where Marika did not return. Another friend, András Jakob, also perished, together with his parents. One day, when I attended a degree ceremony at the university with my mother, a virtual stranger approached us and claimed that he had seen my father dying. He heard my father say that he knew that he was going to die; and how he kept talking about his family, worried about our fate. The informant then slid into casual gossip, which I had no wish to hear.

With so many hours spent wandering and thinking, outside school hours, book-reading remained fitful. At any rate I read less in this year and a half than either before or later on: just a few historical novels including *Quo Vadis* by Sienkiewicz (we were all steeped in Roman history at the time and I sympathised, from the opening, with Petronius who found it very difficult to wake up in the morning) and *The Talisman* by Walter Scott (seeing Saladin as a noble Muslim hero against Richard the Lion-Heart and the crusades as something of a waste—like all wars). I also read *David Copperfield*, tending to identify with David, especially when he loses his luggage and possessions. I resumed reading poetry, both Hungarian and Latin, with some German, as before deportation; I developed an increasing love of the lyric at the expense of the epic, partly because a rival classmate happened to excel in the epic hexameter—a verse form that remained a compulsory component of the traditional syllabus. Daily learning by heart was still practiced and to this day I can recite verses memorised at that time, some of them haunting, others hypnotic like a trusted sleeping pill, for example:

> *Este van, este van, kiki nyugalomba*
> *Feketén bolingat az eperfa lombja*

> Nightfall, nightfall, time of rest for all,
> The mulberry tree's foliage broods darkly
> (Arany: *Családi Kör / The Family Circle*)[5]

I also started reading plays, especially comedies, as if to balance my tragic views. I delighted in *Midsummer Night's Dream*—Puck muddling up the lovers sounded all too lifelike—and Molière's *The Miser* performed at the local Csokonai theatre. Although I had few opportunities for going to the theatre, I found the stage and the whole theatre experience highly stimulating. I refused to call that 'entertainment'; it was much more than that, more like participating in a significant ritual.

I read newspapers avidly (including an English language paper published in Budapest) and non-fiction, especially biology. I resumed my earlier interest in the brain, a much more engrossing part of our anatomy than the organs of reproduction, I argued, to counter my schoolfellows' sexual obsessions. I was fascinated to discover that the brain kept running

---

[5] My translation, as are other citations of Hungarian poetry except Radnóti, p.172

down rather like a battery, for example before sleep. I already sensed that a well-functioning brain could suddenly degenerate into something pathological: drained of the last ounce of energy, without any known reason, even when seemingly one was in a good physical condition.

Some of the books I mentioned I took from the remnants of my parents' library—perhaps a few dozen books which, when found, I proceeded to sort and catalogue. But no furniture survived (other than the found items I have mentioned) and the two little offices we occupied, at the back of the bank building by the large yard, were bare indeed. We used the bank's lavatories and washroom and mother somehow succeeded in turning another tiny room into a virtual kitchen. In former times all this would have seemed a primitive kind of existence but, after the dehumanising extremes of the deportation, our accommodation was supportable—a modest return to civilisation. Living in the bank building, as it were parasitically dependent on the bank's good will, brought some unexpected encounters. We met, for example, my father's successor and his family who seemed to be doing very well indeed in all respects—an experience my mother found painful because it instantly made here think of 'what might have been'. I also tended to indulge in 'might have been' thinking but tried to become stoical: see the situation as it is without feeling too strongly. I gradually came to realise that if we allowed every occasion to remind us of father's death and our reduced circumstances—or else the horrors—life would become unbearable. Without accepting that our loss was inevitable, I decided to concentrate on 'new life', as far as possible. At the same time, I also tried to shed the protective detachment I had developed in the year of terror—and be attentive to whatever came my way.

One day I got into a very friendly conversation with a self-educated soldier from the garrison that had occupied the bank building. He enjoyed reading aloud to me, especially reading from *Peer Gynt*, in a German translation—the sad monologues of Solveig waiting for Peer's return. He read in a gentle but unsentimental voice, utterly absorbed. On another occasion he thought it fit to instruct me on the best way of coping with a woman lusting after you (after him, not me): pour a bucketful of cold water on her. The commanding officer of the same regiment, a major, also became friendly in a more formal way. The outcome of this unexpected camaraderie was that he permitted me to hitch a lift in an army lorry—all the way to Budapest. It so happened that my mother was just then staying in Budapest, with Uncle Miklós, and I took it in my head that it would be fun to surprise her with my sudden arrival in the capital. But there was a complication: by the time I got to Budapest, dropped by the good soldiers somewhere near the centre, my mother had left. And all I had achieved was to give her a shock when she found out about my escapade. Meanwhile, I went to see the ruins of Buda again—those stark reminders—and got distressed once more. Before leaving, I managed to give my uncle, who accompanied me to the East station, a final headache: I chose, out of some whim, to climb right across the tracks and then across the buffers of a train—stationary but ready to start any minute. The adventure did not enhance my reputation in the family.

Soon it was decided that we should move to Budapest permanently—if there was such a thing as permanence, which I doubted. We were, however, not moving at the same time. My sister Eva was first to leave to take up her place at the university to study chemistry—to become a research chemist, not a science teacher. She had actually been warned against choosing the teaching profession by father (presumably because grandfather remained fairly poor, if over-worked, even after a lifelong career as a senior teacher). Eva stayed in temporary lodgings until mother found a flat suitable for three of us—in the outer Hungaria Ring, beyond the well-known City Park. My mother resolutely packed up all our worldly belongings, all that was left, and set out late one evening, seemingly without regret. I remember waving her off as she sat beside the driver of a loaded lorry that looked far from robust; I was afraid that she might not arrive safely as she set off into the night.

The whole post-war sojourn in Debrecen (about a year and a half) had just been another transit, a word I connected with our transit camp, *Durchgangslager*. I kept meditating on life as a movement from transit to transit. At the same time I was waiting for my own exit. I continued going to my old school while I missed my mother and sister. In the interval, I went to live with the Eisler couple (mentioned earlier) who turned out to be very caring people: childless, they took a kind of foster-parental interest in my doings and in my future. They had returned from deportation to their old flat, which was in fairly good condition, though I missed the budgerigars that could once be heard chattering in all their rooms. We spent hours together discussing the past, the present and the future. They were rather concerned when I talked about my interest in politics and literature, shaking their heads and trying to guide me in a more practical direction. They were also critical of what they saw as my 'aristocratic' attitudes, a serious charge when even ordinary bourgeois attitudes were under attack. But their criticism was always friendly and caring. We found time to go out together: we saw recent films and plays, like *Zola* and Priestley's *Dangerous Corner*—recent Western culture had reached us quite speedily. We listened repeatedly to the rhapsodic rhythms of Liszt's *Les Préludes*, perhaps by chance, until the music crept into my ears for all time. Sometimes I even showed them my homework, including an essay on the poet Vörösmarty, commenting on his line 'reason forbids love after vanished hope'; in high style I had evoked the pains of Tantalus and Prometheus and much else. They advised me to 'cool it', lessen the rhetoric. Aged fifteen I was far from ready to follow their advice.

The time came, one autumn day, when I said good-bye to the Eislers sadly. I consoled myself with philosophising about the transitory nature of all things.

25. Budapest, 1947—*Annus Mirabilis* or Illusion

As soon as I arrived in Budapest I started school. The challenge of a wholly new school was enhanced by diving into a strange classroom at the deep end: Class VI for 15 to 16-year-old boys, half-way into the school year. I don't remember being nervous on that occasion but that might have changed had I known how many outstanding boys there were in that class, in a school that prided itself on excellence. Its famous alumni included Lukács (leading Marxist philosopher and critic whom I later came to study, but not from a Marxist point of view) and von Neumann (contributor to pure logic and set theory as well as to the hydrogen bomb). It had scholarly teachers, some members of the Academy, as in the leading Parisian *lycées*. It was run by the Lutheran Church but everybody called it, from its location, the Avenue or Fasori Gymnasium, near the still elegant Andrássy Road, the site of the Opera and some palatial buildings, but also the headquarters of the secret police under the Fascists and later under the Communists. Boys of Jewish origin—many came from converted families like myself— formed a marked proportion of the class; and several scions of professional families, including the Lutheran bishop's son, attended. There seemed to be few, if any, poor boys and very few from the provinces; I can remember only a studious boy from Debrecen who kept talking reverentially about Selma Lagerlöf, the Swedish novelist. Although my old Debrecen school was itself famous, I immediately sensed something distinctive in the new school—ambivalent yet palpably superior attitudes. Even the surface was different: most of the boys were very well-dressed (wearing suits and felt hats outdoors), conspicuously carrying leather briefcases as if set on some important errand. In the breaks they talked about books, theatre, concerts and opera with the confidence of young connoisseurs. They improvised debates, for example on the nature of evil (dismissed by someone as 'fairy tale stuff', an astonishing view so soon after the war atrocities); one boy wondered aloud whether any of us was going to turn into the next Nietzsche (he himself, Moravcsik, became a professor of philosophy in California). The talk was loud but the manners were polite.

Soon after arrival I was surrounded and virtually cross-examined in a way that resembled friendly dogs sniffing out a new dog. I must have passed the test for, within a surprisingly short time, I acquired three life-long friends: Ivan, Gabi and Paul. Chance would have it that Ivan's step-father knew my mother's family from Gyõr and that—coupled with my fervent declaration of an interest in drama—acted as a kind of password or shibboleth. I became a member of a class within the class. It is a rare experience to form several lasting friendships so quickly. Ivan Barko eventually became my closest friend. Relatively small (nicknamed the Little and teased but not by me) with a round face and neatly parted hair, he would talk excitedly and almost incessantly about the two subjects that became my main interests too: literature and the theatre. Gabi had thick dark facial hair, so he had to shave at least twice a day to keep up his smooth, fashionable appearance; from him came a stream of lively comments on music and art and on his still privileged and snobbish social set; he also had a go at contemplating the ways of girls but not from experience. Paul or Pali excelled less at school, partly because he did not feel the need to exert himself, being somewhat plump and already playing the part of a nonchalant man-about-town.

Just as unexpectedly, I found the required academic standard easily attainable. This was partly thanks to sheer luck for sections of the syllabus were already known to me from my previous school: so I recited the (American) Declaration of Independence—making a splash—and effortlessly translated part of the first Canto of the *Aeneid*—another splash. I did not reveal my secret previous knowledge until later, so I got some unearned credit in the meantime. My old habit of frequently asking, and eagerly answering, questions also seemed to go down well in an environment where modesty was, evidently, not a virtue.

Such heady success led to over-confidence (and later to my mother's disapproval). Early on at the new school, a large group of boys went to see an educational film on Edison. There was a lot of excitement and hilarity so that, minutes before the film started, the PE master came up to our group and peremptorily ordered us to be quiet. I classified this man as an impertinent intruder and a spoilsport and, turning round, told him to buzz off. At that moment the house lights went out and I felt utterly safe. However, my features seemed to have got engraved in the master's memory: he tracked me down and the following day I was summoned to appear before the headmaster, accompanied by the aggrieved master. Then inspiration came: I explained, after a humble apology, that I had no idea that the gentleman concerned was a master at our school, as I was a new boy who had not yet attended gym. There was enough truth in this to save me from serious punishment and the scene ended with my renewed apology and a nod of acquiescence from the headmaster and the master. Then I told myself to calm down.

The city itself stimulated me as I went around exploring it, usually on my own. I took an overcrowded tram to school (sometimes hanging on, precariously clinging to the bars of the entrance); often I walked all the way from our suburban boulevard Hungaria through the City Park, an elegant villa area where Paul lived (as did one of the dreaded Communist leaders, Gerö.) After school I went on long walks, mainly driven by curiosity but perhaps also as a getaway from our confined two-room flat where my mother and sister had one room and I the other, an unfair share due to the segregation of the sexes. (Later, after the Communists came to power, it was an advantage for my mother to live in such a modest flat that had no trace of bourgeois luxury). Inescapably, I returned to the ruined quarters of Buda meditating on the horrors of war, as after our return from deportation. But when I started reading about the history of the city, I gained a certain perspective: I saw ruins under the ruins and further layers of ruins—back in time to the Turkish occupation, to the Renaissance, to the Tartar hordes, to the Romans and so to prehistoric times. That was to play the role of Schliemann excavating nine cities on the site of Troy. And I knew, even cherished the knowledge, that no city, no civilization, could last. At the same time I began imagining the restoration of the ruined royal palace and the exquisite Danube bridges, and the rise of new houses to live in.

Meanwhile in Pest, much less damaged though almost every building was pockmarked by bullet holes or worse, there were signs of an astonishingly energetic renewal. The neon lights were being restored and lit up everywhere. The shops of the inner city were loaded with luxury clothes and jewellery as well as with mouth-watering delicatessen. So I became a window-shopper without ever buying a thing. With so much walking on the streets it is not surprising that I soon came across streetwalkers—for the first time. I eyed them with a mixture of fascination and horror, especially a tall, blonde, dominant woman in a fur-coat carrying a large black leather handbag, who patrolled one of the inner city streets as though she owned the place. When she spotted me, at some distance, she slowly walked up to me and abruptly asked whether I wanted to come with her and—after muttering something about my being very young—mentioned the price for both the night and the morning. There was nothing attractive in her manner or even her appearance in close-up, and I fled making an excuse—no money. Further on I stopped outside a dancing club and, peeping in through large windows, watched for a long time the young pairs glide—or rather gallop—across the well-lit dancing floor. Gabi, my new musical friend, frequently went dancing in such an expensive club and I envied him somewhat, though I had no real desire to join the dance, having neither the money nor the talent for dancing.

When winter came I kept going down to the Danube to watch the mutations of the ice. At certain points the ice was so thick that it must have been possible to walk across it to the other bank without the risk of falling through a crevice. But I never tried it. I just stood there meditating on the fortunes of that great river, once more connecting it with the Fascist atrocities only two years earlier—murdered Jews and resisters flung into its waters. Towards Spring the ice began to thaw and island-sized blocks floated speedily downstream, or got stuck and stacked on top of each other, grey mountains of ice in a local Arctic.

It was still winter when I became an avid theatre-goer. The theatre, first explored in Debrecen, now became a passion, although I could not foresee my future dedication to drama. My new friend Ivan had thoughts of professional training as a theatre director. At that time the two of us formed a habit of discussing every production we had seen—*Pygmalion* or *Of Mice and Men*, Sartre's *La Putain Respectueuse* or even *Arsenic and Old Lace*—a habit kept up for years in our correspondence, even after exile had separated us. I was not alone in being spell-bound by the performances of Gizi Bajor, a leading actress at the National Theatre: her every movement and intonation communicated fluctuations of emotion. Her contralto voice and fragile-seeming yet wiry body found a perfect role in Cleopatra and in Camille. In both these parts she made consummate the art of twisting and writhing in pain, sensitively, without melodrama. Seeing Bajor in *Antony and Cleopatra* coincided with my reading and reciting Shakespeare in English (*Hamlet, As You Like It*) at school and at home; I also saw *Julius Caesar* performed in English, with a Hungarian accent, by the students of Sárospatak College (where my parents once wanted to send me to perfect my English). It was about that time that I began to see the inseparable connection between political and erotic, public and private, tragedy. (Bajor herself later committed suicide). I treasured the tragicomic interlude when the Egyptian peasant or clown offers Cleopatra the lethal asp from his basket, like some delicate fruit. The suicidal Queen enters into the naive spirit of the scene and asks: 'Will it eat me?' Before his exit, the peasant says with deadly good humour: 'I wish you joy o'th' worm.'

I saw *La Dame aux camélias* more or less at the same as its haunting operatic version, *Traviata*—with arias so catching that I went on whistling and humming them in the street and in the bath, as if born in Milan. Going to the opera came to be fraught with some conflict with my mother. Although I usually bought the cheapest seats (for the equivalent of a few shillings) and paid for it from my meagre pocket money, the time came when I had to ask for extra money for my indulgence. By chance Paul, my new friend, insisted on my company for Verdi's *Don Carlos*. I hesitated, explaining that I had no money, but he stubbornly walked me back all the way home so that I could collect a subsidy from my mother. I sensed that there was something wrong with this plan but saw no way of stopping the expedition. When we arrived and rang the bell, my mother opened the door conspicuously dressed for housework (apron and headscarf); it was morning and of course we no longer had domestic help. Paul greeted her with 'Good Day'—a greeting that conveyed a social code addressing somebody who was not the lady of the house—perhaps a housekeeper or a servant. A lady would have been greeted with 'I kiss your hand'— mimicking the old Austrian etiquette—however strange that might seem on the threshold of the Communist take-over. I found the scene acutely embarrassing, as my mother must have done, especially as she had to find fifteen forints for a good seat, a sacrifice at a time when we were hard up. I never quite lived down my reputation for extravagance as an aficionado who could not stop opera sinning—it was not suitable for the son of a now poor mother who had survived slave labour. Even so I excitedly discovered Wagner (though I knew that he was Hitler's favourite composer): *Walküre* and *Siegfried* as well as *Lohengrin*—again attempting to sing snatches of the key arias. There followed quite a repertory of Italian opera: *Don Pasquale, Rigoletto, Un Ballo di Maschera, Don Carlos* (with the embarrassing personal prelude), *Aida* and *Traviata*, again, *Tosca, Pagliacci* with *Cavalleria Rusticana* in succession and Gounod's *Faust* added. Strangely, there was no Mozart or modern opera at that time. I tended to follow up my visits to the opera house with a long discussion of plots and themes or the function of opera as an art form, the supreme combination of theatre and music as *Gesamtkunstwerk* or total art—another dangerously intoxicating Wagnerian idea. My mother could see that I was heading for excess—opera being only one example. But she tolerated my expensive hobby (for me 'sacred art') in the hope that it was just a passing phase and she probably realised that this was one reaction to the year of terror. However, we did not talk about that. All seemed well between us when, in midsummer, we went out together to see a performance of Ibsen's *Peer Gynt* on an open air stage in the zoo. That play obsessed me for years; (it must have contributed to my later choice of Norway as a country of work and residence). I went on thinking about 'Peer Gynt be true to yourself!' and how that anti-hero stripped the onion only to find that there was nothing at all at the core, nothing.

Such was the power of the stage—plays and operas in turn—that the cinema enticed me less at the time. Two films I valued beyond all others: Carné's *Les enfants du paradis* —that haunting, sad, white-powdered Pierrot face (the young Barrault) and his vain search for his lost lover in the milling carnival crowd— and Orson Welles's *Citizen Kane* —the non-glory of a press tycoon's social power portrayed in black and white cinematic art (technicolour was not yet widespread and did not attract me except for the yellow road in *The Wizard of Oz* .) I could not have known at the time that just those two films were to become cinema classics for all time.

In the same three seasons, Winter, Spring and Summer 1947, I also became a concert-fan. Concerts were surprisingly cheap at the time, especially the open air ones in the gardens of the former Károlyi palace where I heard a fairly extensive repertoire of popular classics, including Haydn, Mozart, Beethoven, Brahms and Tchaikovsky symphonies, Wagner and Richard Strauss but, again, no modern music for some reason. The principal conductor of the orchestra there was a show-off: before the first beat of the work about to be performed he would ostentatiously send the score flying over the orchestra pit, presumably aimed at infinity, just to demonstrate that he had mastered the score by heart. On one occasion I sneaked into the famed Liszt Academy (one-time musical home of Bartók and Kodály among others) without paying, with the help of a kindly corrupt usher. The older Oistrakh was performing a violin concerto; I remember feeling spellbound, though I cannot recall the music. My mentor in music was Gabi who played the violin himself tolerably well whilst his mother was a professional violinist to be heard on the radio; she would not play privately when I visited their age-old, cavernous, dark, labyrinthine flat in Honvéd Street, full of antiques and valuable art works, including Renaissance and other originals, collected over some twenty-five years by Gabi's handicapped father, Mr Bedö. Part of that valuable collection was sent to England for safety before the outbreak of the war but later confiscated by the British government as "enemy property" (and followed by prolonged international litigation.)

Soon I became interested in the visual arts as much as in music, and spent days rather than hours in the (Szépmüvészeti) Museum of Fine Art; its rich collection had survived the war in surprisingly good condition; El Greco's was 'my' discovery with 'The Despoliation' alongside the same master's 'The Apostle St Andrew'. Time spent in that museum initiated me into years of gallery-going worldwide and deepened my interest in painting and sculpture to such an extent that I would have chosen history of art as a main subject had I not anticipated family opposition fiercer even than opposition to the study of literature.

For half a year I lived in a hothouse of all the arts, where literature was only one way of stirring the mind. I read almost any book within reach or recommended by one friend or another, mostly English and French history (including *The Miracle of England* by André Maurois) and several classics of fiction in translation: from Homer to *Le Rouge et le noir*, *La Peau de chagrin, Fathers and Sons, Crime and Punishment*, works by Anatole France, Stefan Zweig and Franz Werfel among others; in bed with influenza, I devoured *Les Thibaults* by Roger Martin du Gard, a multi-volume family saga at that time still famous and discussed. Although I started reading poetry (including Shakespeare) in English, for the sake of speed I read the Hungarian translation of English language prose works: Dickens and Thackeray, Wilde's *Dorian Gray* as well as *The Importance of Being Earnest*, H.G. Wells's *The World of William Clissold*, Huxley's *Brave New World* and even *Gone with the Wind*. All that reading was part of an effort to repair the damage caused by deportation. At that time reading had a different quality from reading habits developed later: it was faster, more random, and effortless. Later on, after I had lost the art of rapid reading for ever—perhaps as one of the side-effects of changing my language—I could only look back at my early speed reading with some self-envy: over forty pages in an hour, sustained for six hours or so. The randomness came from reading with others, as if in a spontaneous book club, with some inevitable competition. The lightness came from not yet being burdened by any clear literary aim or ambition. Reading was as natural as breathing; and the novel was a form of drama, steeped in history and philosophy, and experienced as personally as my own life. I would pick out a scene or a quotation—say the satirical lament on 'vanity' at the end of Thackeray's famous novel—and see vanity everywhere, certainly in my friends and in myself. Then I went on to link social vanity to universal vanity in the Hebrew Bible—all is in vain, all action is in vain. Or I would brood on how the First World War could have been avoided—after reading a relevant chapter in *Les Thibaults* —and then go on to further brooding on how the whole of (my) history would have changed if... I paid less attention to character in fiction, except in Dostoevsky; I practically identified with Raskolnikov not because I was about to murder an old female pawnbroker but because he kept asking tormenting questions about the value of a life: is a man or a woman worth more than a mouse or a louse? A streak of literary criticism did reach me when I read a good History of World Literature by the Hungarian poet-critic Babits, supposedly better than the literary history by Antal Szerb, the book my friend Ivan happened to be reading at the same time. I may have emerged from that study with an almost encyclopaedic list of famous names and works but with no strong influence on my outlook except a bias in favour of 'no literary frontiers' and ceaseless 'comparison'. That was partly a matter of reading works more or less simultaneously: after I had read *Dorian Gray* I was told that I *must* read Balzac's *La Peau de chagrin* on a similar theme—a man's ugly, sin-laden ageing transferred to an ass's skin instead of onto a picture as in Wilde's novel. At that point the two works were held up to face each other in a mirror but without any serious attempt to place them in a ranking order. We really were young and free from prejudice then.

The arch-reader in our little community was Ivan Nagel. He was Ivan the Great who did not become a close friend. He looked and sounded grown-up, even a touch elderly, at sixteen. He had a fine long, white-skinned face with dark eyes and wisps of black hair falling on his forehead and you could see that he was engaged in the act of thinking all the time—he had the lineaments of the Thinker. He tended to create a solemn aura around him as when, on a visit to his home in an old apartment near St Stephen's basilica, he played a recording of Wagner's Wesendonck songs in a holy hush, with eyes shut. Our conversation consisted of sage comments, mostly inspired by his reading. To an open air performance at the Zoo he brought the poems of Keats in English; at the swimming pool he was reading the avant-garde novel *Der Tod des Vergil* by Hermann Broch and discussing that work's mythology. He shared my interest in the analysis of the mind (the self) but was much more drawn to Freudian psychoanalysis than I. As he was not in my class at school I did not see all that much of him. I probably considered Nagel too literary, too far gone into the realm of 'pure intellect.' (Later, when he had settled in Germany and I in England, he proposed a sort of literary correspondence between us—a project that sounded too much like imitating Goethe and Schiller, a self-conscious exercise between men of letters—but that's another story.) I inherited something of my mother's distrust of abstraction, even while, from her point of view, I was too intellectual already. I intuitively realised that Nagel was more advanced and more committed to literary study at a time when I was not yet ready; but I thought I could take things at my own pace, postpone Broch or even Thomas Mann, Proust and Joyce for a while. Both Ivans were ahead of me, I knew. (Eventually Barko became a university professor of French in Australia, Nagel a distinguished 'dramaturg' in several leading German theatres and Professor of Aesthetics in Berlin's Hochschule der Künste). Meanwhile I was still afraid that, as one result of time lost in my concentration camps, I would lag behind my gifted contemporaries for ever. But could it be that I felt more deeply? Did they know, I wondered, what it felt like facing death daily?

Ivan Nagel was not alone in bringing books and ideas to the swimming pool—we all did. Two or three of us were actually swimming in the indoor pool when I improvised a variation on 'the meaning of life'. 'And what do you think all this is for—what is the meaning of our life?' asked Ivan B suddenly as we turned round at the edge of the deep end. 'Well', I said as if prepared, 'the meaning of life is to find a meaning.' After that we dived in at the deep end. All through the long hot summer we kept going to that pool, out on Margit Island surrounded by the Danube, which was never blue but green or grey-green. We frequented the indoor or covered pool, as it was known, but I much preferred to be out in the open air pool on the same site where one could sunbathe and philosophise at leisure and go on little tours of inspection observing *homo sapiens* as a peculiar species of animal: tribal, gregarious, noisy, sprawling, unnecessarily hairy when half-naked, with frequently repulsive, oily, ill-tended patchy skin, but seemingly at peace around the water, for a time, and therefore much to be preferred to the monster revealed by the war. Ordinary curiosity about human beings proved a good antidote to distrust or misanthropy.

That summer was further enriched by a few excursions and parties. Gabi and I spent a day picnicking up on the hills of Hármashatárhegy (Three Borders), presumably so called because on a clear day you could see far beyond the city towards three 'borders'—or towards infinity. Only just above the city, the place still felt rural and remote, with grassy hideouts and wooded paths. The ramblers were relaxed; a postman stopped to talk to us in a leisurely and friendly way about the flora and the fauna, dropping his postbag for the time being—an example of the decency of some ordinary survivors of the war. Once I joined a group on a rowing trip on the Danube—towards Old Buda—only to find out that I was incompetent. True, I had never before tried rowing but then I added a dose of native clumsiness to the learning process, steering the boat across the river rather than downstream. That provoked not just laughter but a sharp rebuke from one of my companions who ironically asked how on earth I was going to earn my living when I grew up. 'Because I doubt whether you can do anything—unless you want to be a professor'. It was an insult.

I also felt somewhat out of place, socially, at the opulent garden party given by the Biró sisters in a splendid villa on the Hill of Roses—a band playing, lanterns hanging from the trees, merry laughter (not far from the recent ruins of Buda) cakes and drinks galore for all those spoilt teenagers—I kept seeing them as the luckiest survivors, without envy but conscious of a distance between us. I had, no doubt, been invited only because Ivan was a close friend of the younger sister, Zsuzsi, and I was perhaps the only 'single boy' present. Getting paired off was a kind of fashion, sometimes serious and sometimes not, nearly always Platonic as far as I knew. I took my singleness for granted without special regret but I found it awkward to negotiate a throng of revelling strangers in close encounter and being greeted by my hostesses with the condescending courtesy the Budapest bourgeoisie practised so skilfully.

It so happened that I liked the Biró sisters very much, but they were both 'engaged' and the few other girls I met all seemed to have some defect in my perception. They were bluestockings, wanting to impress people with their 'culture' and they struck me as trendily sophisticated rather than authentic. In any case, they tended to be inaccessibly guarded within a refined kind of matriarchy. One admirably educated girl could not be prized out of her salon where her mother hovered around our formal interview as a conscientious chaperon and conducted the conversation, without a baton but gently accompanied by Grieg's piano concerto on the gramophone. Another girl displayed uninviting bony knees under shorts while pointing out the exact spot on the balcony from where she had thrown herself down a few weeks earlier—seemingly proud of her attempted suicide.

The only young woman who attracted me as a woman was our neighbour's maid—my second adventure with a maid. (Our neighbours were Communists who could afford a maid, another sign of the times.) I am not sure about her name, so I will think of her as Ilona. She was probably under twenty, a blithe, good-natured country girl free from any affectation—and free from any inhibitions. She was buxom, the exact word for her, with a slight squint which only added to her somewhat mischievous look. First she wanted to know what I was studying and told me in turn that she was fascinated by Gorky's *Mother*, a book she urged me to read (I didn't). Later she confessed that she had sex with a Russian soldier: it had been a very pleasant experience, she stressed, presumably speaking as a consenting partner. After that she escalated. Once she asked me to touch her neck and I followed her bidding but somehow managed to snap her necklace of pale blue glass beads which got scattered all over the floor of my room and could not be restored. Then she wanted us to hold hands. On another occasion she stopped me in the common hallway wanting a passionate embrace. She was about to go further in generous abandon when I warned her about the sound of approaching steps, which she wanted to ignore; but I was not hallucinating. That was the end of that experiment. Next she wanted me to arrange an excursion, perhaps to the idyllic hills I mentioned earlier. I agreed without agreeing, a tactic I am not in the least proud of, *but* it is not surprising that I hesitated: on her side were the employers, the far from trustworthy Communist couple (the husband had some official function like being an area warden, that is, spying on all the tenants, guarding their moral and political correctness); on my side were my vigilant sister and mother. Mother, already disappointed in some aspects of my post-war development, might have had a fit if she had detected anything between Ilona and myself; my mother had many fine virtues but she did combine old-world prudery with traditional snobbery.

In short, I thought about 'it' until the opportunity passed. At the time so many other things were happening—all the arts, pending emigration—that I hardly minded my retreat. But years later I saw in this episode a regrettable pattern of dithering and delay, a variation on a theme from *She Stoops to Conquer:* going for the maid again while spurning the cultivated young lady.

26. High Summer and Decline

The long summer seemed to get brighter as it went on, with something of interest happening almost every day. A rare euphoric mood kept many of us afloat, while very much aware of darkening political skies. In the long vacation I intensified my study of both English and French by taking frequent private lessons. My English teacher was a former landowner who had once been married to an Englishwoman; he was a complete amateur as a teacher—his main method consisted of asking me to translate excessively word-rich literary texts from Hungarian into elaborate English—but I liked his relaxed, debonair manners and I sensed that his pronunciation was good. We went on to discuss 'our situation' in tolerably fluent English. I decided to start learning French at the same time, perhaps to keep up with Ivan. My French teacher was a small woman of mature years whom everybody called Boci Néni, Aunty…, an untranslatable, affectionate nickname that she seemed to like. She was a perfectionist when it came to pronunciation, patiently drilling me for hours in elisions and semi-silent sounds (for example the '*de*' syllable.) Each language lesson was punctuated by bouts of lively but serious advice from Aunty. For example, she urged me to read Thomas Mann but not before I had acquired a deeper knowledge of Freudian psychoanalysis. Whenever we paused in the lesson, or the discussion that accompanied it, we gazed thoughtfully at the gaping ruin of an apartment block that faced her window—quite a common feature of the cityscape at the time. My teacher and I ended up as friends and I made tolerably rapid progress in French, despite so many competing activities. She was the first person to warn me explicitly: 'if you are going to leave the country of your mother tongue you might as well give up any hope of becoming a writer'.

My mother fully supported my language learning itch, no doubt seeing it as more useful than collecting opera arias. I think that about this time my mother was beginning to emerge from the trauma of deportation and father's death, at least to some extent. I do not know what she really felt because she seldom if ever confided in me at that time. But outwardly she had regained some of her former spirits. She had put on weight (and later was to put on too much weight as if to compensate for a hungry year); she also started dressing up again and looked good and relatively young at forty-six. We occasionally went out together conversing in good spirits—like seeing *Peer Gynt* with her—or else I would visit her in one or another reconstructed cafe in the city centre, where she met her friends. Cafes were not expensive, though it is mere legend that you could reserve a table for half a day ordering just one glass of tap water. Not that my mother took a relaxed view of the present or the future—she never did. On the contrary, she viewed the new Hungary pessimistically—with good reason—and my own future with anxiety. My sister told me what her main concern was: 'you couldn't keep your mouth shut and were a danger to yourself and the family: so politicised that you started tearing down (Communist?) party posters.' The two anxieties combined in her decision to 'export' me to England, and so she became the prime mover of my destiny at the time.

Meanwhile my sister was having a hard time. The deportation year had subdued her spirits and affected her health for a long time. She told me afterwards that, during the bright summer I have been presenting, she spent weeks unwell and bed-ridden. She also found studying chemistry at the high-pressure Budapest University so challenging that she had to postpone one of her key exams. The loss of more than a year of schooling, and the transfer from a provincial to a metropolitan environment, became an underlying difficulty. However, as she seldom complained—unlike other members of the family—I did not at the time fully realise that she was struggling or suffering in our new life.

Aunt Agnes also struggled with the consequences of the war and in a sense never recovered. Although she still managed to look elegant, conjuring up the vanished world of a *grande dame*, her new-found poverty reduced her existence to basics. She continued to live in a rented bed-sitter, not too far from her once luxurious apartment at a stone's throw from Parliament Square, and she had to be economical with every single purchase, even daily food. A stronger, more determined person might have reclaimed some possessions: her apartment and part of the value of agricultural machinery from the country estate already divided by land reform. But she lacked my mother's practical enterprise as she faced a complicated predicament that must have seemed desperate. From riches to rags—she lived a sad tale of loss, the turning of the wheel of fortune.

My other aunt, Janka (the wife of Miklos), fared much better. Her relatively humble origins had been a much better preparation for hard times and she soon set up a makeshift grocery, which, apart from providing her with income, was a source of cheap food for her husband and others. Keeping the little shop going was hard work, as I witnessed when I accompanied her early one morning on a bargaining and buying errand in the covered market: an overcrowded and turbulent bazaar where customers were pushing, vendors shouting and the pungent cumulative smell of supposedly fresh food tickled one's nostrils. Meanwhile, some of Janka's relatives were among those who profited from the opportunities of the short-lived free market—whether through fair trade or on the black market—and lived in style in a sumptuous villa furnished with books they never read. No doubt these *nouveaux riches* were scorned by the newly impoverished bourgeois citizens, like my mother. But that was unfair prejudice for such upwardly mobile people were far from idle and also tended to be generous. For instance, they invited me to a skiing trip in the hills near their villa, fitted me out with skis and appropriate sportswear and then coached me on the beginners' slopes, more exactly tried to coach me, for my ankles resisted instruction as once they had resisted steadiness in skating. After that fumbling attempt at skiing we were served a feast of titbits, from expensive salami to caramel Dobos cake, as though the war had never taken place.

The sun kept shining, all the arts flourished, the swimming pool was an oasis of delight, and in the inner city as well as on the Danube embankments people promenaded as if the summer could never end. Meanwhile 'darkness at noon'—to appropriate Koestler's title—had come. There were ominous political developments. The popular prime minister, Ferenc Nagy (whom I had watched arriving in a grand black limousine for an Easter service at the Calvin Square Reformed church) was implicated in a staged conspiracy—and forced to resign in late May. Earlier, in February, an influential Smallholder party leader, Béla Kovács, mysteriously disappeared. He was arrested in the street, they said, and the rumour turned out to be true. The police acted under pressure from the Communists (still formally a minority in the coalition government) who were in turn under Soviet pressure—that too turned out to be a fact. Yet we did not experience the kind of panic that marked the regime change under the Nazi invasion. Things changed slowly, almost imperceptibly. New 'democratic' elections still left the extremists in a minority, and the centre was divided into a mosaic of small parties to replace the once mighty Smallholders—a cunning strategy, beginning the notorious 'salami tactics': taking one slice at a time. But somehow there was still hope in the air. There was a certain sense of economic stability—ever since the new currency was introduced in August 1946, when 400,000 quadrillion *pengö*-s could be exchanged into one forint, so ending the 'system' of paying one basket load of banknotes for less than a basket of food. Small and medium-sized shops and manufacture were still allowed to function in a limited free market. And the sun was shining, yes, and I was young and almost wilfully clinging to the few good things around—a not so grand illusion.

Incredible as it may sound, I was not all that keen to prepare my departure for England. These preparations took months rather than weeks and at first I resolutely distanced myself emotionally from the whole procedure—a soft variation of the necessary detachment that had helped me to survive our crisis year in the war. I dutifully followed instructions while making a number of serious if unintended mistakes. First I kept queuing outside the British Consulate to make a formal application for a visa. But entrance to that imposing place was controlled by a good-looking and wily Hungarian commissionaire who made sure that it was indeed very difficult to get inside His Majesty's legation, at least until the required bribe had reached him—stealthily. When I finally gained access, after several attempts, I was interviewed by a friendly official who saw me as the right sort of candidate: a victim of the Nazis, a half-orphan to be looked after by an uncle who was a British citizen and a medical officer in Hertfordshire where I had been accepted by a local grammar school as a promising student, etc. If getting a visa to Britain went smoothly (I later heard that the British could be very tough and negative in matters of immigration), applying for a passport made me hit the new political ceiling for the first time. Interviewed by a stern, seemingly hostile, young police officer, I blundered. When he ended his brisk cross-examination with 'your father's occupation?', I instantly confessed that he had been a bank manager (a 'director', in Hungarian, sounds even more sinister.) I could see the officer draw a diagonal line right across my application and I was summarily dismissed. Within a few days the written rejection duly arrived: 'studying abroad is not a justifiable reason for travel'. My family was convinced that I had blown the interview; but somehow my mother managed to buy me a passport: the price was fixed in dollars to be paid to a certain lawyer who would contact a certain official who knew another official higher up…

While obtaining a passport was still in considerable doubt, Uncle Miklós arranged for me to see an orthodox Jewish organization which was making arrangements for the emigration of young people to (still British) Palestine. I was interviewed by a rabbinical figure who did not find me 'suitable', probably because he divined my ambivalent sympathies towards Zionist youth. So my application was refused and there was no question of my being legally shipped out of the country as a Jewish boy. My uncle was very cross when he heard of my second failure, making a speech on the lines of: 'I bet you made the sign of the Cross to that rabbi and talked to him superciliously about Cicero.' The episode showed that I did not 'belong' in that camp and probably belonged nowhere at all.

With the passport in my hand, I still had to apply for visas: to Austria, Switzerland and France, one by one. For I was to take the train to London via Paris and Calais, in itself an exciting prospect which allowed me to delude myself that I was just a lucky world traveller, beginning with a little grand tour of Europe. I would return when the time was right. And mother would come and visit me within half a year. Meanwhile, I kept meeting friends and so discovered that they too were planning to go into exile: the two Ivans and Paul (but not Gabi who was kept back by his mother's emotional blackmail, a suicide threat), and a legion of others, a generation of migrants soon to be seen as refugees or displaced persons.

Time passed and the visas were slow to materialise; at least one visa was still missing by the time I should have been in England to start my new school. So the train journey had to be called off and it was decided that I should fly, for the first time in my life, via Prague, Frankfurt and Amsterdam—towards an emigration I still had mixed feelings about. My mother remained the prime mover in all these preparations but, after I had become aware of the general exodus and the deterioration in politics, I finally had to suspend my doubts. To the end I thought of the journey as leaving behind one transit and heading towards another transit.

At the airport—where all the surviving members of the family had come to see me off—I waved good-bye, without tears. I took my seat on my first ever flight, still playing the role of the young apprentice—just starting, leaving for a while to collect more experience. England was waiting for me. So I opened an English language newspaper and, forgetting the context of death in Hamlet's soliloquy, saw myself as setting out for 'the undiscovered country'.

Part II

27. England, 'Demi-Paradise'

My arrival at London Airport was botched through my own enterprising spirit, and the confusion left lasting traces. Uncle Laci, my dead father's younger brother, greeted me at the inner city terminal, accompanied by aunts Anni and Gizi and my only cousin, Renée—the entire family settled in England, all of them refugees from 1938. A great reunion and celebration might have been expected; unfortunately, it was instantly marred by the discovery that my luggage was not on the plane I had travelled on. Perhaps it was lost. This brought immediate trouble for my uncle, with headache and sore eyes, as he had to spend about four days recovering the lost property, with innumerable phone calls and two extra car trips from Ware, Hertfordshire, while my luggage was being shunted to and fro between London and Northolt airports, in an elaborate game of found, lost again, found again. Meanwhile, I knew something nobody else in London knew—it had all been my fault. I had somehow guessed what had happened from a cryptic message in Dutch, relayed by a crackling loudspeaker at Amsterdam airport: my luggage was left behind in Prague. In a chain of errors, it and I got separated, after I had arranged with a smart B.E.A. stewardess to swap planes so that I could use the four-hour interval, before my next flight, to view Prague's architectural splendours by taxi. But the plan had failed and I was brusquely bundled back onto the original plane minutes before take-off, leaving behind my hand luggage on the runway—also found later—while my checked-in luggage was to travel separately towards London or to an unknown destination. Losing my luggage did not seem to me anything exceptional after my wartime experiences; but my uncle had assimilated the orderly rhythms of English life and was not amused. I therefore censored the Prague story, not wanting to be seen as a deranged spoilsport by my new family from the start. In any case, I must have looked a sight after all-day flying on old propeller planes—three stops at Prague, Frankfurt and Amsterdam—tired after bouts of severe travel sickness that prevented me from retaining any of that marvellous Western food. On the last lap I had the benefit of sitting next to a German woman who ordered me to keep back the vomit: *zurückhalten*! she shouted in my ear against the noise of the plane, 'and learn to discipline yourself because that's the most important thing in life.' *But* if I looked pale and distracted, perhaps distraught, my new-found relatives made no comment other than 'in England nobody wears such suits, such padded shoulders, except spivs.' When I asked what a spiv was, I was treated to the first of many, many lessons on the ways of 'the English', essentially designed to teach me new ways, new manners, new morals—a new decency.

The following weeks proved to be testing as I tried to adjust to wholly new circumstances both in my new home and in my new school. It turned out that I was not just ill-prepared for the changes, but not prepared at all. Aged sixteen, I had been given no advance information about what was expected from me and it did not help that I had developed a superficial nonchalance towards my future in the final months of waiting in Budapest. Also, I had arrived well after the start of the autumn term and missed all the orientation given to those well-informed boys at Hertford Grammar School. In other words, I had to dive in at the deep end. Within a day or two I was asked to perform experiments in physics—in hydrostatics, measuring liquids—and to work on integral calculus with the aid of an obscure-seeming English textbook. In the chemistry laboratory I fumbled until I managed to make such a stink, with H_2S, that finally some attention had to be paid to my doings. Meanwhile, I had to ask myself: 'what exactly am I doing here? What is this strange new pain or bewilderment? Am I going to have a life in this place or was it a mistake to come here at all?'

I put these self-probing questions to the River Lea, my steady companion on solitary walks. The dark green currents in the water reflected the image of a boy/young man who was undergoing a major change—undermining the brief spell of confidence that had lasted only a few months, two years after surviving the camps. Beyond my big new dilemma—the choice of study and career—my new environment also made me feel uneasy. What was I doing in a small town, Ware, without culture, stimulus, amenities and friends? Why did everything seem so bleak after Budapest, even in London—except for the major sights, the theatre and the art galleries— those dark streets, poor shop-windows and grey people. Soon I was told it was called 'austerity': rationing of bread, meat, coal and clothes, shortages and lack of housing, slow recovery from the long war followed by an economic crisis and the severe winter of 1946–7—the winter before my arrival. 'You might think we had never won the war', someone said. I took all this in, and it helped my historical understanding but it did not diminish my personal bewilderment.

The personal questions kept coming and multiplying. Why did they look at me as an exotic refugee?—at school and in town—when I was not a refugee. A victim of the Nazis, yes, but I had survived, I had come through, I was a visiting anglophile and scholarly schoolboy wearing grey flannel trousers. Why did they patronise me?—the headmaster and the physics master who stood over me grinning when my experiment had failed—did they not know that all my life I had obtained top grades, distinction? Why did they keep asking how I liked England, how I liked Ware, how I liked Vicarage Road (my uncle's house) or what I thought about baked beans and tapioca pudding. And why did they keep congratulating me on my command of English just after I had mispronounced a word? Why were my relatives so obsessed by them-and-us—the English, always the English versus the foreigners—their speech, their habits and ways of being, their superior or inferior attitudes? After all, I felt no strong sense of difference between nationalities or tribes, English or Hottentot, all I cared about was the difference in people's interests, their minds, their sympathies and intelligence. And why did I have to carry a document stating that I was an alien?

Officially I was a stateless person, classified as an alien according to a little grey book (in addition to the then standard Identity Card) to prove my identity: it had to be shown to the police from time to time. About a year later, on the occasion of Tito's visit to Britain, I was summoned and questioned by a police inspector, as if suspected of being a potential trouble-maker or assassin. I expressed a sneaking admiration for Tito's anti-Stalinist policies and was promptly sent back to school with a smile.

Six characters (including myself) took part in the autumn drama of deciding my future. My uncle initiated the whole plot by placing me in the Science Sixth Form, blithely assuming not only my readiness for that advanced level but also that I would unquestionably want to specialise in science in preparation for—what? doctor or scientist or accountant, some sensible career fit for a mere foreigner. Uncle had forgotten to inform me about the decision he had made on my behalf; nor did he tell me about the school system that required a boy to make a life choice, between science and arts, at age sixteen. (Over and above my own problem, I considered that educationally unsound, and I still do.) When I started to express serious doubts about the scholastic arrangements I have landed in, uncle responded by warning me that all my future prospects would be ruined and I would end up earning nothing, i.e. starving. He offered me variations of this scenario, calmly but steadily and almost daily. One day he wanted to persuade me to choose dentistry, arguing that a dentist could earn enough money in the morning to buy leisure for the rest of the day, and so write in the afternoon. I pointed out that I had three problems: I couldn't see straight (my eye-sight was, in fact, deteriorating along with my hair, my teeth and my nerves); my hand tended to tremble (I held out my hand unsteadily); and, finally, I had an aversion to a gaping mouth.

The Headmaster, Mr. Bunt, fully supported my uncle; or so my uncle informed me, for I never had a face-to-face interview with that powerful man who remained lofty and aloof. The opposition to this hard-line coalition, so to speak, came from my friend Ivan in the first place. Ivan had emigrated to Brussels more or less at the same time as I arrived in

England, and he seemed to have achieved a soft landing in his new country, at least in the continuity of his education. (But he had financial difficulties and a fierce, on-going battle by correspondence with his stepfather). Ivan had signed on to intensive courses in French language and literature in preparation for advanced study at the Université Libre de Bruxelles. We exchanged a whole series of searching long letters that focused on our respective new orientation; and suddenly I could see that a life in science need not be my manifest destiny. It should be possible to find a viable alternative, to be worked for with diligence and determination, in fear and trembling—yet guided by fearlessness. This correspondence was, by the way, in danger of getting censored by my uncle after he had become aware—perhaps because I had blabbed—of the existence and drift of those letters. My friend was then cursed as an enemy of sane living and duly nicknamed Ivan the Terrible, whilst we two arranged a secret code whereby a letter sent by Ivan to me would be preceded by a postcard saying nothing.

The other supportive voice came from an English master who, unfortunately, left Hertford soon after he had unwittingly intervened in the struggle for my soul. The occasion was an essay class for science students. The master was returning a whole package of essays he had read and marked, a routine occasion, with appropriate commentary. Suddenly I heard my name, incorrectly pronounced, followed by words to the effect that the best essay had come from someone whose mother tongue was not English. (On an earlier occasion the same master asked me whether I had really written an English essay all on my own; he was also surprised to hear that I, alone out of that large group, have been listening to Shelley's *The Cenci* on the Third Programme). Now my essay was quoted at some length to illustrate how to argue logically yet stylishly. I was a little embarrassed, partly because I did not relish being singled out as a phenomenon in front of all those English boys, and partly because I thought that the master had made too much of my verbal tricks—for instance, my use of the Latin tag *panem et circenses* (the masses needed bread and circuses) and the alliterating phrase 'a remainder and reminder from the past' to justify 'Rites and Rituals'—the subject of the essay. I saw that as a good debating topic, fortified by having just witnessed the wedding procession of Princess Elizabeth and Prince Philip. I had queued for hours outside Westminster Abbey to see that manifestation of pomp and ceremony and I naturally wove the experience into my essay—to make a point. I did not think the essay was all that good. Yet the master's praise was singularly well-timed because it helped to restore my flagging self-confidence. I had been wondering whether I had suffered some brain damage, in transit, as the cumulative effect of the 'big dilemma' and the virtual humiliation lasted a term or longer.

My mother—from the far side of continental Europe—took part in the conflict calmly and wisely. Of course all exchanges were by correspondence; long-distance telephone calls were practically unheard of for ordinary people and my mother was not due to visit for about half a year. When my uncle started to express to her his disappointment over my unsatisfactory outlook and behaviour, my mother responded by comparing me to a plant—the boy needed time to get properly rooted after transplantation. Meanwhile, she and I exchanged a number of long letters (which survive). In one letter I argued with close reasoning, point by point, for my firm decision to choose science for study and for my future career. In another letter, written soon after the first, I argued, again with close reasoning, the opposite case: my firm decision not to choose science but arts subjects for long-term study, leaving the question of my future career to—my guiding spirit.

That is a simplified précis. The actual letters (somewhat reluctantly examined more than fifty years later) show a process of painful twisting and turning. In a letter dated 25 October 1947, I first evade the issue with a prolonged metaphor on why I felt stuck: 'I definitely find myself on some kind of track. But the track is so poor that the carriage can hardly move, it is starting so slowly, its wheels need oiling, they are creaking. Or am I just imagining all this? Has something else gone wrong? The horses have stopped, not knowing which way to turn. The coachman is scratching his head. The tracks divide [pointing] in different directions. The coachman has no idea how to start, which way to drive, left or right... He doesn't know the destination of either way: where is it going and how far. Perhaps he doesn't even know where he wants to go and why.

The greatest dilemma of my life. By Monday I have to choose and reply [the words have the same opening syllables in Hungarian]: science or art? That's quite simple, there's no need to explain: this way or that way?'

At that point the letter breaks off and is resumed in a different, more confident tone, a day later, as if somebody else had written it, arguing in cool logic and with seeming conviction that there is no alternative to choosing science: it would lead to a career in medicine. Nobody could dictate such a decision... the same or a similar decision might, indeed surely would have been made by me 'at home' sooner or later... 'You can't make a living out of art but you can make art out of living, surely! And the way to professional writing—provided I master the English language—the way will always be open. Ha.' That letter was not sent for a week. A note called Official Report is attached on a slip of paper: 'I am, without cogito, I am around. I am, in some sort... [untranslatable form of the verb 'to be']. I seem to be somehow. I live, I seem to be living, vegetating (I am still breathing, eating, sleeping, etc.) Apart from that, in *Westen ist nichts neues'*, no news. Re-reading that letter, I suddenly realised that the pages of affirmation, reporting my clear decision, are written in the voice of a ventriloquist. Around it sprawl the words of deep-rooted hesitation and despair.

The subsequent letter is even more winding and full of self-irony. Occasionally, the letter is plain enough: 'some kind of well-meaning blunder has taken place—I would be the last to blame my uncle—as if they had played dice with me, an easy game considering the irresolute and unprepared state in which I suddenly tumbled into this whole farrago of intrigue. For weeks I had no idea what was going on and why, in the end, such a start did not exactly bring the fullness of grace to my spiritual state, nor /did it help/ the functioning of my brain'...'Perhaps I am allowed, as the reward of sleepless nights, to write down on the margin, a modest observation: I do not believe that the logic /of the previous letter/ is my logic.'

Such meditations were accompanied by an attempt to explain to my mother the complexities of the English Matric and Sixth Form system. There is also an attack on imagining that there 'always' might be a career alternative—changing course after five years or so of scientific training— and a mocking commentary on the wisdom of studying something one is not interested in while embarking on a career for which one has no talent, all the while supposing that 'there' leads to 'where?' After ten quarto pages of close writing, a note to my sister thanks her for sending me books (probably mathematics) which instantly illuminated dark areas. In other words, I was still struggling with the science curriculum two and a half months after my arrival; no wonder I expressed the fear that I was going to waste the entire school year in England.

Whether it was the success of my English essay or the impact of my new-found resoluteness or just the passage of time, towards the end of my first term at Hertford the fog of my dilemma lifted. The headmaster, Mr. Bunt, finally realised that there was, after all, nothing to stop my combining three major subjects (English, German and History) for the Higher School Certificate (later A level) with two subsidiary subjects, (Latin and French) for the School Certificate (later O level) and so fulfil the requirements for eventual university entrance. That was a goal from which I never swerved even in the midst of my deepest doubts about the future. It was a simple but seemingly ingenious solution. Why it had taken three months to work out my salvation, remained a permanent puzzle; at times I felt like cursing Mr. Bunt who, with a little more attention, could surely have untied the curriculum knot sooner. In fairness, the headmaster may have been 'destabilised' by the conflicting aims of my uncle and myself, while he probably found it impossible to evaluate my Hungarian education and my actual aptitude. As I said, no proper interview took place during the whole term. I was probably the first foreign student he had to deal with—a complicated case—and he probably felt like cursing me at times.

The Lent Term of 1948 marked a return to seeming normality. I had little or no difficulty in concentrating in my newly chosen field and I started earning good to high grades with my frequent essays on a great variety of topics in all three major subjects. I seem to have got on well with my teachers and my contemporaries who accepted and corrected my accent and likewise accepted, without correction, my strange ways. Nevertheless, the word 'seem' is justified because, under the surface, certain fissures were opening, barely noticed at the time and for a time. Socially I did not really become integrated. Several boys were friendly towards me—and I responded to them—but there was no question of making new friends with the intense personal and intellectual involvement I had experienced on arrival at my school in Budapest; now it was mutual toleration rather than admiration. The boys probably continued to see me as an oddity— an eccentric—whilst I regarded them, with one exception, as not 'true devotees' of culture. They kept disappointing me with superficial attitudes: one boy responded to our first looking into King Lear by expressing the opinion that 'all this happened a very long time ago, things like this no longer happen'—in reference to the violence and cruelty in that tragedy; I thought that much worse things had happened recently. Another time I overheard a boy laughing at the sight of a Goya 'Horrors of War' etching, the image of a man being castrated. Meanwhile, I also thought that my teachers were, though likeable, somewhat superficial in the way they were prepared to spend an entire period just dictating notes or else making us read aloud from a set book, say *Henry Esmond*—without discussion or shared interpretation. We were supposed to be advanced yet there was too much fact-learning and routine spoon-feeding. In short, I ended up by judging my school, while I was no doubt being judged, as not quite adequate. And that was one way towards my later isolation.

My reading itself became a factor in my isolation. The more intensely I read—and I did little else apart from writing essays almost every night— the more I experienced a new and profound inwardness, a drive into solitary thinking, in part intellectual, in part prolonged introspective brooding. I selected certain texts from a wide range of set books and made them my own, through extra study and personal writing, in a process of identification. One such book was Thomas Mann's *Tonio Kröger*, the fine novella about the alienated youth whose need to become an artist, a writer, turned him into an outsider, set apart from the everyday bourgeois world, burdened by estrangement, a feeling of guilt or bad conscience. I re-read that story again and again, finally annotating it with some far from brilliant verses of mine and then informed my German teacher that I could not possibly return the book (which belonged to the school) but offered to pay for it instead. The poem began with something like a wish for sanity:

'O let me still remain a bourgeois
Delight in the daylight that does not blind'—

I wanted less vision, without the light 'that X-rays the light in search of further light…' Later, in contradiction, the poem asks for the gift 'to see the Beyond, Before and After' and ends by praying 'for some reconciliation' of opposites. Those lines must have been written before the onset of a crisis but the feelings expressed there began early, in my first year in Ware/Hertford and remained with me for many years, a source of constant conflict. I entered a split state that could not be healed as long as the relentless outer pressure for conformity (from uncle & Co) and the growing inner need for growth—in spirit, in language, in expression—clashed.

Meanwhile, I did make an attempt to behave like a 'normal boy' at school and tried to join in various activities. I enjoyed the relatively impersonal rituals of the school, such as morning assembly with the Protestant hymns—including one sung to the Haydn tune originally written for Franz, Emperor of Austria, and Bunyan's 'to be a pilgrim'— followed by the resonant tragic triumph of Beethoven's Egmont overture. The bounty of the British welfare state impressed me: free bus passes, free textbooks, free meals and half a pint of free milk (with a tricky bottle top that made me splash milk all over the place when first trying), all for a foreign boy treated as an equal. I also liked the orderliness of the school: the regular timetable, the rhythm of classes interspersed with breaks: a time for solitary wanderings around the school premises, which contributed to my later isolation. Once I gave a talk on recent political developments in Hungary to the school debating society, mostly on 'the salami tactics' of the Communists, earning some curiosity and some praise. One social evening I also impersonated, on the school stage, Chaplin's impersonation of Hitler in *The Great Dictator* haranguing the German masses in a crescendo of shouting, all the while holding a black comb above my lips for the infamous moustache. That too seemed to go down well though I accused myself, after the event, of having enacted a grotesque scene. Perhaps it was an unconscious desire for catharsis through mockery. Later, in a modest contribution to Shakespeare studies, I played the miniscule part of the Keeper in the jail scene near the end of *Richard II*; attacked by the suddenly aggressive king, the Keeper cries 'Help, help, help!'—a good therapeutic cry.

I mention such external events mainly to re-trace my early struggle not to get isolated, not to become—in words people started to whisper behind me—a highbrow and an introvert. But there were strict limits to adapting myself to the new environment, given my earlier formation. For example, I never really took to school games. Though participating was not compulsory for sixth formers, it was expected and prized; only much later did I realise just how seriously sports were taken by teachers and students alike—indeed by the general English public. I tried rugby but I did not feel like emerging with a broken neck from under the carapace of the scrum. My lack of skill in the game did not go unnoticed and one day the captain came to me with a long face and, expressing his sincere regret, diplomatically advised me to absent myself from the Wallace House team for a while. I pretended to be really sorry to have disappointed the team but inwardly rejoiced at quitting. Long-distance running, across muddy fields in the spring term, was another trial: as a natural sprinter I tended to run out of steam after a few hundred yards and I altogether doubted the merits of nearly killing myself for the sake of finishing a few minutes earlier than some other fellow. In fact, unable to give myself wholly to physical exercise, my mind would start working in hyper-active ways while running, usually coming up with a stream of negative thoughts: 'this is ridiculous, this is futile'—like a mutinous soldier in Napoleon's army when driven to death through the snows of Russia. Such thoughts threw me back into a wartime mentality, with an urgent need to escape or evade, accompanied by a mercifully still brief fit of depression. As for cricket, I did not even attempt it though I liked to watch, for approximately ten to fifteen minutes, the ballet-like movement of white figures on a green cloth; and I appreciated certain silly sayings like 'a true Englishman prefers cricket to culture.'

Throughout my two years in Ware/Hertford I took part in hardly any out-of-school activity (apart from frequenting the London theatres and art galleries on my own) and met very few people of my age. No doubt this was partly the penalty for living in a new country and in a small provincial town. At first I was fully conscious of my isolation but, as that isolation grew, it seeped into my mode of being as if natural. My mother tried hard to bring me together—her letters acting as go-betweens—with the grown-up children of her old friends, who had emigrated from Hungary to London. So I dutifully met Peter Kalman, a gifted and hard-working part-time Physics student at Imperial College, several years older than I and—incredible as that may sound—much more pessimistic than myself, in a cheerful 'scientifically informed' way. He predicted that one day soon an atom bomb will be carried to England in a suitcase by a terrorist and that Hungary would be politically annihilated by the Soviet Union; he soon came to regard Orwell's *1984* as an accurate blueprint for a horrible political scenario that was already becoming real. The other legacy of my mother's concern was Agnes Rapoch, also older than myself; she had a strange, dark, almost Indian face and would have liked to involve me in amorous adventures, but not yet. She presented herself as a literary person (the type of blue-stocking I used to meet in Budapest); she wrote poems in Hungarian and her letters contained profound quotations from Nietzsche and Proust. As Agnes was obliged to work full-time for her living as a nurse (though she came from a rich family including bankers as well as the producers of Hertz salami), she envied and admired my free status as a student and went so far as to state that I was the only *homo sapiens* she knew. I instantly realised that the compliment was based on an erroneous view of evolution and I remained ambivalent about both her personal and cultural approaches towards me. These budding and not fully maturing friendships were, in any case, shadowed by my secret determination to cut, or at least reduce, the Hungarian connection. It was a secret even from myself at the time for I had not yet formulated it as a definite intention or doctrine. But the process of distancing myself from things Hungarian—including people and the language—had begun, inevitably deepening my isolation from 'normal' social life.

Apart from Agnes, there were no girls on the scene. I did my best to keep at bay the few girls who somehow surfaced outside the monastic celibacy of a gender-separate school. I am thinking of Sylvia, still in her teens. She had large appealing eyes, a full figure and a soft voice rising to high notes when singing the flower aria of Gounod's *Faust*. She did her best to tame my fundamental estrangement and I shall never know why she failed to take me beyond polite, friendly exchanges. One reason may have been that she was 'over-sold' by her older sister, my German teacher, a kind and considerate, happily married woman (who also wanted me to become a scholarship boy in German literature) saying 'you and Sylvia have so much in common' or 'you are both intellectual types'. Such remarks froze me. For, apart from hating to be labelled an 'intellectual'—adding to my Tonio Kröger apartness—I may have been getting paranoid about people who were too kind to me. What did they want?—those amiable parents who invited me to their Tudor cottage and talked about the virtues of Sylvia, her interest in literature and the theatre. What was my role? Was I supposed to court Sylvia? Much later I saw that my non-relationship with Sylvia had in it the makings of a Chekhovian tragicomedy. By contrast, another 'no girl for me' episode was fleeting and farcical. A whole contingent of sixth formers were invited to the annual dance of teacher training students, all young women, a little older than we were. I watched them dance from a safe distance—my old habit ever since I escaped from my dancing school—until one boldly walked across to me and asked for a dance, presumably as 'the ladies' choice.' I consented and endured being dragged around the dancing floor, listening to what sounded like unwelcome personal questions and insipid general comments. At the end of the dance, when ready to bow out, I was astonished to hear my partner invite me to walk around the college garden. What for? Did she really want a kiss after our failed dance? (For a classmate had tipped me off about the vulgar custom of 'spooning' in the garden). I made some excuse and extricated myself from that seemingly soulless English girl in search of a foreigner.

At that time I probably found it safer to make frequent love to my pillows.

Living with my uncle and aunt also developed into an alienating experience, literally so since they were so keen on stressing our foreign status—the gap between the English and the aliens. I was constantly treated to anecdotes, cautionary tales and forebodings concerning refugees. But materially my situation was comfortable: I had a little room supplied with a bed, a small desk and, most importantly, a good radio; a room with a view over a quiet suburban street and a garden with a towering monkey-puzzle tree to centre my wandering mind. I was well fed and my clothes were gradually replaced to look decent by the standards of the time; I was even given a double-breasted blue suit with a waistcoat, which I considered far too formal. A mackintosh, woolly underwear and carefully selected shirts and ties were supposed to bestow on me something like an English appearance—but I wanted the essence, not the appearance. By essence I meant the language and ways of being.

My uncle and I spoke Hungarian to each other, my aunt (born in Bohemia before the First World War) spoke exclusively German and my beautiful cousin Renée spoke English—received pronunciation and lady-like. The lingua franca of the family tended to be German, which seemed natural under the circumstances but underlined the dominant role of my aunt. She had a tendency to aggressive or menacing outbursts, walking with heavy tread, for she was over-weight, up and down the stairs until the house trembled; and she would raise her voice to shouting pitch whenever annoyed. Early on she had made it clear that she/they had been through hell after the Nazi invasion of Austria—the forced escape, the internment of uncle on the Isle of Man as an 'enemy alien', years of joblessness and hardship, worry about the rest of the family and feeling altogether at a disadvantage in England, professionally demoted and faced with real or imagined hostility. So now, in her forties, aunt Anni was impatient and did not suffer fools gladly. She saw me as a fool because of my appalling choice of arts subjects and because I had failed to conform to English and domestic rules. Not that I did anything outrageous, but just the way I went about things irritated her; once she summed it all up as my 'unpleasant personality', *deine unangenehme Persönlichkeit.* She particularly objected to what she saw as my unrealistic expectations as a foreigner: 'for all I know you may become a Goethe, though I very much doubt it, and in the meantime we expect you to behave like a decent schoolboy in England.'

Uncle had a much softer voice and a softer approach. He did his best to be paternal towards me, taking the whole task of my 'upbringing' seriously, as a debt to my father—victim of the Nazis—whom he had respected and loved, though we never talked about that. Hardly a week passed without a pep talk, mostly concerning the perennial subject of my orientation—my progress at school, my career plans and, above all, my long-term prospects, or lack of prospects. He regularly handed out precise small sums of pocket money to me (the source of which turned out to be a fund set up by my mother) and he responded generously to my intellectual and artistic interests, though he thought they would end in disaster. My Christmas and birthday presents included a 'folio' edition of Shakespeare and The Desk 'Standard' Dictionary of the English Language (Funk & Wagnalls)—I went to sleep with that dictionary. I was also given a subscription to *The Times Literary Supplement,* accompanied with the advice: 'don't carry it in the streets of Ware for people will think you are a pretentious foreigner.' Come Saturday, uncle frequently gave me a lift to London in his little black Morris, on his way to the Great Ormond Street children's hospital where he tried to keep abreast with developments in paediatric clinical practice. Uncle's obsession with our/my being foreign seemed to intensify with the passage of time and was ultimately harmful to me. However, I had empathy for his fears: a mirror image of real or imagined xenophobia. I also understood his fear of studying arts, with literature as the ultimate pit of decadence; that fear had its roots in something he claims to have witnessed in Vienna where rich young dilettantes wasted their time chatting in cafes and dabbling in this and that, kept going by family handouts. Uncle really thought I might turn into one of those feckless bohemians, even though I was—for the time being at least—sober and hard-working. He had very little patience with 'the inner life', distrusting anything provisional or potential, in other words anything fed by sheer ambition and hope, or worse—imagination.

My cousin Renée sided with her parents in the great argument over my destiny but moderately so, accompanied by many smiles and teasing remarks and a certain underlying flirtatiousness. I had to be on guard about what I said or did in her presence. Just to say 'I was in a sad mood' would be met by a riposte: 'only artistic types have moods.' If I wanted to change the time for a meeting, she would admonish me: 'never break an appointment'. Indeed, I was treated to a whole repertoire of don't commands, from the accumulated stock of English etiquette stretching back to Edwardian times: 'don't ask personal questions; don't praise just one dish when invited out to dinner; don't walk too fast or too slow', etc. But Renée had her own problems: difficulties with landing a good job without a degree (she probably thought that she too was handicapped by her foreign background though she spoke English without an accent) and difficulties with men, especially after the sudden and painful breakup of a promising engagement with a publican's son. So Renée's seeming serenity—emotionally at the opposite end of the spectrum from her mother—was hard-earned.

In addition to the family disagreements over my career and temperament, something like a battle of life-styles also sprung up 'at home' within a fairly short time. My uncle and aunt liked listening to radio entertainment, especially on the BBC Light Programme (ITMA, *Much Binding in the Marsh*, etc) while I just wanted to withdraw to my little room to listen nightly to the Third Programme, especially to philosophical talks that I could later read in *The Listener*. I never missed an opportunity to listen to Wagner though very much aware, again, of the controversy surrounding both his music and his anti-Semitic obsessions. I tolerated my uncle's middlebrow tendencies on condition that he would occasionally talk to me about performances at the pre-war Burgtheater in Vienna, paying special attention to Schiller. At school I was reading *Kabale und Liebe* as a prescribed text and I immediately added, feeding my interest in historical tragedy, the far more interesting *Don Carlos* and *Maria Stuart* and even the somewhat absurd version of the Jeanne d'Arc legend *Die Jungfrau von Orleans*, prompted by Shaw's mention of it in the preface to his *Saint Joan*. So my best communication with uncle at that time was through his old culture, or what was left of it. I had little or no taste for the immediate popular culture around me, another withdrawal symptom, parallel to my neglect of team sports at school. That too was something of a departure from my previous ways, for as a boy I had effortlessly absorbed pop songs and shows together with chunks of junk. In other words, my growing isolation excluded more and more of the 'real' world—living in a tranquil corner of England and turning into something of an aesthete, as if inviting the world to reject me. But I simply could not understand why the good people of Ware objected—according to my relatives—to my having the light still on in my bedroom at midnight ('is the boy ill?' they asked) or to seeing me run to catch a bus ('hasn't he got a watch?').

Privately I did try to connect. For instance, reading *Saint Joan* was followed by seeing the play unforgettably performed at he Old Vic (with Alec Guinness as the Dauphin), then seeing and reading several other plays by Shaw and finally sending the revered writer (who lived so near, in Ayot St Lawrence) a congratulatory telegram on his ninetieth birthday. But I sent that telegram anonymously, thus giving up even the remotest prospect of an interview, letting a whole set of questions concerning plays and the art of the playwright go on buzzing in my head.

About half a year after my arrival in England, my mother came to see me on a visit we thought of as 'normal', just a long journey to be repeated, as we could not foresee the immediate future. I was among those who did have some forebodings at the time and I even predicted that the Iron Curtain would keep getting thicker; and I wondered why my mother had not applied for a longer-term residence permit in England, to be joined by my sister, perhaps as a student. All sorts of objections, risks and uncertainties were then recited, starting with the fact that my sister was just then in the middle of her university studies as a research chemist in Budapest. Nobody paid much attention to my questions and so, in a virtual re-play of my parents' hesitation about emigrating from Hungary before the Second World War, my mother returned to Budapest after a brief visit—in time for the Communist coup in Czechoslovakia. From then on the pessimistic forecasts about the future of Central Europe were fulfilled. One unforeseen personal consequence of the rapidly worsening cold war, so soon after my mother's visit, was our ruthless separation: for nine years I was not to see my mother again.

The main purpose of my mother's visit was not to consider her future, but mine. The debate over my studies and my possible career choices had to be re-opened, to become the subject of repeated argument in the evening hours. If I have hardly any memory of such discussions, it must be because by that time I had virtually switched off; I had made my choice—having gained new self-confidence and a sense of direction after the prolonged dilemma of the autumn months—and nobody, not even an alliance between my mother, my uncle and the headmaster was going to deflect me. In any case, my mother had once more taken my side. She shared the family's fundamental distrust of the arts yet she must have realised that my choice was intuitively—existentially—authentic and she was not going to try and force me to change course. (She might have tried because it was she, and not my uncle, who had control over the remaining assets of the family after the war. So she might have vetoed my choice, as other parents had done in that age when minors had hardly any rights).

I was very glad to see my mother and tried to make her visit as pleasurable as possible, even showing her London: wandering around Westminster Abbey proudly as if I had privileged access to the kings and poets of England buried there—after all, I had become a resident of the kingdom and was in process of transforming myself into an acceptable future British subject if not an Englishman. A street photographer snapped the image of mother and son at Westminster Bridge, looking quite happy together. Nevertheless, my mother complained that she had not seen enough of me, unfortunately underestimating the time needed for my new and total commitment to study—at scholarship level in English and German, among other subjects—just then preparing a report on the novels of George Eliot: reading *Adam Bede* with delight, and F.R. Leavis's critical commentary in *The Great Tradition* with less delight but some benefit. I was afraid that mother tended to measure my love towards her by the length of time I spent with her, as distinct from the quality of our being together, by analogy with King Lear's wrong-headed quantitative love-test for his daughters; but I dismissed that potentially damaging comparison. A certain amount of tension was created by these conflicting expectations but I hoped that my mother had left relieved to see me not yet heading for disaster. Her visit was over all too soon at a time (to repeat) when we could not anticipate the future of total separation awaiting us.

There followed a springtime of hard work and relative calm though the political situation in Hungary—another 'faraway little country', after Czechoslovakia in 1938—was deteriorating all the time. As a result, my own sense of isolation gradually worsened and the Hungarian connection weakened to a point of nullity, propelled by a historical fiat that only fortified 'the way that I was going'. My immersion in English accelerated, somewhat paradoxically timed as it was only a short while since two of my articles were published in *Magyar Nemzet,* a leading liberal newspaper in Budapest: one discussed the astonishing Van Gogh exhibition at the Tate Gallery, the other the English Bible as brought to life at the National Book League. At the age of just seventeen I stopped travelling along that 'native' creative way altogether, apart from letters to my mother and Ivan and (about a year later) experimenting in a soft porn fantasy on the dalliance of Adam and Eve in paradise, and then writing a long, desperate poem on

155

death, in an intolerable month of crisis (see p.165 below).

While consolidating my studies, I drifted further away from my external anchoring. In late spring it was decided that I should go and live as a lodger in a Hertford house that was owned by a fairly prosperous grocer and his teacher wife. It was a friendly enough environment: the family included a delightful four-year old boy with whom I played games in the garden, and the location had the benefit of being near my school. Still, I felt uprooted by the move, probably more troubled than I knew while pride presented the move as 'ordinary', just a change of address for everybody's convenience. Meanwhile, I suspected that my aunt—impatient with my presence in her vicinity—had been the prime mover. Fairly soon after settling down in my new transitory residence—I had dropped the word 'home' long ago—I became aware that the landlord, Mr. Bryant, also found my literary bent objectionable. I did not advertise it deliberately but occasionally I listened to talks on the Third Programme, on their radio and with their permission. One day Mr. Bryant overheard a brilliant lecture, probably on Donne by J. Isaacs, and became very irritated: 'I can just about understand English poetry but not a word of that highfalutin gabble'. And now he knew where I got my big words from so that every time I opened my mouth he, a trueborn Englishman listening to a foreigner, had to fetch the *Concise Oxford English Dictionary*. The landlord's wife—with whom I once read aloud a few Shelley poems and who let me listen to the *Electra* of Sophocles on her radio—was much more in tune with my ways. Later it occurred to me that a touch of jealousy might have fuelled the landlord's anti-literary anger. Then I knew that my days were numbered in that house too and soon I would be on the trek again, a nomad, a refugee.

Before my next move, the summer vacation brought further isolation, this time linked to a strange and revelatory experience. I found myself in a cabin near the beach off Great Yarmouth under the care of a family I did not know—presumably hired by my uncle to feed and guard me for a fortnight. I had absolutely no interest in any person, action or object in my immediate environment but gave my total attention to books and the sea, and let the flow of words and water flood me with their wave-like motion, at times disturbing, at other times illuminating. I started reading Virginia Woolf's *To the Lighthouse* and I soon felt immersed in the rhythms of its language:

'to see the same dreary waves breaking week after week, and then a dreadful storm coming, and the windows covered with spray, and birds dashed against the lamp, and the whole place rocking, and not be able to put your nose out of doors for fear of being swept into the sea...'

I was moved and disturbed by the rhythm as much as by the sense of that prose, and by a consciousness of self, more than by the sound of the waves which I could hear all the time while reading, whether in the cabin or outdoors. I had tended to be introspective from an early age but here, in those long hours of solitude, I kept probing and questioning myself most of the time. I dwelt on my situation, perhaps for the first time since arriving in England, as a survivor of the Nazis, and as a refugee from Stalinism, though one who had made no effort to escape. My life was a gift. I saw myself as having been spared for some unknown reason, for a task I had to identify and fulfil. I should have to pay, of course, with further homelessness, be lonely and poor (my uncle would be proved right), keep turning my back on what the majority of people valued: a home, money, material goods, a proper job, sex, love and marriage and just go on, walk on, as I have walked into the incoming sea from the littered sands.

Out on the sandy beach I found a sort of alcove in a dune-like formation of the sand. There I hid from my guardian family, who did not seem to mind my failing to participate in their holiday hobbies. Meanwhile I just read and read. Mostly I read from *Paradise Lost*, entire books in one sitting and long passages aloud, as this one from Book VII:

On heavenly ground they stood, and from the shore
They view'd the vast immeasurable Abyss
Outrageous as a Sea, dark, wasteful, wilde,
Up from the bottom turn'd by furious windes
And surging waves, as Mountains to assault
Heav'ns highth, and with the Center mix the Pole.

Again, the sound as much as the sense was intoxicating and the experience contributed to the sometimes almost pathological, but ultimately benign, growth of my obsession with words, the English language. And that was soon to lead to a new choice or revolution.

When my hosts heard that I was reading Milton all day and all that week—not as a set book, not for an exam or a scholarship but only for the delight of it—they shook their heads in disbelief that looked like disapproval. I could not confess to them, or later to my family, that I doubly or trebly enjoyed 'useless' reading, just because it was not something I was required to do; it was, as my mother would have said, also with some disapproval, *l'art pour l'art*. After that I settled down to getting through large sections of my set German literature syllabus (from Lessing to modern poetry) with concentration but with less enthusiasm. And again it was the extra texts, chosen voluntarily, that had the strongest effect on me, such as Goethe's *Die Leiden des jungen Werthers*; I duly identified with the sufferings of that famous young hero but I was already somewhat sceptical about the necessity of suicide for the sake of unrequited love and also aware of the irony of my own infinite longings—at that moment directed at the waves, being unable to summon any female presence. Then Rilke's Orpheus sonnets came to guide me, especially the one beginning with the line:

> Wolle die Wandlung. O sei für die Flamme begeistert[6]
> Will the change. O let yourself burn with the flame
> (my own free translation: 'change, I understood, had
> the strong sense of a personal metamorphosis').

Much of my reading accompanied me—amid reflections on my present and potential state—on long walks. It was on one such walk that the idea of changing—from German to English literature as my eventual major university subject—began to crystallise. Perhaps it happened on the walk when I got soaked to the skin, as they say, my green tweed jacket, inherited from my father, dripping wet in the chill wind. I felt wretched and exalted at one and the same time, once more confused about my destiny yet caught by renewed trust in my inner direction. For days I hardly spoke a word to anyone, continued my reading and my walks, and finally left that static place on the seaside with the feeling that perhaps I had been travelling through ‚a vast, immeasurable abyss'.

The train journey back bored me, and so did much else for months: my everyday life at school and in my lodgings.

London never bored me, the theatre never bored me. When in London, I would walk for miles alone, from St. Paul's to Kensington, tired and hungry, and sometimes with aching feet and head as I had not enough money left to eat in the hours between early morning and night. Those solitary walks kept drawing me back to the ruins in the City: I would stare at the grass and the weeds that grew out of the bomb sites, not far from the saved dome of St Paul's. I compared those ruins with those of Buda, with a sense of affinity, and I kept brooding on the common destiny of so many of Europe's cities. I re-created the war: I sought out photographs of the London blitz and the shelter drawings of Henry Moore and I joined T.S. Eliot in a chant of the haunting lines:

> 'London Bridge is falling down falling down falling down...'[7]

---

[6] Rainer Maria Rilke, *Die Sonnette an Orpheus*, 2:XII

[7] T.S. Eliot, *The Waste Land*, V, 426 (New York: Boni and Liveright 1922; London: The Hogarth Press 1923)

When, by way of contrast, I walked through the well-preserved magnificence of Whitehall—past the Banqueting Hall and the Horse Guards to the great ministerial buildings—and when I stared at the statues of conquering British generals of the imperial past, I was filled with thoughts of decline and fall, partly prompted by the end of British rule in India but even more so by my personal experience of history. I imagined the future with an almost eager sense of doom. I thought I could foresee the end of capitalism altogether and, beyond it, the end of Western civilisation as we had known it since the Greeks, in so far as it depended on a known political and economic system. The luxury shops of Bond Street and the swishing cars on the Mall only added to my forebodings. All that—with the great dome of St Paul's, the Wren spires and towering Big Ben—would be annihilated in the coming third world war. Meanwhile, I took comfort in certain signs of enduring England: the memory of victory and the commemoration of the war dead, even the singing of the National Anthem before a performance in the theatre. It became my clear intention to get assimilated into the life of England, undeterred by the unfortunate history of my parents and grandparents, death or failure after long assimilation as Jews in the life of another country.

After a full day in London, I would return to Ware exhausted but still reading on the bus—*War and Peace*, for instance—unable to understand how my fellow-passengers could just sit there with dull or closed eyes, seemingly oblivious to the accumulating horror as well as to the wonder of our time.

28. Crises: Books, the English Language and Death

Early 1949 marked a difficult season in my life. It still had days of normal work (studying for my Higher School Certificate) and enjoyable distractions (the London theatre and opera), yet it vividly engraved on my memory a succession of crises.

The supposedly simple choice of a book in a famous London bookstore, Foyles—intending to cash in a twenty-five shilling book token given to me by aunt Gizi—engulfed me in a sense of bewilderment and nausea. My initial indecision escalated into a total incapacity to choose, as I moved from room to room and from floor to floor, and from subject to subject, until the stacks became threatening like walls about to collapse. The multitude of books around me surrounded me with their physical persistence: books I ought to have read, and which I longed to read before entering that menacing place, suddenly turned to dust. Not only did I lose all interest but I was tormented by questions: why take one book rather than another? why books at all when my family lost all... and my old school library was looted. As I survived, perhaps I was entitled to read—a few thousand books—but what for? All those books will end up on a huge rubbish heap or in a bonfire. I faced the ocean and I could not begin to swim. I started to remove one book after another from this or that shelf, wandering around the labyrinthine store, and I hastily returned each one or put it down somewhere, anywhere, without attention, as my state of paralysis deepened. Finally a young assistant, a young woman, noticed me and came up to me: 'Can I help you?' she asked in a voice that conveyed deep suspicion. I muttered something about finding it difficult to choose a present; the assistant was pacified and smiled, 'Sorry, I confused you with somebody else'. Then I almost felt tempted to steal a book and finally stumbled out of the bookshop dazed and depressed, having bought *The Short Stories of H.G. Wells* and thinking that I would never read that book, or any other, again.

Soon, changing languages became a traumatic experience too. It need not have been so, for it all started as normal learning. I have been relatively well-prepared linguistically before coming to England; my first essay in English was singled out for special praise soon after arrival at my grammar school, as already related; I had experienced no particular difficulty in speech and even less difficulty in reading and writing: having devoured a shelf-load of English classics in a few months and writing at least two essays a week, usually returned with good to high grades. Nor had the sustained learning—English as a second language—prevented me from reading quite a lot of German and some French and Latin, or from writing those articles for the Budapest press alongside long letters in my mother tongue.

But it was no longer my mother tongue. Somewhere around spring 1949 I decided to separate from my mother tongue. At least I began to distance myself from it, to grope towards a final disconnection, suppress it and simultaneously intensify the search for some unattainable perfection in English. I wanted to be born into the language or at least to be re-born in it, make it a language in which I could retrace what might have been: sing and recite nursery rhymes and proverbs, revel in idioms, talk nonsense (the least difficult target), quote scenes from *Alice in Wonderland* and limericks from Edward Lear, come out with quick repartee, jokes, insults and swearwords, count (do multiplication and division) and dream (yes, the language of my dreams must be English, I decreed) and write, above all, write.

This desire to grow up in the language became an overgrowth. I absorbed and started to imitate all the styles of English that came my way, starting with Jane Austen (I wrote an episode for her unfinished novel, *Sanditon*, in a competition), and proceeding to imitate the language of the nursery, the great English prose writers and the daily press. 'Humpty Dumpty had a great fall' reached me about the same time as Milton (above); other word-intoxicated writers included Jeremy Taylor and Thomas Browne, de Quincey, Carlyle and Pater, all masters of an eloquent or ornate style, aesthetically inspiring but hardly fit models for a young man from Central Europe. I acquired new expressions like 'upsidaisy' and 'bugger off' more or less simultaneously with fascinating rare or archaic words, picked up straight from one of the many dictionaries I slept with or at least treated as a paramour (another new word): anfractuosity, desuetude, tergiversation, and so on. I also became bewitched by complex syntax and the sound effect of words. My sentences in English were getting as long and complex as in German or in Hungarian (that is, my somewhat twisted version of Hungarian, especially in certain personal letters) until one of my teachers remarked, in red ink: about twenty-five words are usually sufficient for an English sentence. The incantation of Milton's verbal music spread; I sought it in poetry and prose and indulged in it, often at the expense of sense, making up verses like

Humming and lulling dull lugubrious lullabies.

That was the time when I began to sink or get sucked into the quicksands of the language.

The new language, when I thought I had mastered it, started to break into fragments. More exactly, there were separate language compartments for things, ideas and feelings. The names of things were like a catalogue learned by rote: the names of tools I had never used or seen in use (awl, auger, angle-jaw, windlass); the names of flowers and trees not recognised, herbs and spices not tasted (cinnamon from Keats or mandragora from *Othello*) all concrete words without a corresponding object for my senses. Ideas were simpler in that so many abstract words are derived from Latin and international, but as I advanced, I also regressed—for the split between ideas and feelings grew. It became more and more difficult to express felt thought and the more I wanted to communicate the less I was able to do so—a painful paradox.

I suppose everybody who is learning a language has found, even beyond the stage of parroting, that one has become a ventriloquist. You can listen to yourself speaking fluently—it may sound good, even convincing—and all the while it is not just a foreigner speaking but another, an alien self. It goes well beyond play-acting in speech, and it goes beyond unconscious pastiche in writing. Then self-expression becomes self-betrayal, a sort of breathing through ghosts. That happens when the mother tongue has been cauterised. It is like the after-effect of a certain kind of dental surgery: a nerve has been removed from the tooth and at first there is intense pain, then just a dullness, no feeling at all—the drill can be heard but not felt.

Eventually this led to a total writer's block—but not yet. The rehearsal for the later trauma (some four years later) also came in that season of trials, in spring 1949. I had to sit for a scholarship examination for Cambridge, St Catharine's College; I say 'had to' because it was my only chance of being accepted by that university in the same year, since, as a non-British subject, I was not required to spend two years in His Majesty's armed forces, nor would my family allow me an extra year at school to reach scholarship level in English with real confidence. The prospects for that exam were, therefore, 'not brilliant' from the start. But what tilted the balance was, I think, the task of having to write an essay on a precarious subject—'Illusion'. Now that was a subject in tune with my preoccupations: I had been brooding on it endlessly, meditating on the illusory nature of faith, hope, love and vision; I had recently read Pirandello's *Six Characters in Search of an Author* with its bitter ironies on the confusions of 'reality' and 'illusion' (I read that in the school yard, to the disapproval of the headmaster who leaned over me to see what I was reading, tersely commenting 'I see!') and I had interpreted my own life as a ceaseless performance on a shaky stage. I was also going through a prolonged crisis just that spring, questioning the solidity of everything; I was left with a sense of 'empty air' all around me, an illusory or meaningless existence hurtling towards extinction. I saw death at every corner. (I wrote a long poem on that theme, in Hungarian—p.165). So when I had to write on illusion, that infinite-seeming topic, within strict time limits—probably summoning a galaxy of ideas with an ambitious excess vocabulary—the result can be imagined. I never saw my script again and I had made no draft, but I am sure that the essay was a prime example of over-reach; those good, perennially sane, English examiners must have wondered what had hit them.

Not winning that scholarship was a serious blow, and it was to have a lasting and damaging effect on my development. But by the time I had to absorb that particular disappointment, I no longer cared about anything at all. As if slyly attacked from an unknown direction, I walked about in a state of lethargy, in a permanent stupor. I had come to see all action as totally futile. From the beginning of the day—putting on clothes, a tie, getting on a bus to school—to the tedious routine of bedtime followed by miserable, broken sleep until the next dismal dawn—every single hour brought more dejection. When I went out to the fields, all I could see were the cows being driven to the slaughterhouse, even though they were grazing peacefully. In my third transitory lodging place—the vicarage at Ware, a spacious house—I could smell death in every room. The grandmother of the house, whom I hardly knew, was dying a slow death and I extended that death to include all the members of my host family and myself. I saw everybody as dying, dying soon. What did a gap of a few years between now and my death matter? How can anyone possibly do any work, be creative, concentrate for a single moment in that knowledge? It was spring but I could only see rot and decay in the garden, the lawn and the flowers blotted out by a moribund copper beech. One morning, on the way to school, I saw some old graves in the nearby churchyard and, after that vision, I could see nothing else. Somehow I crawled through the weeks, coping with my lessons and tasks up to a point. People did not seem to notice my state, partly because they did not notice me at all. Once in a while somebody, a virtual stranger, would ask whether I was 'all right'—having probably noticed how I hung my head and dragged my feet—but that was all for weeks. One of the worst moments came one afternoon when I was trying to read in the well-stocked County Library. I picked up a volume of Tennyson (not on my syllabus) and, turning the pages without any conscious choice, lighted on 'The Two Voices'. I practically ignored the voice of life but listened to the voice of desolation and death-consciousness—an echo of my own condition:

> Again the voice spake unto me:
> 'Thou art so steep'd in misery,
> Surely 'twere better not to be.'

....

'Some turn this sickness yet might take,
Ev'n yet.' But he: 'What drug can make
A wither'd palsy cease to shake?'

The long poem ends by trying to cheer itself up, with a forced Victorian repetition of 'rejoice', but I was struck in every way by stanzas like this one:

'A life of nothings, nothing-worth,
From that first nothing ere his birth
To that last nothing under earth!'

All I wanted to do was to precipitate my own death, but I did not know how. After a few weeks, as my nameless sickness got worse, I made an attempt to communicate. I asked to see the Anglican vicar, Mr. Ferguson, in whose vicarage I lived, thinking that a 'man of God' might be expected to know something about a troubled soul. Well, after listening to me for a while, the reverend suggested that perhaps I was suffering from indigestion: 'it is surprising how often a spiritual crisis is due to dyspepsia'. My uncle proved to be just as much a Job's comforter; hearing that I was disturbed by thinking about death, the death of everybody and the consequent meaninglessness of life, he said: 'that's not a problem, when you die you will be buried'. I marvelled at the metaphysical simplicity as much as at the callousness of such answers.

However, my uncle suddenly came up with the idea that, if I was really so troubled, I should consult a certain Dr. M. Rather reluctantly, I took his advice and went to see that supposedly eminent psychiatrist—another refugee from Central Europe, like so many others in my uncle's circle. The door of his apartment, somewhere in South Kensington, was wide open when I arrived and Dr. M stood there waiting crossly, and immediately started reproaching me for being late. I had nearly lost my way in finding a difficult address—a black mark for starters. There was little dialogue between us before Dr M abruptly informed me that he could see that I was suicidal, and understandably so; he too had wondered, shortly after arriving in England, whether it might not be best to throw himself on the tracks of a tube train. Then he proceeded to diagnose 'poor self-control'— on the basis of my handwriting, which I thought was not a worthy diagnostic tool—together with 'low feeling power' or rather a split between intellect and feeling. Therefore, despite a high IQ, I was destined not to succeed in anything in the higher sphere. That was a pity because if I had brought intellect and feeling together, he went on, I might have become an eminent don at least, like Sir Maurice Bowra—a name he mentioned with reverence. I thanked Dr M for his consultation and, plucking up courage, added that he told me nothing I had not known before. Dr M angrily retorted 'but I am telling you all this, and that's what matters.'

My dark state endured all through that spring, starting to sabotage my preparations for the Higher School Certificate. I willed myself to fulfil the curriculum requirements but, considering my long-term aims, that was hardly enough, in fact minimal. My uncle seemed to sense that my work had slackened—even though we were no longer living under the same roof, in fact we rarely met—and he gave me a pep talk along familiar lines: 'promise' of poor results, failure, hopeless career prospects with attendant poverty and 'don't count on the family's continued financial support.' He talked to me on one of my very low days, in his black Morris, which had a somewhat sick-making car smell. I think I nodded automatically to everything he said, inwardly knowing that I would react by slowing down further, not out of spite but as a reflex of my temperament. Only some chance impulse, perhaps a splendid or funny line from *Twelfth Night*, would re-awaken my desire to study.

I did not reveal the depth of my despair to anyone except to Ivan, in a long letter; and some time in that season I wrote the dark Hungarian poem already mentioned:

> As the wry smile of the sun
> crept across the airless space,
> a host of loose balloons
> swollen with fetid air...

danced a macabre, rhythmic dance of balloons. Some fifty almost untranslatable lines ended with a recognition: there is nothing out there but airless space with bits of coloured balloon skin drifting. Someone is watching the dance of balloons from a theatre plunged into darkness. Finally,

> A long silence no longer conspicuous,
> With no pain, no turbulent rage,
> acknowledged what you have become—
> the equal of a shrivelled-up amoeba.

The burden of that darkness was lifted as unexpectedly as it had descended, after about two months. It is useless to look for a cause. It might be asked—

as I did later—whether my intolerable awareness of death was not a direct after-effect of my Nazi deportation experiences and my father's death. But at the time I did not consciously make such a connection. I had never experienced anything like that before—so prolonged and so intense—and when my 'fit' returned, more than two years later, I could barely cope.

One side effect of my troubled months was a further increase in my sense of isolation, this time justified by the discovery that nobody could help me. I did not resent that fact, I just recognised to what an extent a deeper sympathy or empathy was beyond all people in my environment. In future I was not going to count on anybody, even less so than I had done in previous years, already devoid of 'great expectations'. The way the vicar let me down was particularly disappointing, given a certain trust towards the clergy inculcated in my old religious college in Hungary (though I had cause to be disillusioned then, as already told). Meanwhile, the vicar's coldness towards me seemed to increase, as if my 'confession'—followed by my attendance at one of his services—had been offensive. At least he remained polite, more so than his wife who started to make hostile remarks like 'English people don't appreciate showy things'—her response to a gilded Parker propelling pencil my mother had given me. On another occasion, when I referred to the procession of the Seven Deadly Sins in Marlowe's *Doctor Faustus* as medieval, my pious landlady remarked to the vicar, in my hearing: 'he thinks sin is in the past. You see, Andrew is a humanist!'—giving that word the colour others would give to words like 'fascist'. Even more alarmingly, I witnessed her anger on hearing some lines from the greatest religious poem of our time—the Good Friday sequence from Eliot's *Four Quartets*, beginning:

> The wounded surgeon plies the steel...[8]

The whole family was listening to a radio recital of the poem; it was brief, direct, moving and majestic, I felt. But it angered the lady of the house, possibly because she did not like modern poetry and/or just because I had been listening so attentively. (I later recorded this episode in an essay called 'A Young Man's Eliot'.) Not for the first time, hostility towards 'a foreigner' became associated with explicit anti-literary and anti-art feelings, with a possible undercurrent of anti-Jewish feelings, thereby adding to my split state, homelessness and resultant defensiveness. Nor did it improve my view of certain sections of the English educated classes. The vicar, an alumnus of Trinity College, Cambridge—where he had managed to place

---

[8] T.S. Eliot, *Four Quartets* (New York: Harcourt, Brace & Co. 1942; London: Faber and Faber, 1944): 'East Coker' IV.

his son, Robert as a choral scholar—strongly disliked intellectuals, found Victorian novels 'too harrowing' to read and preferred Gilbert and Sullivan to Verdi. Throughout my stay at the vicarage he made not one remark that could be seen as illuminating in a religious or spiritual sense.

Soon it was summer and my transit in Ware and Hertford came to an end or, more exactly, fizzled out. There was no ceremony and nobody said good-bye either at school or at the vicarage or in town. I moved all my stuff alone, discarding lots of things just because it was difficult to store them for a few months. Once more, then, I was reminded of wartime emergencies. And I still had no idea where I was heading.

Two comforts counteracted that bleak departure. I had done tolerably well in my final school exams: 'good' in scholarship level English and German, 'excellent' in History, with further good grades, at a lower level, in French and Latin (something of a joke as I translated my unseen text more through sheer guesswork, coupled with some general linguistic intuition, than knowledge). I knew my results could/should have been better but, in view of having started a term late—as 'a foreigner', again—and having recently lost two months through my crisis, I could live with the results. Nobody, not even my uncle, felt inclined to dwell on my failure to gain distinction at scholarship level as my grades satisfied university entrance requirements. And, confronted with new problems, I tried to shrug off the partial failure.

The second comfort was just quitting that place. I actually began to look forward to the future, even if apprehensively in view of glaring uncertainties: not knowing what I would study and where, whether I would stay in England at all. Perhaps I was facing another big mess. So be it, I thought, that would be another challenge. Meanwhile I would go on walks, read and think. Just before leaving Hertfordshire, I went down to the river Lea again to meditate, mostly on questions of universal existence, my existence as part of it, perhaps significant, perhaps not at all. Against all the difficulties I had experienced, I again pitted the surprise and the gift of my surviving the Nazis and the Stalinists. Thinking of those totalitarian extremes made me see my struggles in 'exile' in proportion. I then began to see the people who had been responsible for my recent fate as often well-meaning but blundering. My reflections left undiminished my general love of England, based as much on history, culture and language, together with an abstract idea of Englishness, as on actual encounters. I wrote to my mother that I'd rather settle in England than anywhere else in the world, including continental Europe—the prospect of an eventual return to Hungary was fast receding—or in America or Canada, a real possibility at the time. I gave implicit thanks for all that I had received and I tried to shut off firmly the valves of complaint. 'That passed' I thought, after the Anglo-Saxon complaint poem *Deor*, 'this also may'.

The Censored Version

In writing about my first two years in England, I kept a deliberate distance from the surviving correspondence between my mother and myself. But when, having completed the above narrative, I finally opened the torn old cardboard box that contained my letters to mother and read a good proportion of them, I was startled to see that I had treated her to a completely different version of some significant experiences. What I remember as the torments of my death-consciousness, in spring 1949, gets no mention at all in letters written at the time. On the contrary, I tell my mother not to listen to possible rumours about me (presumably from my uncle) and not to go in for forebodings and anxious anticipation of things that might or might not happen. I ironically ask to be protected from people who get pessimistic presentiments about this or that. And I quote— more than once—the Hungarian folk song: 'the horse has a big long head, let the horse be sad'. Why this omission? And why, in later letters, did I present my months of residence at the vicarage as a singularly serene and happy period of my life—in a house where I was well looked after? Why no mention at all of any felt hostility towards me as a foreigner, except remarking, by-the-way, that Englishmen seem to think that foreigners pollute the air, though soot and smog are home-grown.

No doubt I wanted to save my mother from fresh and serious anxiety about me—after all she had gone through in the war and while struggling with the new difficulties created by the deepening Communist dictatorship in Hungary, including our enforced separation. At the same time I probably wanted to counteract any reports sent to mother by my uncle, whom I came to regard as a sort of family spy diligently collecting black marks or negative information about my state of being. So I started to impose self-censorship on reporting personal experiences just as it had become inevitable to censor any 'subversive' political remarks or, later on, any reference to love's confusions. Beyond that lay something else, something I have hinted at before: I had achieved, if that is the word, a split state of mind over a prolonged period. Fits of deep despair were followed, after a while, by a kind of forgetfulness, dipping into that river where things are not exactly forgotten—as in the Greek myth of Lethe—but rather diluted to the point where they seem unreal. Then something experienced by A-me would be belittled by B-me and even treated with impatience by C-me until the original experience was almost buried.

Those letters are, generally speaking, full of precise detail about events and dilemmas—for example, concerning the choice of Canada versus Europe, McGill, Montreal, or Bristol (if no longer Cambridge)—contrary to my mother's charge that I kept feeding her abstractions. It is true that I would follow up a close analysis of practical possibilities for university entrance with a somewhat grand declaration about my state of being, which must have puzzled or irritated my mother: 'the probable equation is 50:50, one side of the balance being mostly emotion and the other loaded with reasoning motivation, not that those two can be separated all that simply. Besides, if you know me, emotions are often stronger guides for me than what the world, rightly or wrongly, calls commonsense. Truly—and why not write this down in ink—a deep crimson thread runs through my vision of the world and my ability to judge: I must give my inner spirit to a universal human spirit that had infected me and fructified in me at one and the same time. It is an inexhaustible source.'

29. Another Transit—Limbo

Waiting for my destination took up the rest of the summer until October. I coped with the uncertainties by not thinking about them too precisely, in a sense allowing 'destiny' to take its course, an attitude contradicted by a simultaneous need for making a rational choice and proving my will-power (as in the choice of arts subjects against strong opposition almost two years earlier). For four weeks I managed to escape to France, on a school trip. On the beaches of La Baule, in Brittany, I became both adventurous and solitary. One day I went swimming and, as if carried on the back of friendly waves, swam far out and across the bay, without informing my group; when I finally returned to base camp, our leader greeted me with real anxiety for I had apparently disappeared from view for a long time. After that I spent entire days lying alone on the sand, eating little and hardly communicating with my fellow-travellers from the school (I can only remember the boy who had an epileptic fit one afternoon), doing nothing except reading as many French books as I could get hold of: Maupassant, Benjamin Constant, Anatole France, André Gide and—the one that mattered most—Rimbaud's 'A Season in Hell'. Its poetic prose spoke to me, especially the lines that seemed to echo my spring obsession with death in a not too melodramatic but sardonic way:

'Comme je deviens vieille fille, à manquer du courage d'aimer la mort!'
'What an old maid I am becoming, to lack the courage to love death.'

In a lighter vein I tried to prove my still limited competence in French by addressing a pastiche love letter, full of superlatives, to a French girl from another school party: 'vos yeux ont une clarté lumineuse et mystérieuse', I wrote among other hyped compliments; the girl replied, by return, that her parents had found the tone of my letter very funny indeed and that she herself had been wondering whether I had eaten too many artichokes— cœurs d'artichaut—a vegetable that was supposed to be an aphrodisiac (I discovered this only years later).

From Brittany to Paris: where I linked up with my best friend Ivan, in a well-co-ordinated plan that felt like a conspiracy—after our two-year separation and an intense correspondence plotting my change to study Arts subjects. We stayed at a rundown but, to us, exotic hotel in St-Germain, in the rue du Dragon, from where we emerged for some twelve hours of sight-seeing daily—exploring the wonders of the city for the first time, arguing and philosophising all the way, while virtually ignoring the presence of three photogenic Hungarian girls and spurning the supposed temptations of a night club. We chose, instead, higher pleasures, like a good night's sleep before visiting Versailles with Trianon. We ate very frugally but had coffee in Café Flore, where Simone de Beauvoir and Sartre were supposed to appear, but did not; we discussed existentialism ('everybody' did) drawing on minimal reading; we went to see recent or new films like *Le Silence de la Mer* (based on the then famous war story about French-German relations by Vercors), Cocteau's compelling transformation of the fairy tale *La Belle et la Bête*, and a stirring import from England: *Henry V* with Olivier roaring at Agincourt, in a climax of post-war triumphalism, 'God for his Harry, England and St George!' We marvelled at the sculpture of Rodin (the monumental, not the erotic) in the museum named after him, and we went to see the latest Picassos, a new explosion of light Mediterranean colour. We sampled wine cellars, sang popular chansons, read pamphlets and newspapers like Sartre's *Les Temps moderne*s and the Communist *Humanité* (Ivan remained a Marxist despite the Communist dictatorship in Hungary). We moved in an exhilarating environment as if Paris were a superior Budapest that somehow belonged to us.

Returning to London meant returning to reality. I struggled to shape my still uncertain future from a tiny bed-sitter in NW3, found for me by my infinitely caring aunt Gizi, who fed me daily on tomatoes and cucumbers and insisted on my dressing like a perfect young English gentleman, in a blue suit and polished black shoes. For two months everything was provisional and difficult again. Nothing had been settled about my university entrance, although the choice had narrowed down to either McGill in Montreal or Bristol—with neither/nor still a distinct possibility. In early September the Canadian option seemed imminent: I had been accepted to read modern languages after several interviews at the offices of the Canadian Pacific in London; I was going to be funded partly by Hertfordshire County Council and partly by my family; I had been duly and painfully vaccinated against various diseases and, to prove how real it all was—though I never quite believed it—I had a cabin booked on The Empress of Canada, which had to be cancelled when the time ran out; then a difficult second booking was again cancelled due to further administrative delay. Nobody had foreseen the sudden and drastic devaluation of the pound by Sir Stafford Cripps (I could hear fragments of his historic speech through the open window of a stranger's house); in the ensuing currency crisis the Bank of England refused permission for the transfer of my scholarship funds. So that was the end of that possibility. I took the disappointment lightly, all the more so as

I had been expecting some kind of major obstacle all along, for the scheme was getting hyper-complicated. My ambivalent heart was not committed to that journey. 'Love of England' pointed to Bristol, but I was not yet ready to forgive Bristol for not being Cambridge. I seriously expected that the third world war would break out before long, incinerating the whole of Europe. I therefore rushed to see as many English cities as possible: took trains to Stratford-on-Avon, Oxford, Canterbury and York. Those short trips were part of a larger attempt, after Paris (and Vienna represented by the Kunsthistorisches Museum as well as the Albertina and Munich displaying the wonders of the Alte Pinakothek in a superb conjunction of London exhibitions) to see, to witness what Europe was like before doomsday. More than half a century later that may sound strange or silly, but at the time I was at least as troubled by the pending end of European civilisation as by the immediate uncertainties of my university career. I merely glanced at the latter, feeling almost light-headed in face of another mess.

I think that kind of levity was a defence against another collapse. An escape into lightness was, not for the first time, my drug, accompanied by much heavy reading and thinking. It was in those weeks in London that I read, slowly and carefully in German, Thomas Mann's *The Magic Mountain*, a novel that inevitably re-opened the jaws of death in a dominant compartment of my mind: Hans Castorp viewing the X-ray films of tuberculosis patients or struggling with his own gnawing awareness of death in the snow. All that reached me powerfully but, mercifully, I did not relapse into my spring crisis. On the contrary, I soon switched back to 'lightness' quoting Mann's not all that brilliant sentence 'Tod und Liebe ist ein schlechter Reim, 'death and love do not rhyme'. (They are closer in French, at least phonetically: *la mort/l'amour*.) I also returned to reading Hungarian poetry: cut to the marrow-bone by the last poems of Miklós Radnóti, written before he was shot by the Nazis on a forced march. Those poems were found in the coat pocket of the murdered poet, and they had the terrible simplicity of a death sentence:

> I fell beside him. His body—which was taut
> As a cord is, when it snaps—spun as I fell.
> Shot in the neck. 'This is how you will end,'
> I whispered to myself. 'Keep lying still'.

> (31 October 1944)[9]

---

[9] Miklós Radnóti, *Forced March*, translated by George Gömöri and Clive Wilmer (Manchester: Carcanet Press 1979, p.58)

30. Maturing or Else

I arrived at Bristol University, late again and as unprepared as before my arrival at Hertford two years earlier, to be met by unsettling peculiarities. I had nowhere to live (neither in a hall of residence nor privately) as the university administration had confused me with somebody else. Perhaps my application had not been clear enough, or perhaps they simply concluded from my name, still resoundingly Kárpáti, that I must be a temporary foreign student not reading for a degree course. I had to summon my remaining powers of persuasion to convince the authorities that I was not a 'foreign student' in their sense (they had classified me as 'overseas') and that I had no intention to read for non-degree courses, nor for a certificate of attendance, nor for a diploma, nor for a General Degree. What I wanted was: a full B.A. Honours course… no, not in Modern Languages, and not in English Honours either, but in the Joint School of English Literature and Philosophy. Admittedly that choice was an improvisation on my part, dictated by a sudden insight: I was 'destined' for such a course. After such a clear-sighted intuition I was not going to be deflected by a few raised eyebrows—from a tutor and an administrator—nor by the prospect of my uncle's disapproval (I had ceased to care by then, even though I was still dependent on him to an extent that became evident later). I readily accepted the precondition of entry to the Honours courses in English and Philosophy: good grades in my first year.

After these ructions, which I saw as a climax to the recent months in limbo, I eagerly plunged into reading for my several courses. For a time I managed to shed my tendency to melancholy and concentrated on the melancholy of Hamlet instead: writing a first essay on the thesis that Hamlet's mind was totally paralysed by his obsession with death: seeing man as 'the quintessence of dust' and meditating on the earth-covered yet witty skull of poor Yorick in the churchyard; it was inevitable that he would lose his capacity for action. That essay brought praise from a tutor for its 'originality' balanced by her observation that more preparatory work was required. In reality, I had done hardly any preliminary work and wrote that essay in about two hours from my head, in long hand, using my subjective experience as a source; I had not bothered to read critical texts other than Bradley and a recent book by Salvador Madariaga, and I even proclaimed that too much study was not good for writing an essay, suggesting that certain Shakespeare critics should be punished with the bastinado for writing too much. My tutor was too polite to comment on that. Perhaps I had reached a moderately manic stage. Soon another initial success came my way: the distinguished professor of Philosophy, J.C. Field, singled out my essay on Plato's *Republic* in the presence of an audience of a hundred or so students. Something had appealed to him in my essay, probably the fact that my approach was homespun—as in the essay on *Hamlet*—a direct reflection of my first reading of Plato without any reference whatever to existing scholarship . Also, as a refugee from what had become a totalitarian state, I had an instant grasp of questions of political power versus justice, and simultaneously appreciated and distrusted government by an elite claiming moral or ideological pre-eminence. Anyway, my Hungarian name was read out aloud; though the professor's voice was somewhat husky it had sufficient resonance to attract the attention of Paul, Prince Odescalchi, another refugee who happened to be among my fellow students.

Paul greeted me warmly and soon became my first friend at the university. He was older than myself, a tall, strongly built, virile man with thick dark hair and prominent traditional moustaches—every inch the aristocrat but impoverished. His name was barely known to me even though his family was related to almost 'everybody', including the Apponyi and Károlyi families who had played leading political roles in the history of Austria-Hungary. He once pointed out that there had been an Odescalchi pope, the Blessed Innocent XI, intrepid opponent of Louis XIV. He was proud, but not too proud, of these connections, holding his head high but in conversation always approachable if not intimate; later, in a time of trouble, he tried to help me. He was married to an aristocratic Hungarian woman (related to Kállai, the prime minister who had tried but failed to take Hungary out of the Nazi alliance); she seemed sad, possibly suffering the pains of exile or so I thought until I realised that she was also caught up in an unhappy and childless marriage.

By coincidence, my other early, and somewhat strange, friendship was with an upper-class German, Götz von Boehmer. Nobody introduced us, we simply found ourselves sharing a room (I could not find a single bed-sitter for several weeks.) I took to him and wanted a German friend, in the name of reconciliation; but this formal young man, with a stiff body language, turned out to be a descendent of the enemy, not because he was German (his language and the culture were partly mine) but as the grandson of Hugenberg, leader of the right-wing Deutschnationale party who had helped to bring Hitler to power. Admittedly his family was in the habit of scorning Hitler's low-class manners and Austrian accent! We argued a lot, from the start, as Götz had preserved hyper-conservative views about his nation and shook his head vigorously when he read, in my leading article in the student newspaper, a reference to jackboots that might kick again (arguing against German army participation in the Western Union). Our curious partnership, but not our cohabitation, lasted the whole academic year and climaxed in a walking tour in the Lake District, at Easter 1950, when Götz displayed a supposedly un-German inefficiency in failing to take account of those subtle contour lines that mark altitudes on the map; consequently, after a long day's walk, we would end up in a swamp or in a thick dark pine forest at nightfall, instead of a selected youth hostel or some other well-lit shelter. By way of compensation, he would recite Goethe's 'Prometheus', calling on Zeus to darken the heavens, about once every mile on our long walking tour.

One day, reading in an intimate turret room of the old university library, appropriately gothic with shelf-loads of Italian classics, a girl student appeared, chatted to me casually but sweetly and disappeared. It was more a vision than a meeting. I kept seeing her at different lectures and perhaps we talked a little from time to time, spread out over the following months, years. Her image haunted me incessantly. She was Joy Wingfield Digby of Sherborne Castle, but it was not her name or breeding that moved me, nor her brightness—she was an average student—nor even her striking good looks. She had a gentle yet strongly etched face framed by short blonde hair, seemingly proud and shy at the same time, not the type of feminine beauty I would instinctively be drawn to. So what was it that stirred my imagination beyond anything I had experienced before? It must have been the total effect: her voice—somewhat husky with a perfect enunciation, worthy of a trained actress—together with her graceful bearing and self-possession, a little mannered but not affected, controlled yet friendly. Still fumbling in presenting her now, I feel that her appeal remains indefinable, even ineffable. A cynic would scoff at such words, dismissing them as infatuation: why fall for a quintessentially 'English' English girl, an aristocrat to boot, an utterly remote and unattainable maiden? Yet her presence felt real enough. It took me half a year to summon up enough courage just to write her a very long and passionate letter rewarded with no answer. One day I heard her say about me, in my presence: 'Andrew writes good poetry but talks a lot of nonsense.' Ages passed before I took the plunge to ask her out, to see a French film, *Le Colonel Chabert*, followed by dinner and our first shy but truly personal talk. No sooner had I overcome my prolonged inhibitions in her direction—some thirty months after first glimpsing her—than she was being hotly courted by an ex-serviceman student, Bernard Harvey, my rival in every other field as well: in philosophy seminars, in leading the Literary Society, in poetry, in debates, in our current and future writing plans and in more than one student friendship. So just as I thought that I was getting close to Joy, she withdrew; and I felt compelled to write a valedictory sonnet, and withdraw. The day came for our last meeting. I was petrified by shyness again and held back when she came down to the gate at Manor Hall (her university residence) and asked, looking at me tenderly, 'shall I close the gate?' as if asking for a farewell kiss.

Seeing a vision of a girl is not a relationship. I hardly ever saw Joy outside public places like lecture rooms, always at a distance. I treated her as a *princesse lointaine* with all the patient adulation of a troubadour, on the far side of the moat of her castle, practising the medieval art of courtly love. I did suspect that there was an element of sheer illusion in my feelings towards Joy but that did not weaken those feelings; on the contrary, I had become 'passion's slave' to such an extent that a year or so later I could not fully return the love a young woman who really cared for me.

Meanwhile, I had found a few new friends. John Watts, another ex-serviceman and budding poet who was to marry a gifted and beautiful girl, Elizabeth (student marriages were still rare at the time, usually to legitimate a pregnancy); he taught me not to underestimate Jane Austen when I would not stop talking about Dostoevsky and helped to reduce my self-consciousness about being different from my English contemporaries. Donald Patterson, a Canadian physicist, inspired me with an interest in cosmic ray research and shared my enthusiasm for the frescoes of Giotto. We also shared the friendship of an older man, Dr. Jablonski, a Jewish refugee from an earlier generation, an eye specialist with a passion for culture. He was very direct, almost naïve, in displaying his literary interests. Soon after our meeting he showed me his holy bookshelf—set apart in a corner of his room—where you could see, displayed in a row, Homer, Horace, Dante, Shakespeare, Goethe and Schiller... 'All these I carry with me', he said, 'omnia... meum porto'. He balanced this grand gesture with constant serious conversation, questioning the younger generation (Donald and myself) as though we had some priceless hidden information that we would impart when cajoled. He was red-haired and thin-faced, and his voice was thin too but compelling; he died within a few years of our meeting. I recognized in this ageing doctor a certain Central or East European type and felt affection and affinity.

Otherwise I remained very much on my own most of the time, but seldom felt lonely. Apart from anything else, the two years of real isolation in Hertfordshire had probably given me some immunity from later outbreaks of the solitary disease. I found myself in an environment that was generally neutral to friendly, with a lot of smiling and polite people; so the absence of close friends did not torment me. Life at the university was liberating, as has been claimed by a number of British writers, like E.M. Forster, when they felt free after public school—different yet comparable experiences. Add to that my dislike of games and gregariousness, especially in the form of drinking and pub-crawling, together with a genuine craving for solitude needed for dedicated study—up to ten hours a day every day of the week—and for my newfound involvement in journalism.

Early in my first year I just walked into the offices of the thriving student newspaper *Nonesuch News* and I was immediately asked to start scribbling. In a surprisingly short time I became a regular reviewer, mostly covering theatre at the Bristol Old Vic and the Dramatic Society but also reviewing poetry and art (encouraged by my article on Van Gogh for a good Budapest newspaper) and even political leaders (for instance on the risk of re-arming Germany, already mentioned). Almost invariably, I gave strong support to aspiring student actors and directors while tending to be severe in my criticism of the mighty. Thus I grumbled about the production of the *Antigone* of Sophocles by Kitto—already famous as the author of *Greek Tragedy* and of the newly published *The Greeks*—writing that he had turned the tragedy into a Handel oratorio. I also faulted Glynne Wickham (embarking on a brilliant career as theatre historian and soon to head the first School of Drama in Britain) for the way he directed Auden's rarely performed verse play *The Ascent of F6*—it had offended my love of Auden's poetry and my youthful enthusiasm for the verse drama of Eliot and Christopher Fry. (That article was probably not printed). Criticism of my betters did me no good in the long run, for when I needed the support of just those two professors, I was punished with their indifference. But at the time I probably told myself that it was authentic criticism to treat an aspiring student actor or director more kindly than a famous professor who was expected to live up to the highest professional standard. My distrust of authority was itself a hangover from the war years. My rebellious impulse extended to one of Professor Kitto's lectures on the *Oresteia*. He went on and on eloquently stressing the paramount principle of *dike* (justice) in that magnificent blood-soaked trilogy of retribution: identifying justice with order, divinely ordained order. The word 'order' instantly reminded me of Ordnung—*Ordnung muss sein*—and provoked me to write a short poem on the spot, beginning:

Then let us rather in chaos live…

(Come back Nietzsche, I thought, come back Dionysus, spare us this Christianised Apollo.)

My writing for the student newspaper and the annual magazine Nonesuch (which I came to edit in 1951–52, in another year of severe crisis) was a sustained, four-year activity that I took seriously but lightly. In other words it was work without felt strain, a spontaneous record of my involvement in the arts, especially in the theatre. At one time I wondered whether I might not embark on a journalistic career but I realised that those contemporaries of mine who harboured just such an ambition were more practical or worldly people. I also saw that I was probably too slow. I heard from Alan Dent, the critic of the *News Chronicle* (talking to him outside the elegant eighteenth-century Theatre Royal) that he would dictate his review by telephone immediately after a performance; whilst I might take hours over polishing a copy. I further thought that journalism was yet another career where my foreign background would be a disadvantage; I had picked up a few hints on that score, suggestions that I 'sounded a bit foreign' even in writing. So I wrote articles and reviews almost as an art for art's sake exercise—an attitude my mother had always disapproved of; and one of our lecturers mocked: 'who is art to have a sake?' I might have countered with the Kantian principle of 'purposive purposelessness', an aesthetic approach that grew stronger in me in those years. With hindsight, my student writing was clearly no waste of time, even though it did curtail the time set aside for obligatory essay writing.

One advantage of my regular reviewing was that I tried to write impartially about plays and playwrights not on my personal wavelength, away from Sophocles, Shakespeare, Ibsen and Anouilh. I publicly discussed or reviewed less than excellent plays like Flecker's *Hassan*, Pinero's *The Magistrate*, Saroyan's *The Time of your Life*, an adaptation of Steinbeck's *Of Mice and Men* and even the melodrama *Maria Marten*. I thus became quite professional, especially when I began to review productions at the Bristol Old Vic; however, my complimentary tickets to that august place were stopped as soon as the box office manager twigged that my reviews, even the good ones, did nothing to boost student attendance at his theatre. Extending my Bristol reviewing, I wrote about an open-air performance of Schiller's *Wilhelm Tell*, seen by chance at Interlaken. Overall, my published writing remained impersonal and detached, at least in the first year. My first contribution to *Nonesuch* magazine was an ornate and humorous traditional essay, perhaps pastiche Charles Lamb, a dissertation on beards called 'De Barbis Barbaris'. At least one of my contemporaries greeted the appearance of that article with head-shaking disbelief—it seemed to contradict my 'serious' image. And it is true that I seemed to be avoiding serious as well as personal writing—not a hint about my wartime experiences or about being a foreigner or about Jewishness or about my struggles with or for Englishness. The nearest I came to personal writing was at the end of my second year when a few of my poems, selected by Professor D.G. James, were printed in the magazine. Even then, what I offered for publication were ironic and masked poems:

I shall never be able to face the world,
Never trace back the track that slipped me, whirled

178

Me, raced me, routed me reeling, to this place,
Withered me hither via vacant space...

Lines like this earned me the lasting contempt of Bernard, the 'rival poet' already mentioned, long before our hidden rivalry over Joy. However, it was impossible for me to please Bernard on any level. When I invited him to share the wonders of the Festival of Britain, he remained sulky. When he stood behind me in a lunch queue, he asked whether I was a Slav, because he had heard that Slavs had vague minds. Once he abruptly interrupted our conversation and left saying he wanted more congenial company—the Cambridge Platonists. None of this bothered me much at the time, but I had no idea how I had aroused so much hostility in someone towards whom I felt only a kind of sympathy. Given my indoctrination in Hertfordshire about the precarious status of foreigners in England, I assumed that such unprovoked detestation could be a mark of xenophobia—an assumption I could not verify despite that remark about Slavs. (Anyone who knows anything about Central Europe knows that Hungarians consider themselves 'immeasurably superior' to most Slavs excepting the Poles).

My most committed writing never got into print. In my first long vacation I wrote a novella about a girl who wanted perfection in everything and so remained loveless and unmarried; the narrative included a story-within-the story in which the characters enter Botticelli's 'Primavera' only to find spring transformed into a wintry and nightmarish scene of utter desolation. Professor James read this story with approval—was he sincere?—but he advised me to concentrate on my degree work and not to dream about becoming a professional writer: 'you could never earn a living wage', he said. 'What about Balzac?' I muttered, quite inappropriately as I knew that Balzac's genius included titanic energy: writing through the night on strong coffee and re-writing his galley proofs with abundant strokes of barely legible thick ink. My other major writing venture came towards the end of my second summer vacation when I embarked on a full-length play—in prose despite my passing reverence for verse drama—concerning a politician or minister fatally weakened as a man of action by his sensitivity and artistic inclinations (shades of Marlowe's *Edward II* but without the homosexuality). I was forced to stop working on that play, in the third act, when term started. I stopped writing and soon I was heading towards a total breakdown—but that is a later story.

Some time during my first year at the university I began to feel almost at home, growing roots. I did not exactly fall in love with Bristol but I certainly liked the city—especially the streets of Clifton with those imposing stone houses, a second Bath, the well-kept front gardens (magnificent magnolia in bloom) and Brunel's wonderful suspension bridge: my new place for meditation or brooding to regain access to the sublime, after some event, perhaps a hostile act, had damaged the privileged moments of experience. It was much later that I discovered that many of the mansions of Clifton had been built out of the profits of the slave trade.

If I felt relatively relaxed about my environment, for a short time, I nevertheless remained aware that I was regarded by several of my contemporaries as an outsider. 'They' stressed a difference—foreign or Jewish—something I had tried to forget and conceal. When somebody called me 'eccentric', I was surprised for I thought I had made an effort to adjust if not to conform. From time to time I would get a comment about my accent—which I thought I had shed—or about my appearance: distinctly 'not English'. It is one of the ironies of life that I began to look more foreign and Jewish after arriving in England—hair, nose, general profile—having lost my youthful blond and smooth image, and lost the visible inheritance of my father's and paternal grandfather's gentlemanly looks. That was nature's revenge for my trying to appear more English or, failing that, physically anonymous. No doubt my short-lived prominence as a student also worked against invisibility, for I would get comments on being a 'culture-vulture' or 'hyper-critical' or even 'frightening'. I interpreted remarks like that as signs of moderate hostility and on the whole went on smiling amiably, somewhat like Malvolio when failing to see the illusions of his love or self-love.

Most of the first year in English Literature concentrated on the Seventeenth Century, a period I revelled in, reading well in excess of what was recommended. In drama: all of Shakespeare and most of the Elizabethan and Jacobean dramatists from Marlowe to Ford ('Webster was much possessed by death', and so was I); in poetry: returning to Milton with delight and discovering the Metaphysical poets. I found an immediate affinity with Donne both in the love and the religious poetry, but I expressed the opinion that Herbert was a 'country parson preaching platitudes', shamefully wrong but I had become inflated by conceit—in a double sense. I felt then that poetry and drama were my prime elements. Since there was little appealing fiction in the seventeenth century, as distinct from 'prose', I turned to European literature outside the curriculum, reading Tolstoy and Dostoevsky (*The Brothers Karamazov* with total absorption) and a fair selection of Penguin classics from Homer to Chekhov. Soon I got verbally intoxicated when reading and reciting the *Divine Comedy*, canto by canto in the Temple parallel text, while learning Italian in preparation for my planned journey to Italy, partly inspired by Burckhardt's *The Civilization of the Renaissance in Italy*. As I was planning to write about the decadence of our civilisation (its decline and pending fall, a project that led to two published essays), I plunged into the weighty works of Spengler's *The Decline of the West* and Toynbee's *A Study of History*. For tragicomic relief I relished the story of Spengler and Toynbee going on an inspection tour of a hospital for civilisations: the former announces, at each bed in succession: 'dead, dead, dead, dead, dead'... while Toynbee, in a rare fit of optimism, diagnoses 'dead, dead, dead, dead, dead... maybe, perhaps, not yet, not sure'. The last patient was our Western civilisation responding to the supreme challenge of totalitarian Stalinism. Of course, all my thinking concerning history and culture was deeply marked at that time by the growing gloom emanating from behind he Iron Curtain, the brutal dictatorship in the new Soviet empire accompanied by the hysterical witch-hunts in the United States during the inquisition-like trials led by MacCarthy. The extent of my general anxiety—about the world during the Cold War—was probably shared by few of my student contemporaries and consequently I tended to consider some of them lightweight if not frivolous or mediocre.

Whoever devised the English curriculum—no doubt strongly influenced by Professor D G James, a devout Christian—had the inspired idea of asking us to read the Authorised Version, with detailed study of The Book of Job. Thus, under the heading of 'the bible to be read as literature', I came to study religious writing seriously and renewed my once rooted (pre-deportation) spiritual quest. The Book of Job was supremely appropriate. First of all, it re-connected me with the Old Testament/The Hebrew Bible and its often magnificent language. It also connected the drama of a soul with the theme of inescapable suffering and the temptation to denounce the whole created world and its Creator out of sheer despair. I was haunted by many of the unforgettable verses of Job, not least his sudden lament:

'Wherefore then hast thou brought me forth out of the womb' (10.18).

At the same time, I remained unconvinced by God's final rhetoric, a voice out of the whirlwind, aimed at subduing the rebellious protestations of Job by an appeal to the wonder and mystery of the universe. But then Milton—justifying the ways of God to man in his theodicy—had not cured my scepticism either. Nevertheless, from this time on, I would wince when somebody labelled me a 'humanist' (as about a year earlier, in an incident at the vicar's house). For I could not share the humanist's confident assertions concerning human perfectibility and I increasingly felt

181

the need to contemplate religious hopes and doubts more deeply. That is partly why Donne's 'divine poems' had such a strong appeal:

> Take me to you, imprison me, for I
> Except you enthral me, never shall be free,
> Nor ever chaste, except you ravish me.[10]

At about the same time I re-discovered Eliot's *Four Quartets* which became my constant companion as a text and as a memory following a reading in a small, extra-curricular group gathered together by one of my tutors, Virginia Browne-Wilkinson. She had the gift of turning a casual-seeming tea party into a challenging encounter with Modern writing. Those readings—after Eliot, Virginia Woolf—may have done more for my later development as a literary critic than most formal lectures and tutorials. There is a world of difference between criticism springing from study (or 'appreciation', a now outdated word) and criticism intertwined with the rhythms of one's inner life. Certainly, several of the texts we read 'privately', never examined and never part of our curriculum—which ended with the nineteenth century—pursued me all my life.

---

[10] John Donne, *The Complete English Poems* (ed. A.J. Smith), Penguin Education (1971), p. 135

31. Zenith and Nadir

I had a year or so (1950–51) that was almost trouble-free, before the next crisis. My good second year at university was preceded by writing (the novella already mentioned) and travel in the long summer vacation: a journey full of discovery that took me from Provence and the Côte d'Azur through Central and Northern Italy to Geneva. I will only briefly mention here, on top of the expected 'grand tour' sights—Genoa, Milan, Florence, Pisa and Siena, from Rome to Venice, Vicenza, Verona and the lakes—a galaxy of marvels found more by chance than by plan: above all the Giotto frescoes in Assisi and Padua and the Byzantine mosaics in Ravenna. Such awesome, life-enhancing experiences tempted me to embark on a formal study of art history but I knew that opposition from the family would be unremitting. The journey itself had some ambiguities on the personal level. First of all, I was stateless, travelling with a document—enriched by numerous visa stamps—that gave me much less security than a passport and indeed earned me a rebuff at the British Consulate in Paris (when I eventually needed a short-term loan). I had also failed to reveal the scope of my route to my family and indeed to myself; I invented the journey as I went along, driven by an ever-increasing desire to see. I set out without enough clothes in my rucksack and without enough money: I tried to stretch a sum meant to last three weeks into a journey of seven weeks, living on less than ten shillings a day (about 50 pence in post-decimal terms.) I did, however, win a day's living expenses at the casino in Monte Carlo; I slept in youth hostels and, when I could no longer afford them, in open fields and once, in Domodossola, in a monastery where I paid for the hospitality of the monks with prayers, followed by a sermon on the Virgin Mary, at six o'clock in the morning. I ate at cheap *mensa communale* set up for pious pilgrims (it was the Holy Year, Anno Santo) and I managed to eat less and less—bread and cheese with a few pieces of chocolate, for instance. When in Vicenza, two generous sisters invited me to a meal consisting of one egg—the one and only egg they possessed, a gift I could not accept.

And all the time I was given lifts and treats. In Vicenza, apart from the sisterly hospitality, I was invited to a performance of the *Antigone* in the famous Teatro Olimpico by the company of Tomasso Salvini who then treated me to a private recital of Richard II's prison monologue and a lively discourse on the theatre. In Rome, a violinist, met by chance on a bus, took me to see *Aida* at the Terme di Caracalla, enriched by camels and elephants, and he wrapped me in his own jacket when the temperature dropped at nightfall. In Venice a floating grocer took me on his barge and

I became his assistant in delivering dried fish, baccala, in a multitude of little winding canals. Near Lago di Garda a nubile girl showered me with art cards as I woke, at sunrise. I travelled alone for weeks yet never felt lonely, except on my fifth day in Venice when a stranger stopped me to ask, out of sheer curiosity, whether it didn't feel lonely travelling all alone. I had company at the youth hostels—casual and ephemeral company, more than once leading to long discussions with German students (Germans outnumbering all other nationalities in travel): I needed to satisfy my urge for understanding and reconciliation with the children of my persecutors. Every conversation made me conscious of the wonder—the inexplicable chance—of my being there at all, in Florence or anywhere, as a survivor.

The journey ended in Paris where I arrived with a high fever and completely broke (I had to borrow the fare for the Channel crossing from a friend.) I felt so low that I took no action when, at the youth hostel, I witnessed someone stealing my pocket knife, covered in mother-of-pearl and much valued as it used to belong to my father. At one point I thought I was going to die and as I had no worldly goods to bequeath to anybody, I wrote a verse testament ironically ending with 'messieurs, dames, la visite est terminée'. Not surprisingly, on my return to England I was greeted with much head-shaking and I also received a rather sharp letter from my mother who, far from appreciating my spirit of adventure, scolded me for wanting to swallow life all at once; she pointedly wondered why I had not stopped at the Prado in Madrid on my return journey from Italy. I excused myself from such criticism but remained acutely conscious that I was 'living it up' in the West whilst my sister was having a hard time—both in study and in her circumstances, with travel to the West forbidden—in Budapest.

Back in Bristol, for a short time I was guided more by sense than sensibility, enjoying eighteenth century studies from Pope and Swift to Fielding and Dr. Johnson. Appropriately enough, it was the Fielding connection that managed to expose me to public ridicule after I had privately asked Henry Gifford (the future professor and Russian literature scholar) whether he could point out the most reading-worthy chapters in the endless picaresque saga of Tom Jones. A week later, the lecturer retold this story to his student audience, in my absence, to general mirth that prompted Gifford to add 'actually it was quite an intelligent student who asked me.' It is true that I already thought life too short to read a long digressive novel if it did not illuminate something quintessential. I found the spirit of the Enlightenment congenial—especially satire and irony— though my heart remained at home among the Romantics (Wordsworth and Keats) and my critical and writerly interest focused more and more on the Modern (not part of any formal curriculum). This was also the year when we concentrated, in addition to Descartes, on English philosophers from Bacon to Hume; overnight I wrote a dissertation-sized essay on Bacon, which was very well-received; but another essay brought the curious comment from Professor Körner: 'you write too fluently, I can't get my teeth into your text'. With hindsight, it seems clear that a period of Reason had strengthened the empirical/sceptical strain in my mindset, later to be challenged by a time of trouble and a search for a mystical dimension. The Enlightenment zone is a comfortable place to be in as long as its tendency towards megalomania, undermined by fits of melancholy, is kept at bay.

In the winter of my second year I met Ruth Woollons who became my best friend and, for a time, we were in love spiritually. Our first meeting was as simple, even conventional, as a meeting between two students can be. I went to a Union dance, somewhat against my inclination, telling myself that 'I had to go' to keep up some sort social life, as a public student: reviewer, writer and active member of the Literary and Dramatic Societies. I remained diffident about my abilities as a dancer, as told before. So I arrived late and intended to leave early. Then, in the course of surveying the scene, I noticed a girl—with a fresh and gentle, appealing face—just standing there as a virtual wallflower. Why should a girl like that not be dancing with a suitable partner, I wondered, and asked her for the next dance. Soon we were in deep conversation, insofar as the music, the tumult and our relatively clumsy dancing allowed. It turned out that she was reading French and knew France, Paris, well. That provided not just an enjoyable starting point for our talk but also assured me, in a coded way, that this very English girl from Plymouth was not parochially English: her Continental connection had instantly given her a kind of cosmopolitan dimension; so we could talk of Baudelaire and French wines and songs. I warmed to her immediately and 'confessed' my foreign origins, something I tended to avoid, especially when first meeting 'a stranger'. (On one such occasion, when somebody asked about my parentage, I answered with a broad smile: 'well, my mother was a Hottentot and my father a Zulu'. I don't remember the reaction to that utterance). So that first meeting with Ruth turned fully personal and as intimate as the age (the tranquillised Fifties) and our mutual restraint allowed. By the end of the evening I found Ruth enchanting: her brilliant eyes, her face, her voice, her manner, her laughter, all that. And we started going out as frequently as seemed right, again by the standards of the time. Once she invited me to her student residence, in Manor Hall, where I thought fit to play with her necklace and strangled her. Ruth responded to my theatrical act by reciting lines from Browning's perverse, necrophiliac poem, 'Porphyria's Lover':

and all her hair
In one long yellow string I wound
Three times her little throat around
And strangled her

When Spring came we started going on excursions around the nearer end of the West Country: we cycled to Tintern Abbey where a magnificent ruined arch gracefully framed Ruth while we paid homage to Wordsworth; to the Mendips and Cheddar Gorge; to Bath and Wells, moved by the splendour of the architecture. So we grew closer. Nevertheless, that spring remained the high point of our relationship: we could not take it any further, and I am not sure whether we wanted to. On my part, I realised that I could not experience with Ruth the kind of aesthetic passion (probably adolescent) that plunged me into ecstasy when meeting Joy. Nor did I feel any physical desire for Ruth, though we did kiss, gently, under the orange sodium light of a street lamp and once I tried to kiss her in a railway tunnel, but she refused. When the summer vacation came, it seemed natural for us to go in different directions in our travels. That restraint was again partly dictated by the age (travelling together would have been seen as a virtual engagement to marry) reinforced by our mutual puritanism. As time went on that distance persisted, leading to a potentially tragic separation in the following term.

My second summer journey was also adventurous. Criss-crossing the Alps from Lake Geneva via Interlaken and Lugano to Bodensee, I entered Germany for the first time as a free man. I travelled up the Rhine driven, beyond ordinary curiosity, by a desire for reconciliation—following my study of German literature, my mountain walks with Götz and all those late night talks with German students in Italy. It was a kind of quest. So everything I saw—ruins and signs of re-building—was poignantly felt while certain remarks overheard haunted me: 'no more war, no more army' said the teenager on the back of a lorry that gave both of us a lift. In Heidelberg I re-met Ivan Nagel, the boy genius, who spent virtually the whole night—in Philosophenweg—talking about the literature of the demonic. I spent a rough night in a Wiesbaden doss-house, compulsorily disinfected (memories of the concentration camp). That journey ended in Brussels and my second reunion with Ivan Barko, my best friend; our meeting turned into another symposium—less drinking, more philosophy—accompanied by the revelation that Ivan had a mistress. What, a mistress? I instinctively knew that I was not going to have one: contemptuous of tarts, immobilized by a still burning aesthetic passion for Joy and a deep spiritual affinity with Ruth.

I returned to Bristol still in high spirits, now it would be called 'high'—hyperactive though not on drugs. A crisis was brewing early in the autumn term though I did not know it. By October I was simultaneously writing a three-act play (unfinished before term began), dealing with serious essay assignments, reviewing, and leading quite an intense social life. And I had become restless in my feelings towards Ruth. One day I suggested to her that we need not go out with each other exclusively for a time. I meant to say this lightly without any intention to break off our relationship but Ruth felt it was just that, a declaration of non-love (as she told me much later). I had nobody else in mind yet I began to experiment: I invited a girl called Naomi to the theatre, using my complimentary tickets to the Theatre Royal. At our first meeting, which was to be our last, I got over-stimulated by her distinctly Jewish warmth, wit and her freckled beauty—large brown eyes and a motherly bosom. But I immediately repressed the attraction. My old non-desire to start a serious relationship with a Jewish girl—the fear of provoking another cycle or another generation of suffering—must have contributed to an underlying yes/no emotional conflict. Instead I indulged in an orgy—of talk.

At the time I was unaware of being over-excitable or 'over the top' and Naomi, who did not know me from Adam, was unlikely to have registered my incipient madness. It took a short while for the 'high' to get converted into severe depression. Perhaps the best way of presenting that particular trial is to quote here from my 1951 diary, only started just four months before the darkness came. I only quote myself of long ago because my memory of those two and a half months were weakened or obliterated by the illness itself and perhaps even more so by the violent cure that had been prescribed.

9th November (1951)
It is with the utmost effort only that I force myself to /make/ this attempt at recording my state of mind in these plague-stricken days. But beneath the thick layers of banality and spiritual exhaustion there still lingers a soul—if I still have one—a latent hope that some day the demon of hebetude may be exorcised by a sudden act of grace or by an effort of this kind. I should not have said 'latent hope', I should have called it a minute particle of that blind, biological force that still causes me to vegetate, to eat my meals without appetite, to sleep without rest or even the desire for rest, to move my limbs in the accustomed manner—though I am hardly conscious of these movements—to think no thoughts, to talk without having anything to say. I should like to pray that this heaviness may be lifted from me but I have long forgotten how to pray. I can turn neither to God, nor to love, nor friendship

nor beauty for help; the totality of Life is levelled down to one colourless stretch of fallow, which the birds of the field leave wholly unnoticed and which is shirked even by the earth-worm. The soil is as hard as basalt, rain cannot soften it, ploughshare cannot break it, sunshine cannot warm it. A pneumatic drill would not help either: below the crust of basalt there is nothing left but a stagnant pool of whey—it is doubtful whether even frog-spawn or bacteria can exist there.

I cannot say what has come over me or how I became this bloodless inhuman thing. It is now nearly a fortnight since my very faculties of sense have snapped; since then I am incapable of any truly sustained thought or speedy work, I can respond to nothing, rejoice in nothing, I merely put on a show of existence and all my thoughts and actions seem to be prompted by thoroughly spurious motives. Even while I write what I know is the truth, I lack the force of sincerity.

A kind of mental paralysis—of a degree never before experienced—has deadened my inner life without—to torment me—robbing me of consciousness, the consciousness of vacuity. Today I was scarce capable even of writing a few lines of birthday greeting to my mother. I could only repeat—with infinite, snail-like effort—what I remembered were a short while ago my innermost feelings. In the very moment when I wrote that it is her love alone that brings new strength to me when I am left utterly alone—being incapable of shaking myself off me—I felt this was no longer true. I merely recollected my past experience, as if racking my brain to squeeze out the memory of a mathematical equation learnt a very long time ago. If this is possible it is no longer even surprising that everything in the world around me is devoid of content.

I cannot continue. I have become wholly inarticulate. How long can I carry on like this? I try to will that I should love to love life again.

20th December.

For two months I have tried everything—all in vain. Reading, company, friends, excursions, play, dance, returning to the past, church—but I am only further and further removed from life. All that I once understood and felt—beauty, love, friendship included—has become as incomprehensible as the most recondite elements of differential calculus. I have not enough energy left to record my experiences.

O Lord, preserve those nearest to me from
humiliation through me. O take my life rather
than my ability to live.

It is not torpor, it is not madness.
Everything a symbol of not being a symbol.

I also wrote:
Here where all clatter and chatter must cease
Encased in a forsaken cell of ice
The glacier's new captive prays for release...

And I might have tried to sing (with Hooker):
'I'll never get out of these blues alive'.

When I try to reconstruct what happened between those diary entries and after, I can remember only an initial tiredness made worse by a heavy cold, which naturally slowed me down in a high-pressure phase of the autumn term. As the days went by, I slowed down further and found it more and more difficult to concentrate. The crunch came when I tried to write an essay, an imposed task, on a challenging subject:

'"O for a Life of Sensations rather than of Thoughts"
—Discuss the poetry of Keats in the light of this quotation'.

It was a topic that had an underlying personal difficulty for me as I was conscious of the struggle, or split, between sensation and thought in my own personality. But normally I would have covered the topic with fairly effortless arguments—full of quotations, poetic and critical—and probably rounded it off with some grand conclusion, rejecting either/or in favour of both/and, appealing to the fullness of Keats's creativity. What happened instead was that I could not proceed at all, could not even begin. The sentences crumbled as I tried to formulate them; the words fell apart. While still writing, I kept changing my approach, re-wrote and rejected what I wrote in a succession of desperate hours until I came to a complete standstill. I panicked. When repeated efforts at going on with the work yielded only worse results, I went to my tutor, Mr. Reynolds, to report that I could not finish the essay in time, and asked whether it could be postponed. Next I was summoned by the university health service. That surprised me as I had not asked to be 'seen', and Mr. Reynolds had not told me that he was worried about my condition; he was a dry, laconic man with whom I had no real previous contact beyond discussing essay topics. I duly attended my medical appointment and probably—here my mind is blank—told the truth about my state.

By that time my condition may have become visible or at least audible—I probably spoke anxiously, in broken fragments. I had already tried and failed various personal remedies of my own, like those listed in my diary. The worst thing was to go out in town and see everything in a haze: people at a party—at the Psychology Department, of all places, as Paul Odescalchi's guest, invited to join in the games: Romeo had to find Juliet and the Id had to find the Ego. All those people are mad, I thought, and so am I. Or else I kept staring at ducks—colourful Chinese ducks at Peter Scott's nature reserve at Slimbridge in Gloucestershire, taken there by Donald Patterson on his motorbike, out of sheer kindness. There I confronted Nature with my troubled questioning: why has Creation created such creatures or any other… for what purpose? why not rather end it all now, quack, quack, quack. A parked car caught my attention in a busy street and I wondered how Plato might have classified its form, the car-ness of the car, if he had come across such a man-made machine—and I envied Plato the ease of his task, contemplating a world not yet totally cluttered by artefacts and engulfed by chaos.

So I went to see Dr Smith—his real name, I don't know what his first name was—a consultant psychiatrist. My old suspicion of this man's profession was revived as soon as he started pontificating about 'completely natural processes, chemically stimulated electro-magnetic impulses in the brain'. I was sane enough to realise that the man was inadequate as a healer, obsessed by neurological jargon, which I had heard before at the Burden Institute in Bristol and discussed in a long seminar on 'mind and matter'. However, I was by then becoming dependent on my questioner and I lacked the courage to argue with him, as I would have done when fit. Dr Smith further undermined my confidence when he belittled my sincere worry over having achieved so little—'I know no Greek', I lamented—'well, it's hardly necessary', said Dr Smith; 'and I have forgotten all the maths I had learned'—'good riddance', said Dr. Smith. This man is a philistine, I thought, even while I was getting more and more dependent on him and the institution he chaired. It was a day care centre, a miserable place, quite enough to depress anyone entering: the waiting area was full of shrunken patients, mostly poor old women with frighteningly frightened faces like Géricault's yellow-skinned 'La Folle'. White-clad young nurses flitted about self-importantly, demonic angels.

I must have given my consent to the treatment but I have no memory of doing so. I was afraid of its consequences but also afraid of trying to carry on with my deepening depression. Dr Smith tried to present a case; he said that there would be no pain, perhaps a certain tiredness and blur afterwards. He said that the machines used were brought to England by some clever Italian shrinks and, nobody knew how, a lot of patients were completely cured. No, ECT had nothing to do with lobotomy; it was confusing to suggest such a comparison. It did no damage to the brain. Perhaps some memory loss, but that would be temporary. There was nothing else as effective.

So one day I lay down on a bed, no different from a bed seen in most surgeries, and tried to think of nothing. A youngish nurse carefully wiped some fluid on my temples and placed on them a metallic object, like earphones. Then I lost consciousness. When I awoke they tried to explain where I was and what had happened, and I was told to wait lying down for a while. After that I was escorted out of the day centre. It seems that I walked home, but I cannot be sure about that. How could I have walked? My legs were unsteady and a kind of fog had penetrated my mind. That lasted for quite a long time.

Then the treatment had to be repeated. I think I tried to escape, tried to avoid a repetition by not turning up for an appointment. But I was caught meandering in Park Street: a doctor from the unit recognised me and persuaded me to return. He looked and sounded quite agitated; I suppose it was dangerous to go around like that, with my treatment not complete. So I went through the whole operation for a second time, dreading it more and feeling the after-effects—like a heavy, ongoing hangover—more strongly.

Christmas was approaching and I stayed in that reduced condition in my rented room under the almost maternal care of Mrs. Venning, my landlady, who had bought a chicken and other goodies to mark the festive season. I remained uninterested in anything—in people, music and food— but I ate something every day nevertheless and kept reading, trying to concentrate on certain philosophical texts, for example on Collingwood's *The Idea of History*. I realised that it was easier for me to read something difficult for I could absorb an intellectual argument but could not respond to a poem or a novel; my inability to be moved emotionally (to see but not to feel, as Coleridge lamented) would bring further torment. I remained under self-imposed house arrest over the whole Christmas and New Year vacation, trying not to think, for thinking had become dangerous. Nevertheless, I found some consolation in the messages that reached me: from my mother, from my uncle (who came on a brief visit and gave money to the landlady for the extra care and the Christmas chicken) and from Ruth. She sent a little parcel for my birthday (9th January) filled with homemade bakery and a note 'with the cook's compliments.' Her separate, gentle and deeply reflective letter carried wise counsel quoting St Paul's famous letter on seeing through a glass darkly before…

That letter proved to be providential for soon I felt much better and then, with astonishing speed and intensity, I recovered my faculties just before the spring term began. I noticed that I had slowed down, and I could not remember substantial chunks of what had happened before and after the ECT treatment, but I had begun to feel again and think again and I greeted every new opportunity with anticipation and joy. I went back to my studies as naturally as one goes home (if you have a home) and it was not necessary to be told by Dr Smith: 'as soon as you are better you must start working like stink. And, by-the-way, give up your easy-going liberal-humanitarian attitudes!' I also resumed writing, only reviewing at first. Ruth and I re-established our close friendship and even attended dancing classes together: 'merge your aura in this closeness', commanded our dancing teacher. Despite that almost spiritualistic blessing, Joy remained my aesthetic polestar and Agnes, on a transitory visit initiated by herself, took me to bed wanting to teach me how to do it. If that sounds like a threefold division—friendship/the Muse/sex—that's how it was, a precarious balancing round.

My vision of the world had undergone a transformation, or so I believed. I kept writing endless notes amounting to a re-education of myself towards stronger ethical aims—away from what I saw as excessive emotion or hedonistic sensation for the sake of 'higher pleasures' like art and architecture, poetry and music. And away also from that constant analysis of my states of mind (a habit that started when I was about fifteen) encouraging a degree of self-centredness not too far from selfishness, I now thought. All those notes dwell on a 'new philosophy' (new in personal terms though leaning on Kantian ethics at several points), grouped under headings like: Revaluation — Landslide. Some examples:

Personal freedom—freedom from self
Simplicity—complexity tends towards shuffling and
    shamming
Wisdom—before and above intelligence
    ('intelligence of itself moves nothing'—Aristotle)
The danger: arrogance of ignorance

Oasis in the centre of the desert
Soul (mind) and brain distinct?
If purpose then spirit. Mere refinement of matter cannot
    be purposeful.

Thy will be done.

I was going to work out a theory of mind, combined with my new insights in ethics, aesthetics and religion; I even informed one of my lecturers that I wanted to write about these things but I never got beyond my heap of notes. I had accepted—as I reflected on my clinical depression and the violent intervention that cured it—that physiological, bio-chemical brain functions lay under all ideas: electrons jump and I experience a leap of faith; electrons are praying to electrons. But the language of a computer model for the brain was wholly inadequate for recording any subtle or deep experience. So back to poetry, metaphor and myth: the language I needed. Just as music could not be defined in terms of sound waves and their auditory reception (complexities of hearing) so none of our essential ideas—concerning truth, beauty and spiritual experience— could be defined in terms of psychiatric fundamentals (*pace* Dr. Smith). We need several and different languages to 'cover' reality (one stuff, many perspectives), languages that overlap though they may seem to be polar opposites.

All through those months, and years, I was governed by a new sense of gratitude as well as fear. Gratitude for having been granted the experience of climbing out of a dark valley, thinking of Keats's letter on life and suffering as a 'vale of soul-making'. At the same time I constantly feared a relapse: any morning when I woke up in a low state I wondered whether it was not the symptom of depression returning.

My excuse for writing only notes at that time (though I wrote some poetry and was preparing to edit the university literary magazine mentioned before) was the shadow of the final exams. I realised that I was running out of time and that I could not possibly sustain course work as well as my other aims. So I applied to the Arts Faculty for a postponement of my degree exam and that was granted. But at that point my uncle intervened in a heavy-handed way: he drove down to Bristol, secured an interview with Professor James and managed to talk him into countermanding the faculty's earlier consent to extra time: to allow for a full recovery from my illness and, I hoped, a first class degree. I was actually sent out of the room while this fatal conversation was taking place but, standing outside the door, I could overhear a few keywords:

—Uncle: 'He'll only waste his time'…
—James: 'But he is ambitious'.

My uncle's argument, backed up by a claim to have gained a lot of psychological know-how as a practicing paediatrician in Vienna, had won over the influential professor. I am not sure whether my uncle still had the legal right to control my destiny, after all I had just reached the age of maturity—then 21—but the power balance was like that in those days. I thought the decision would be a major setback and it did affect my long-term career.

So I decided to concentrate on reading for my finals and discarded most of the other things I had wanted to do when well. I gave up the idea of launching an extra literary magazine, somewhat ignominiously as I had already commissioned a batch of articles, among them studies of Thomas Mann and André Gide, and I had started soliciting articles from science professors, beginning with Nevill Mott (the future Nobel prize winning physicist) for I wanted to include the Baconian 'advancement of science' alongside articles on literature and philosophy. My illness had induced a new caution; but I had also underestimated the printing costs—'typical', my mother would have said. Meanwhile I did not renounce editorship of the official university magazine and it duly came out in May; my leader had an exceptionally affirmative tone under the title 'The Age of Synthesis'. My article rejected certain obsessions with cultural decadence and claimed, on behalf of the generation that 'grew up during the Second World War and its aftermath' the need to preserve and expand European culture. 'Some of us had seen first hand what the collapse of ordered life means. Some of us have passed through most maladies of the age. Some of us have been nursed on dissolution and disillusionment. Again we say these have been conditions of growth'… And so it went on. One day I ran into the university doctor who had read that editorial and congratulated me; I instantly realised that he had decoded an underlying declaration of personal recovery.

There were other signs of my return to normal—though not to my old self-confidence and courage. During the Easter vacation I saw Joy again and duly got re-intoxicated, writing a long poem, a sort of dramatic monologue in the manner of Browning, a pastiche poem, dedicated more or less openly to her. She had reservations about the poem at first but then came to praise it enthusiastically, perhaps by way of compensation for her absenting herself for all time. I also recovered my delight in music—a chance hearing of Bizet's 'Symphony in C' on the radio moved me with unexpected force—and Nature. Unable or unwilling to travel as the time of finals approached, I kept walking around Clifton. The river Avon, the mellow stone buildings fronted with exquisite trees and shrubs, were a daily wonder:

'Magnificent magnolia stellata, blossoms as pure as the Madonna
lily, burying the tree under a mountain of bridal whiteness—

194

sunlit petals fold the focal blossom into shadows' (my note from that time).

The recovery meant that I refused to brood over the rejection of my plea for an extra year and I threw myself into studying, more or less non-stop. Revision and new reading took up about twelve to fourteen hours a day, much of the time spent outdoors, lying on grass or sitting on the branch of a tree. The day usually ended with drinking Somerset cider, imported in a barrel by Peter, my flat-mate. All this may seem ordinary enough except that I—having climbed out of the abyss—seemed to enjoy the pre-finals tension: revelling in the inescapable pressures, the immense amount of reading for two major subjects, the pumping adrenalin, the panic of some of my contemporaries as well as my own private fits of fear, the irregular stool and the disturbed sleep. Some of the reading was itself remedial, such as passages from Wordsworth's *The Prelude*:

'There are in our existence spots of time,
That with distinct pre-eminence retain
A renovating virtue, whence, depressed
By false opinion and contentious thought… our minds
Are nourished and invisibly repaired.' (XII, 208–15)

It was not all plain sailing of course. I recall dropping and breaking my spectacles (both glass lenses smashed into smithereens) and losing my Parker fountain pen that had enabled me to write smoothly and speedily, and which could not be replaced in time for the exams. But my demons had retreated and I vowed that they were not to undermine me again. As the 'day of judgment' approached, I took some sadomasochistic pleasure in collecting reports of fear and trembling while circulating, among my fellow-sufferers, lines from Webster about 'going into the wilderness where I shall find no friendly clue'. I also found some satisfaction in denouncing the entire examination system as absurd—to Professor Field, the kindest of all our teachers—arguing that it was not a true test of knowledge or of intelligence but only a test of endurance. 'That's right', said the professor, 'life is about endurance'. Meanwhile, although I judged that I was doing reasonably well through the relentless sequence of exams—about a dozen times three hours, morning and afternoon—I had a presentiment that I would fall short of a first class degree. For one thing I kept running out of time; on one occasion I had just managed one opening sentence on Berkeley's solipsism (the fourth of four questions) when we had to stop writing; after that I came to doubt that to BE was to be perceived and that God will always see me and so guarantee my continued existence, as Berkeley supposed.

At that time if you did not get a 'first' you were finished—your chances of research or even continued study were virtually nil. That was proved to me soon enough when I called on Professor James to discuss my results and prospects. He did not say what I had hoped he would say— that my literature papers were first class but that some of my philosophy grades dragged me down. He just shook his head gently and I dared not remind him of how he had prevented me from studying for an extra year. At a certain point I told him of one of my research plans (I had several): the study of autobiography from St Augustine's *Confessions* via Rousseau to John Stuart Mill, linking changing definitions of the self to changing times and ideologies. 'Well', said Professor James, 'it doesn't begin to make sense'. I attributed his negativity to my failure to get a first; for I knew that D.G. James was particularly interested in combining the personal and the ideological and I thought that such a theme had a future. (I was proved right, for years later an abundance of books began to appear resembling my proposed subject). I was no less lucky when preparing a study of Webster's dramatic language, a topic I had felt enthusiastic about. On the strength of an outline, I was invited by Allardyce Nicoll, then director of the Shakespeare Institute at Stratford-on-Avon, for a conversation (i.e. an interview) at his half-timbered house in Worcestershire. He seemed interested and amiable; yet he decided that I was 'too philosophical' and that he really wanted somebody who would focus on bread-and-butter jobs like sorting Elizabethan laundry bills. He thought that a thoroughgoing study of Anglo-Saxon grammar might have been a better preparation for the vacant fellowship than reading Kant. I privately asked why he had invited me at all as my CV and my synopsis must have given him a clear idea of my qualifications and aims. But in those days there was no point in making even the mildest protest, and I left wondering what I would or could possibly do next.

As an insurance policy I put my name down for Education—for the Post-graduate Certificate, and duly fulfilled the initial requirement: a spell of teaching practice in a secondary modern school. In the middle of a lesson on punctuation—perhaps trying to convey the thrills of the apostrophe to boys with vacant eyes—I was suddenly struck by the utter futility of my teaching anything at all, at that level and to such nice but slow young boys. As soon as I had finished my practice, I abruptly withdrew from the Education course and packed my luggage, intending to leave Bristol for good.

I had little hope of finding a solution to the problem of my career. Perhaps I could try publishing, perhaps librarianship, or just 'wait and see'—live on very little, getting odd jobs while continuing to read and write and deepen... My sense of failure was tamed by a sharp consciousness of at least two necessities. First, I had to protect my family from perceiving my failure as failure, and so avoid my uncle's 'I told you so' responses and my mother's fresh anxiety. Second, and more fundamentally, I had to avoid a relapse into depression: I had to cheer myself up, perhaps like Nietzsche, loving my destiny: *amor fati*. I therefore tried to avoid 'thinking too much' about either the present or the future. One day I walked up to Brunel's suspension bridge for what I took to be the last time, stood there for a long while staring down into the gorge, into the green river Avon. I silently congratulated myself on having accepted another failure and somewhat lightly recalled all the good arguments against suicide.

* * *

32. Reflections

When I first mentioned my attempt at recording memories of childhood and early youth, a retired psychiatrist remarked: 'writing an autobiography is always a narcissistic exercise.' On the contrary, I said, my intention was to portray a vanished age, concerned as much with the age as personal confessions. Those two poles are not opposites but inseparable aspects of one picture, as the personal mirrors a certain place and time and vice versa. Whether what I have written does strike a just balance between the self and the world, I can't tell. But after finishing the memoir, I became aware of omissions. While re-creating the dramatic episodes of living—trying to find my way back to 'how it was' and what it felt like to be a child and a young man in that time—I understated the immediate social contexts of the events recorded.

When I was born, my mother thought that I was too skinny and I cried too much; my nanny-governess handled and hugged me more often than my mother did. This may be connected with the scream re-created at the opening of my story: it may seem like a banal incident but that scream—the fear of getting lost—runs through much of my life. My privileged and, in many ways, exceptionally sheltered early life was soon cut across by a degree of insecurity. My mother's ordinary anxiety—and worrying formed a strong element in her caring love—must have got gradually transferred to me though she once said, in my mature years, that I was born nervous. Possibly so, but I can't remember that! What I do remember is that the historic anxieties of the time—from somewhere around 1938 at least, from the Nazi occupation (*Anschluss*) of Austria on—got woven into our seemingly peaceful home life. Despite all the secrecy, and my parents' conscious attempt to create an appearance of well-being and a zone of safety, our world had a shadow side.

Our home situation was, no doubt, a microcosm of a society hurtling towards collapse. The Jews, including those baptised and fully assimilated but included in the race laws, felt threatened most. Soon after the outbreak of the second world war, the country of my birth was totally surrounded by Nazi Germany and—though there were plenty of Nazi sympathisers—millions of people must have been getting increasingly fearful: men of property feared a revolution; right-wingers feared defeat; school teachers could no longer teach properly, being constantly disrupted and lacking teaching aids and labs; rumours of war dominated the public sphere even before Hungary sent an army into the misconceived war against the Soviet Union after June 1941. Meanwhile—we know this from the research of later historians—political leaders were impotently groping to find ways of avoiding a catastrophe through secret negotiations with the Western Allies.

With hindsight, and through reading the history of the war as it affected Hungary, it is clear that our ultimate fate—deportation with a death sentence—was delayed for two to three years, roughly from 1941 to 1944. The extermination of the Jews of Hungary had become, it is on record, a principal aim of the Nazis and it was only the balancing act of the Horthy regime, particularly under the premiership of Kállai who performed a political czardas dance—two steps to the left and to the Western Allies, two steps to the right and to Nazi Germany—that postponed the evil day. Thus, without knowing anything about the ghastly politics of the Final Solution, we lived on ignorantly in an island of relative normality. And we survived. It was only much later, especially when questioned by my children, that I fully realised how abnormal those years of seeming stability had been: the underlying, half-suppressed fear coupled with bouts of irrational optimism. We would be spared—though, unknown to us, our island had railway lines leading to Auschwitz. So my parents made no attempt to escape either before the outbreak of the war—when it would have been relatively easy—or in the early years of peril when it had become very difficult. No doubt they feared losing everything: position, home and an integrated way of life. Meanwhile, some trust in the 'good will' of our government remained.

Beyond that, traces of the old respect for Germany remained. Like many others, my parents would not have believed that our extermination—as distinct from persecution—had become a war aim of Nazi Germany. After all, they were brought up as contributors to, and participants in, German *Kultur*, a word and a phenomenon still revered. They were children of the Austro-Hungarian Empire with a lasting heritage. Everybody in the family could speak and read German. My paternal grandfather, Emmanuel Karpati, taught German language and literature in a *realschule*. Among other works, he published a searching and enthusiastic long article on the religious and philosophical toleration expressed in Lessing's play *Nathan der Weise* (which survived from the otherwise lost family archives). My father studied Economics in Vienna and read a German-language newspaper daily until deportation (as I recalled). The family bookcases had ample German literary and other works, from fairy tales to Kant on eternal peace—ironically enough admired by a senior German officer billeted in our flat in the early days of occupation (March–April 1944). Conversation with German officers remained relaxed; they probably didn't know about our 'status' though one of them may have guessed. The children had German-speaking nanny-governesses from infancy; we were singing German songs and repeating German proverbs, slogans or lines of poetry. My father read to us from Goethe and Schiller; my mother (as I recorded) talked about Storm's *Immensee* and Mann's *Buddenbrooks* when I was about eleven. All that added to a false sense of security, through culture, right up to our deportation. One of my last memories of my father is seeing him talk to an SS officer not far from the deportation train as it was being assembled—he must have been desperately trying to get some information. There is circumstantial evidence that my father, alone in the family, did know where the deportation transports were destined to take us—and that knowledge undermined his capacity for hope together with his resistance to the illness that killed him.

In a further irony, the Jewish dimension of our family seemed relatively remote—somewhere in the background or just a racist concept. It was seldom mentioned by my parents and I felt integrated in my well-known Protestant school. Certainly, my mother seemed at ease with a number of Jewish women friends—especially bridge partners—whilst less at ease with members of the traditional Christian middle class. That, however, had something to do with her lack of appreciation for the provinciality of the locals in Debrecen, that city of the plains where she was never as happy as she had been in her youth in the hilly West country. My father's distinguished professional life seemed to flourish, though no doubt he had concealed from us areas of conflict; and the habit of concealment must have been a strain. I glimpsed his nervous tension when travelling with him in the country and in Budapest (as I recorded). My own attitude to 'the Jewish question' was quietly concealed yet possibly stressful, half-consciously. In my story 'Falls the Shadow' (2007) I dramatised and extended some lived episodes to bring out the conflict between Christian and Jewish children and the intense ambivalence of living a fully assimilated life as a studious, uncircumcised Protestant boy. But my conscious experience of those years was much less dramatic. My immediate environment offered immunity from persecution and, aged only about eleven, I was already beginning to behave as if I were a mere spectator of life. Quite possibly, that attitude— nothing to be proud of—was itself developed as a response to all that compulsory secrecy and latent fear. I disapproved of anti-Semitism but did not fully absorb the fact that it was directed against me too. It is well-known that Jews, and especially baptised Jews, are quite capable of a degree of anti-Semitism, and my mother took a dim view of Orthodox 'Polish' Jews who were far too different, and far too visible in their distinctive garb in the street; on the other hand, she also felt critical towards certain ostentatious Jewish plutocrats (mostly living in Budapest). Those were the people who caused anti-Semitism, she felt; while the hard-working, modest, patriotic, fully assimilated Jews, hardly Jews, whose ancestors had been living in the country for centuries, were indiscriminately lumped together with those people, in a flood of irrational prejudice and hatred.

We climbed into our deportation cattle trucks ignorantly, blindly. And it was only an accident—a recorded mistake made by an SS-man—that sent us to a forced labour camp in Vienna instead of a death camp.[11] That circumstance will always haunt me. Memory of my survival against the murder of so many—my maternal grandmother, Olga, and two childhood friends, Marika and Andras, among the millions—is always accompanied by intense questioning. Was it mere chance, like winning a round of roulette? If so, a whole range of philosophical or religious ideas remain permanently suspect. You cannot call it Providence because the same 'Providence' is then responsible for allowing mass murder. You may call it fate only in a narrow, fatalistic way—a primitive belief. I can try and think of my survival as destiny but only if that is justified by a life-time of meaningful action and love—quite a burden of expectation to live with. When I am fully conscious of my survival, the question 'what for?' and the command 'live up to your gift!' is never far behind. On one level it is like the experience of Dostoevsky's Idiot based on the Russian novelist's own experience when released from the threat of execution: determined to live so that every minute has value or significance and finding that impossible in practice. Then a certain sense of failure, or waste, follows every achievement and even joy.

Liberation from our last transit camp, Strasshof, not far from Vienna, was followed by confusion for a short time, and a kind of amnesia mixed with ambition—for many years. The short-lived confusion—which is re-lived again and again at moments of crisis—had a core feeling of absence: 'I am not really here, not present, not I'. That feeling might be accompanied by frivolity, a sense of lightness or even light-headedness, as in the intoxicating post-war months of cultural discovery in Budapest (1947), when literature, theatre, music and art took up all my attention—something that worried my mother for several reasons. At that time I was aware of our straitened family circumstances but almost ignored them. I was also aware of the threat of a Communist dictatorship but played it down—until, in my English grammar school, I felt free to give a talk on the 'salami-slicing' tactics, the gradual take-over of Hungary by THE party.

Once in England, I became aware of the messy end of Empire—beginning with independence for India followed by Palestine, each change

---

[11] See footnote to p.78

accompanied by violence and chaos; I was aware too of the ongoing post-war economic crisis, of widespread poverty and the persistence of Disraeli's 'two nations', which the new welfare state (including the National Health Service, in which my uncle had a job as a county medical officer) was supposed to cure. But I did not feel deeply about such momentous events even while I was writing balanced essays on current affairs, on those very subjects. Above all, I put the year of deportation—the forced labour camp and the death of my father right at the beginning of our ordeal—into brackets.

It now seems very strange—it even feels unsound—to recall that the mass murder of millions of Jews was also buried in partial amnesia. It has often been said that people everywhere were afraid to confront the evidence of the death camps—everywhere in Europe, not just in Germany where the psychology of repression was most evident. In my own family and in my circle of friends—some of them survivors—prolonged silence about that past prevailed, amounting to an instance of collective repression. The flood of appalling information—documents, memoirs, historical studies, trials—came much later than the period of my youth I have been writing about. My own deeper involvement in remembering was prompted by a correspondence with *The Observer* while Eichmann was on trial in Israel. I wrote to say that there were survivors who remembered what it was like to be on one of Eichmann's trains, and the editors asked me for an article (1961, included in the memoir). I wrote from experience—detailed memories and feelings came effortlessly after long suppression, almost twenty years after the event. Someone noticed a degree of detachment in my writing even then: Ian Michael, my one-time tutor in Education at Bristol—a man of deep empathy, who was also very responsive to shades of language—commented that there was an 'anaesthetised' quality about my article though he found it moving. I can't remember whether I agreed with this view at the time but I already knew that the emotional strategy of survival does foster a degree of distancing. Later there was less distancing, and I would break down at wholly unexpected times and places—prompted by just a casual word or a place-name, a chance association. Once, walking in the streets of Manhattan, New York, a friend told me about a memorial or a museum to the victims of war in Italy. That was enough to start me crying irrepressibly. I had become vulnerable.

Another aspect of distancing: I followed with 'interest' developments in Central and Eastern Europe, leading to the Communist dictatorship in Hungary by 1949, which brought about my separation from my mother and sister, for nine years (well beyond the time-scale of my memoir). And if 'interest' sounds like a tame word in this context, it is nevertheless just. I struggled with the consequences of my separation—its loneliness and recurrent anxiety—but did not dwell on my condition, at least not on the conscious level.

My main ambitions became—cutting across everything else, including my personal isolation: to perfect my command of the English language, not just the syntax but the rhythms, not just a large vocabulary but the phonetics, with a fair imitation of Received Pronunciation; and to cultivate Englishness, in mind-set and manner, substance and appearance. My ultimate aim—writing—developed into writing in English. I jumped in at the deep end with minimum caution when such ambitions had to be struggled for daily, under fairly hostile circumstances, in the teeth of acute scepticism: 'you are a foreigner here' or 'you came here too old for such ambitions'. That was the dogma preached by my uncle and aunt, pre-war refugees from Vienna. True-born Englishmen and women, from headmaster to prospective employers, gently mocked my endeavour. I chose English as a degree subject in secret, a day before term started; I was convinced that, after the strong opposition to my earlier choice of Arts instead of Science at Sixth Form level, the second choice—of English— would be seen as futile or mad, a passport to no job. The questions would never cease: 'What will you live on?' 'Who do you expect to feed you?' The same profound doubts about my chances for a professional career— concerning anything to do with English studies or teaching, not to mention writing—led my uncle to obstruct my extra year of study at university, after it had been granted by the Faculty of Arts at Bristol. At that stage, still in my early twenties, I abandoned post-graduate literary research for sixteen years. Underlying all these struggles was a profound consciousness of the gulf that, in an age that now seems almost prehistoric, separated 'the English' from 'the foreigners'—a degree of actual discrimination made worse by family prejudice.

There had been a thread of 'anglomania' in my outlook from childhood: it hit me during the war, long before I reached my grammar school. In the Nazi concentration camp I constructed a map of England from plasticine (I don't know how I got hold of it) and placed the little map above my bunk bed—luckily it was not spotted by a guard. But it was after the war, especially at school and university, that my struggle for Englishness (I never used the word 'Britishness' at the time, nor was it much used in public) gradually turned into an obsession. By the early Sixties (again beyond the time limit of my memoir) I gained insight into this condition as an observer of its symptoms. I wrote a full-length play—*How Many Miles to Babylon?*—in which the central character, the daughter of refugee parents, enthusiastically aspires to become a full-fledged Englishwoman, with all the incongruous conflicts entailed in that ambition. The play received public praise (from Peter Schaffer among others) but was not performed. After a while I came to terms with the 'myth' of Englishness, helped by my wife, Judy, a Yorkshire Quaker woman who had a humorously critical attitude towards my hybrid state. She would gladly accept my English vocabulary tips for her cross-words, and she generally enjoyed what she sometimes called my 'rhetoric'; yet she would make fun of my involuntary 'foreign' hand gestures or my over-emphatic intonation in emotional moments. Eventually and ironically, I ended up teaching English as a second language—abroad for many years.

My involvement in literature and the other arts—especially going to the theatre, to art exhibitions and listening to classical music—became a way of life. More than that, Art—with capital A and as a generator of profound experience—became a religion. I had fallen into a persistent aesthetic life— above anything ethical or religious or 'ordinary' in terms of everyday living or search for friendship and love. One or two people in my environment glimpsed my 'orientation' from time to time, but on the whole I have managed to live through more than four years without calling attention to my 'bent' as a monkish devotee of the arts, together with the ideas, the knowledge, required for their pursuit. But even such knowledge was secondary to experience—to virtual enchantment. I only realised what had happened to my mental outlook—I still used the word 'soul' at the time, quite naturally—after a deep clinical depression hit me towards the end of my twentieth year.

My depression was not a direct reaction to any one circumstance. I have presented that dark experience in some depth in the memoir and here I wish to add only one context: the Cold War. After my relative detachment in the early phase, by the time of the war in Korea and its aftermath (from Summer 1950) I had become acutely anxious—anxious every day. The prospect of the Third World War, with nuclear weapons, hung over us and obliterated a good portion of personal or communal prospects—our future. It was as if we had acquired apocalyptic expectations, not like the early Christians who looked forward to the end of the world and ultimate redemption for the faithful, but with unredeemable visions of uncontrollable devastation— worse than Dresden, worse than Hiroshima. On the one hand, the Soviet Union was becoming, in the final years of Stalin, ever more repressive domestically and belligerently hostile to the West. Hungary itself had become a Soviet satellite or colony with deportations, show trials and executions transferred from the Soviet system. My own family did not suffer badly; my mother and sister were classified—by a Communist inspector who had visited their humble post-war flat in Budapest—as 'lower middle class, with no religious images on the wall' (as my sister remembers). On the other hand, the conduct of the Cold War by the U.S. could be seen as aggravating rather than stabilising the precarious situation. Far-sighted diplomats, like George Kennan—whose policy of 'containment' worked for a delicate balance to avoid both defeatism and aggression in responding to Soviet acts—were almost pushed aside by virtual maniacs like General MacArthur who wanted to use the atom bomb against China (1951) and Senator McCarthy who saw Communists in every corner of a threatened civil society. Fortunately, the former was dismissed by Truman and the latter was partly tamed by Eisenhower who could also see the danger of the U.S. 'military-industrial complex'—a vast war machine. No doubt this is not a particularly subtle summary of those times but I think it is a map of my anxious perceptions. I hope that later generations will understand how and why the peace that followed the horrors of the Second World War was no peace. And why those years left us—I keep using the plural pronoun because I was certainly not alone—so frequently discouraged and pessimistic. A contrary hope was provided by Arnold Toynbee's vision, in *A Study in History*: every civilisation has to face a major challenge and the response to that challenge—in intellectual quality as much as in military and economic power—would shape the future of the West.

A puritan attitude to love and sex—in a heady mixture with idealised images of women and late romantic patterns of courtship—prevailed in that period. On the personal level, my inheritance did inculcate a high level of puritan restraint—or repression—through my mother (inherited from her father who, though he died before I was born, was always portrayed as a rich but strict and economical Jewish patriarch). Then my 'brilliant' Calvinist school urged us daily to live up to its motto: prayer and work— the full Protestant ethic. Pleasure was not to be aimed at. The romantic idealism came out of the air as it were—out of the culture—surviving the horrors of war. The war may even have intensified the yearning for high values and ethical behaviour in a seemingly shared communal experience, corresponding to a partial Christian revival in England (the age of Eliot and C.S. Lewis). A personal disposition towards ideal images—was it sublimation?—was intensified by aspects of my reading, among other sources the neo-platonic love sonnets of Shakespeare ('Shall I compare thee to a summer's day?', 18) and Dante's virtual sanctification of Beatrice ('*donna bella e beata*'). I cannot tell why such idealising literature had an irresistible appeal, given that there were blatant counterpoints in my reading as well as in my experience: Shakespeare's sonnets included a parody of the whole tradition of female beauty elevated beyond sense ('My mistress' eyes are nothing like the sun', 130) and the desperate anti-sexual disdain of 'Th'expense of spirit in a waste of shame/ Is lust in action' (129). What is more, I had already read Boccaccio, Baudelaire, *Madame Bovary* and *Anna Karenina*, together with Fielding and the picaresque or bawdy novel. And I had seen a lot of prostitutes in the cities of Europe, in Budapest, London, Paris, Brussels, Amsterdam, Rome. Privately, I lived out a strange split between various needs—intellectual, spiritual, sensual—distributing them in separate portions among the girls I knew.

Perhaps a little more social recall is needed here. Firstly, there was a fairly widespread horror of promiscuity, as our headmaster called it, haranguing the Sixth Form in a special session intended to keep us all straight while improving our minds. Secondly, virginity before marriage was still the proclaimed aim of most women and a certain group of men. That was the ethos of the time (though the statistics may contradict its prevalence). Thirdly, being trapped in a premature marriage was the ultimate fear of a young man, especially in the life of a young scholar who was prepared to give up his yearning powers in full knowledge of his very limited earning powers. One can make light of these things, but the age took all this very seriously indeed and the only wholesome solution was the ultimate good: marriage—something I came to be blessed with, more than five years after the story of my early youth.

The intellectual climate of that time—late Forties and early Fifties—also had a certain purity: concentrating on Art (with capital A) and wide learning. The word culture was still used (at least outside social anthropology) in a general sense of high culture—the summit of ideas, books, painting, sculpture, architecture and music—which called for constant reading, looking, listening, endless discussion and some enthusiastic travel (with limited means, hitch-hiking and youth hostelling). I think it was taken for granted that a student of English literature would read several other literatures as well; know at least one classical and two foreign languages, with a reading ability of others; know a lot of history and quite a lot of theology or mythology—would read the Bible diligently even if not a believer, together with the sacred books of the major Asian religions—would attempt to follow developments in the arts but also in the major social sciences, especially Psychology (including the controversies of psychoanalysis); would also try to find out about the hard sciences, especially post-Einstein Physics even if the mathematics could no longer be followed. The appeal of a wide range of general knowledge—the appeal of the *uomo universale*—was still powerful, with an almost Faustian urgency: 'still striving after knowledge infinite'. The past, especially of European culture, was constantly present: typically, from Plato to Russell and Whitehead and early Wittgenstein (the late work, *Philosophical Investigations* with its 'language games', was not yet published); from Greek tragedy to Eliot's *The Cocktail Party* (1950), seen, and discussed by a group of like-minded readers, soon after its first performance in London; from *The Odyssey* to Hemingway's *The Old Man and the Sea* (also just published) together with new poetry, Auden and Dylan Thomas—recited aloud by a roomful of excited students. No doubt, there were some inherent dangers in the pursuit of excellence: the risk of cultural snobbery (overcome through regard for all human beings where it mattered most: in personal encounter, in everyday living); and the risk of turning into a dilettante (my family's fear—overcome by trying to gain a thorough professional grasp in at least one 'field'. Why not rather a meadow? I would ask, facetiously.) There were relatively few social activities that might compete with those intellectual pursuits: in my case, no sport, no pubs, no girls to go out with (before meeting Ruth in 1951), no television and telephone, living in low-rent lodgings that did not posses such luxuries and, in any case, letter writing was still the main medium of communication—long, mostly hand-written letters, full of speculative thought and private jokes. The 'revolt of the masses' had not yet reached us; we paid little attention to 'mass culture' except to traditional folk songs, music and dancing, jazz and the popular theatre.

As I write this, I am aware that I may sound like a cultural dinosaur. But that could be the point—we were members of an endangered species.

Lightning Source UK Ltd.
Milton Keynes UK
UKOW040505210313

207921UK00003B/51/P